THE BOAT BUILDING BOOK

by
Geoffrey O'Connell

Published by Ashford Press Publishing 1988
1 Church Road
Shedfield
Southampton
SO3 2HW

Text: © Geoffrey O'Connell 1988
Illustrations: © Geoffrey O'Connell and
Ashford Press Publishing, 1988

Printed by Oxford University Press Printing House

British Library Cataloguing in Publication Data

O'Connell, Geoffrey
    The boat building book.
    1. Boatbuilding
    1. Title
    623.8'202   VM321

ISBN 1-85253-013-8

Illustrations by G.R. O'Connell and T. Spittles

Main front cover (Westerly Corsair 36), left hand front cover (Westerly Storm 33) and main back cover (Westerly Ocean Lord 41) pictures photographed at the works and by courtesy of:
    Westerly Yachts Ltd., 47 Aston Road Waterlooville,
    Hants. PO7 7XJ.
and taken by G.R. O'Connell
Cover design by Jonathan Duval

Errors and omissions
Whilst great care has been taken in the compilation of this book, it is regretted that neither author nor publisher can accept responsibility for the use, or consequences of the use of the information and opinions expressed herein, nor for any inaccuracies or mishaps arising from the work.

by the same author
BOAT BOOKS
The Boat Building Book
The Boat Owners Maintenance Book

LOCAL HISTORY
Secretive Southwick — Domesday to D-Day
Southwick — The D-Day Village that went to War

GROC's CANDID GUIDE TO:
Corfu & The Ionian Islands including Athens
Crete, Athens & Piraeus
Rhodes, The Dodecanese Islands, Athens City & Piraeus
The Cyclades Islands, Athens & Piraeus
Samos & N.E. Aegean Islands, Athens & Piraeus
The Greek Mainland Islands including the Sporades & Argo-Saronic

HUMOUR
Divorce Without Remorse

Geoffrey O'Connell, 47 years of age, has a very wide experience of all aspects of boat building and marine engineering spanning some twenty-seven years. A Mechanical Engineering apprenticeship was followed by a period of building up an Inland Waterway hire fleet in the early 1960s and setting up one of the first cabin cruiser production flow lines as well as a marine engineering works in the middle of the 1960s.

Later experience on the North East coast encompassed building steel and wooden inshore fishing vessels up to 55ft in length, yard repair work, marina management and custom boat building.

Production of competition and cruising yachts between 22ft and 34ft, from the lamination of the GRP mouldings to the finished boat, completed a thorough technical and practical grounding in the marine trade.

Geoffrey O'Connell's highly personalised style of writing not only encompasses books on yacht building and maintenance but humour, a series of GROC's Greek island travel guides and a magnum opus concerning the history of Southwick village.

THE BOAT BUILDING BOOK

CONTENTS

ILLUSTRATIONS

INTRODUCTION

"Believe me, my young friend, there is nothing — absolutely nothing — half so much worth doing as simply messing about in boats".   The Wind in the Willows

Apart from building one's own house, surely nothing can afford more pleasure and anticipation than completing a boat, be it a canal cruiser or an offshore yacht.

Even if an owner is not possessed of any soul, the thought of the monetary savings over and above the cost of a similar production craft should be enough to warm the wallet. An 8m yacht fully fitted out and built from a bare set of mouldings will take a total of approximately 750 hours whilst a 10m motor sailer involves some 1500 hours. The effort should show savings as high as 50% of the purchase price of a finished craft. On the other hand, a lot of determination and diligence is required which will be thoroughly rewarded if the project is seen through to its conclusion.

A forerunner of this book was conceived out of a sense of some frustration with most of the literature available to the amateur or home-completion boatbuilder. All too often, a number of books have to be purchased to cover the range of information required rather than just one or two volumes. Additionally, there is a tendency to separate inland waterway craft from seagoing boats and GRP from steel and ferrocement hulls and decks. This appears to be an illogical step as most of the information relating to, say, a GRP salt water craft is relevant to a steel or ferrocement freshwater cruiser.

Whatever, anybody who takes on the task deserves all the assistance he or she can muster and it is to be hoped that this book will make the job that much easier.

ACKNOWLEDGEMENTS

Once upon a time . . . a fledgling representative, who had only just joined a now major chandler, called at a then embryo boatyard on the Grand Union Canal. He was unceremoniously berated for some misdemeanour by the rather large owner who was covered in grease and oil, being involved in hire fleet maintenance. The angry young man was the author and the 'rep', the now well-known and respected, Bob Bingham of South Western Marine Factors.

Years and years later Bob commissioned me to write the precursor of this book. 'There's now't so quaint as life', to misquote a Yorkshire phrase.

As for other books, Viv Hitie operated the word processor and Ted Spittles drew the illustrations from my original drawings.

I would reiterate that I have no commercial connection with any business mentioned in the text other than as a partner of a small Inland Waterways boatyard.

DELIVERY & LEVELLING UP
THE HULL & SUPERSTRUCTURE

For the purposes of this book I have assumed that the owner has run the gamut of the trials, tribulations, agonies and decision making involved in the purchase of a hull and deck, its material of construction, the stage of completion and whether ballasted. To 'Ballast or Not to Ballast' is dealt with in Chapter Five.

Statistically most purchasers of yachting craft buy a GRP hull and deck and Inland Waterway folk, a steel shell. With this in mind, these materials are detailed first with sections to cover plywood, timber, ferrocement and aluminium where the techniques are widely disparate from those used to complete GRP and steel hull and superstructures. Purchasers of a 'Sailaway' craft will be fortunate enough to be able to launch their purchase immediately.

KEEL CONFIGURATION

There are one or two instances where the style and type of keel must be taken into consideration and this chapter covers the most significant of these. Naturally flat bottomed vessels and twin, or bilge, keeled craft, designed to take to the ground, are the easiest of all boats to bank store (Illus. 1a & b). Obviously, they do not require any more than a flat area and a few (railway) sleepers. If the craft is fin keel then it is mandatory to purchase a cradle from the boatbuilder's or make one using the available drawings and details and send it to the factory prior to delivery (Illus. 2a). Ensure the cradle has jacking points fairly low-down on each corner upright to aid unloading and levelling up (Illus. 2b).

It has been known for home constructors to dig up the garden to accommodate the depth of the keel and skeg. This seems rather OTT (over the top) but if this course of action is chosen don't forget to save the turf, store the waste soil and put a plank in the bottom of the pit on which to sit the keel. The main body of the hull can be sunk to ground level and trued up with the use of packing pieces. One other category of keel shape, the long straight through keel, usually found on motor boats and motor sailers, also necessitates a building cradle or cripples (Illus. 3a & b).

Most hull and decks are delivered on a trailer. If the craft is under, say, 8 metres (26ft) in length why not, if possible, employ a firm that has the tackle to be able to self-unload? Over and above that length, and the equipment usually will not be able to cope. Should no such arrangements be available, and the services of a crane are out of the question, then it's back to 'handraulics'. Handraulics aided by a little ingenuity, bottle jacks, or a trolley jack (if one can be scrounged),

Illustration 1   Hardstanding for Flat Bottomed Craft and Twin Keeled Boats

1a Flat bottomed craft

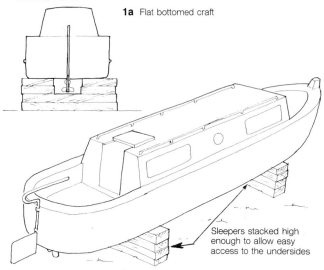

Sleepers stacked high enough to allow easy access to the undersides

some hefty baulks of timber, packing pieces, wedges, padding and/or tyres, a couple of oil drums and four or five strong men. When the trailer load is standing over the chosen area of hardstanding, proceed by jacking up a stout, athwartship beam at both ends, positioned as close to the leading edge of the keels or keelson as possible. Position a pair of padded shores, affixed to the beam and hard up against the sides of the craft, so as to secure the hull when it lifts off the trailer and block the skeg with another jack. The beam must be long enough to allow the trailer wheels to slip through the jacks. Whilst lifting the beam, continually chock the overhang so that should the jack slip . . . ! When the keels are sufficiently high at the front, block securely and commence raising the stern until the keels are completely clear. After which release the trailer and start to carefully lower the hull until it is safely earthbound (Illus. 4a).

If the thought of jacking a newly prized possession towards the sky, tentatively withdrawing the trailer and then ever so slowly lowering the same earthwards, scares the living daylights out of an owner, it will be necessary to arrange for the hire of a crane. And do make sure the operator has soft webbing straps and, if feasible, a frame or spreaders. These latter items are

1b   Twin keel craft

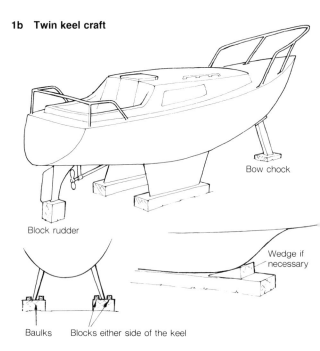

Bow chock

Block rudder

Wedge if necessary

Baulks   Blocks either side of the keel

Illustration 2   Building Cradles

2a   Fin keel hull

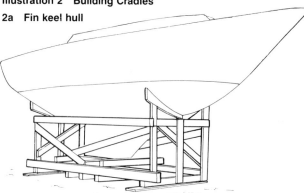

2b   Cradle — Fin keel

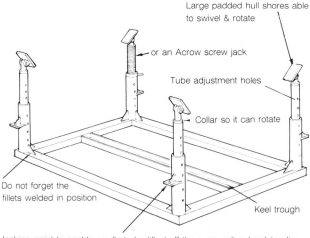

Large padded hull shores able to swivel & rotate

or an Acrow screw jack

Tube adjustment holes

Collar so it can rotate

Keel trough

Do not forget the fillets welded in position

Jacking point to enable cradle to be lifted off the surrounding hardstanding

Illustration 3   Motor Boat and Motor Sailer Cradles

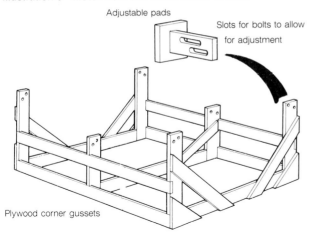

Adjustable pads

Slots for bolts to allow for adjustment

Plywood corner gussets

Material — minimum 150mm x 50mm (6" x 2") softwood to be doubled where the keel sits on cross beams. The frame to be bolted together & angled braces positioned as shown at cross beams and carried as high as possible at the uprights without interfering with the adjustable pads.

3a   Building cradle — for straight through keeled craft

not an absolute necessity but do ensure that the hull and deck are not 'pinched' in the lifting (Illus. 4b). On the other hand, the hire of a crane costs anything between £60 and £300, depending on the locality and availability, so perhaps it might be necessary to reconsider the strong men . . .

3b   Thru' keels

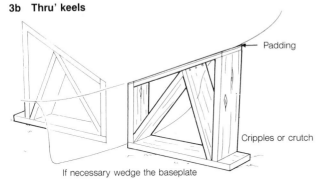

Padding

Cripples or crutch

If necessary wedge the baseplate

Illustration 4   Unloading methods

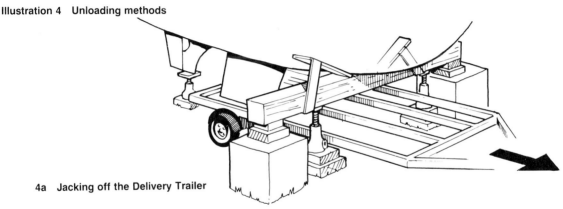

4a   Jacking off the Delivery Trailer

LEVELLING UP

It is important to ensure the hull and superstructure is on a level with the craft's eventual water-line. This warrants that, when the boat is floating, the bulkheads, soles and internal fittings will not only be perpendicular but will be at right angles to the fore and aft centre line of the vessel. Some hulls come with the water-line scribed in but, if this is not so, it will be necessary to 'lift' the fore and aft water-line, measurements of the craft from the General Arrangement drawings as detailed in Illustration 5. To establish the developed water-line place a staging either end of the hull, level with the fore and aft marks but below them by the thickness of the plank placed between the two stagings (Illus. 6). Then run a scribe along the top face of the plank, carrying out the same procedure on both sides of the hull. It is important not only to level up the hull fore and aft but also from side to side (usually by placing a builder's level across the cockpit coamings) as well as to establish the centre line of the craft.

ACCESS STEPS & INSURANCE

Do not skimp on the method of getting on and off the boat. Suitable timber for steps may well come from a demolition contractor and with luck a flight of house stairs can be pressed into service. Construct the steps and platform rigidly so that working on the craft is not a chore or downright dangerous (Illus. 7).

This rejoinder reminds me to mention that a Builder's Risk insurance should be taken out whilst the craft is under construction. This type of policy allows the value of the vessel to be increased as building progresses. It also prompts me to point out that a hull and deck must be covered by the owner's insurance from the very moment it is loaded on to the transport contractor's trailer. And do advise insurers of the additional risks of trailing and craning in case of an accident. Then they won't be able to wriggle, will they!

4b   Craning

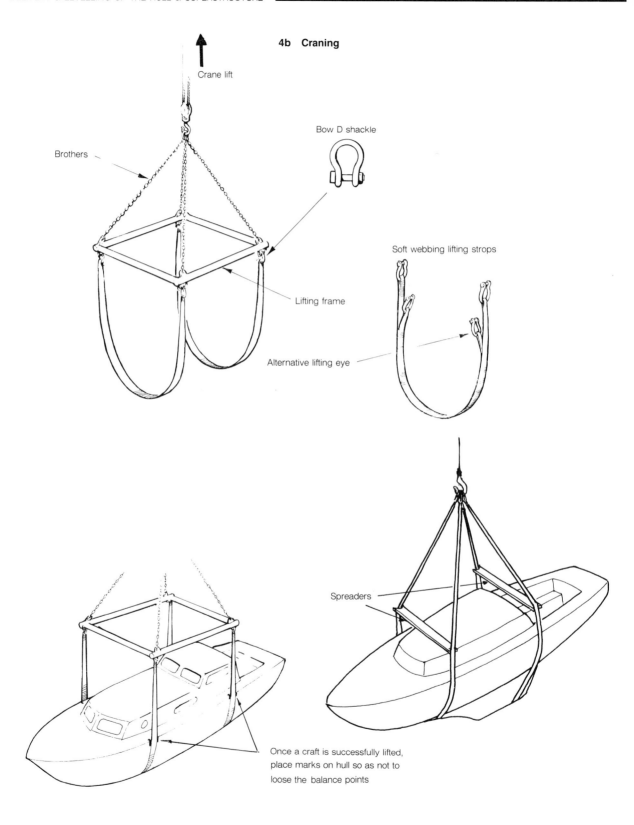

Crane lift

Brothers

Bow D shackle

Lifting frame

Soft webbing lifting strops

Alternative lifting eye

Spreaders

Once a craft is successfully lifted, place marks on hull so as not to loose the balance points

Illustration 5   Levelling Up

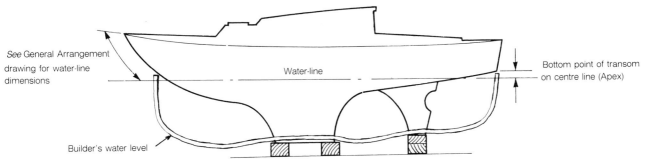

See General Arrangement drawing for water-line dimensions

Water-line

Bottom point of transom on centre line (Apex)

Builder's water level

To level up the craft prior to commencing construction, use a spirit level & builder's water level (a clear polythene tube filled with water which will be level when the water settles at the same distance from the tube ends).

For ease of operation the builder's water level pipe should be clipped at each end to a reasonably stout stake driven vertically into the ground, which does away with the need for six helpers, all with three arms!

Level bow point with apex of transom.

Level coamings or cockpit lockers with spirit level athwartship & or use the builder's water level.

Establish a centre line by plumbing width measurements at various points down to the sole & or ground.

Then all vertical & horizontal items can be positioned & checked with spirit level.

NOTE: Set up the craft on firm ground with blocks — allowing the boat cradle to take the full weight of the keel — use shores for balance and minor support only.

Illustration 6   and developing the Established Water-line

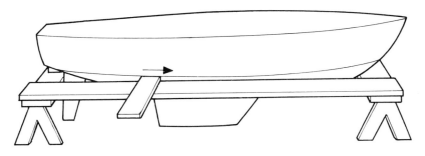

Illustration 7   Access Steps

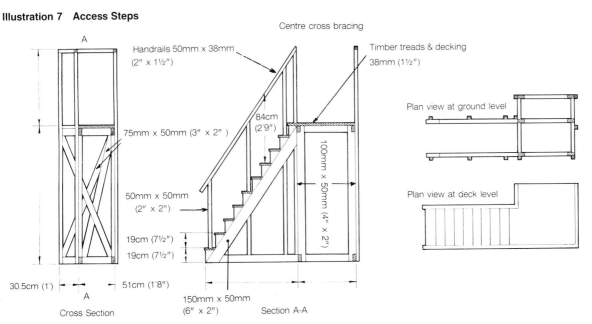

Centre cross bracing

A

Handrails 50mm x 38mm
(2" x 1½")

Timber treads & decking
38mm (1½")

Plan view at ground level

75mm x 50mm (3" x 2")

84cm
(2'9")

100mm x 50mm (4" x 2")

Plan view at deck level

50mm x 50mm
(2" x 2")

19cm (7½")
19cm (7½")

30.5cm (1')   51cm (1'8")

A

150mm x 50mm
(6" x 2")

Cross Section

Section A-A

COVERS

An arrangement to cover at least the cockpit and the after end of the main cabin is worth considering. To save on materials costs, the outline sketch in Illustration 8 offers a fairly inexpensive option. The feet of the frames are mounted on the side-decks and require one or two canvasses measuring 4½m (15ft) long by 9m (30ft) wide. Ensure the frames are spaced at no more than 1.5m (5ft) intervals, are coach bolted and have plywood fillets

let into the frame corners. Do not cut down on the number of fore and aft stringers — they give the structure rigidity. When comparing cover prices, check 'like is compared with like' and resist the temptation to acquire cheap, un-reinforced, un-gusseted, un-eyeleted polythene haystack sheets — the money will be wasted. Remember that the covers and framework will be extremely useful for winter lay-up in the years to come, so don't skimp now and regret in leisure later!

Illustration 8   Covers

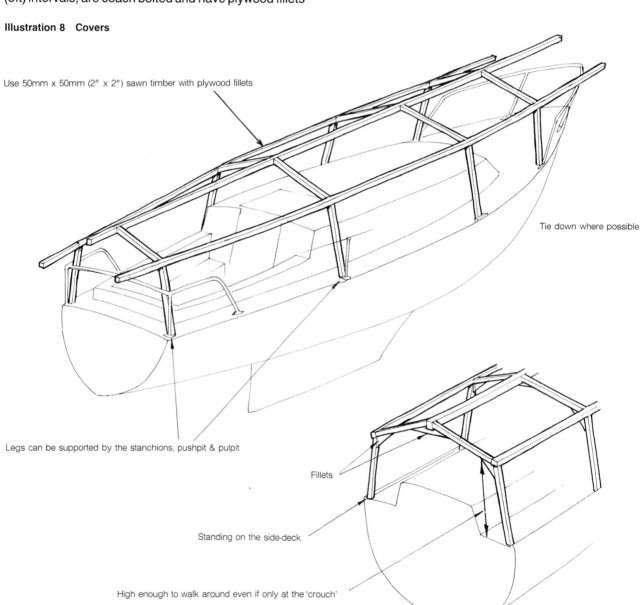

Use 50mm x 50mm (2″ x 2″) sawn timber with plywood fillets

Tie down where possible

Legs can be supported by the stanchions, pushpit & pulpit

Fillets

Standing on the side-deck

High enough to walk around even if only at the 'crouch'

HERE BEGINS THE LESSON
or THE BASICS OF GRP

Prior to launching (oh dear) into the subject matter of fitting out the craft, it is worthwhile considering the 'foibles' of the various materials of which the the hull and deck will probably be constructed.

THE USE OF GRP

Glass Reinforced Plastics (a misnomer this), or more familiarly GRP, is the sole constituent of a set of fibreglass hull and deck mouldings (one hopes!). The necessity to understand the subject stems from the fact that in fitting out this type of craft, the major internal components are best 'Laminated' or 'Glassed In' position.

Technical Terms
include:

Lay-up: Where used in connection with a Glass Reinforced Plastic (GRP) hull and superstructure, is expressed in terms of 'grammes' lay-up and indicates the weight per sq metre of the glassfibre mat, i.e. 450 grammes per sq metre (or g/m²) (1½ oz/ft²).

GRP: Glass Reinforced Plastic, often incorrectly called 'Fibreglass' (a registered trade name), is the term used to describe the finished product which is made up of the following basic materials:-

Polyester Resin: A thermo setting plastic material, popularly called resin for short, which has to be activated by a:-

Catalyst: An organic peroxide in paste, powder or liquid form which cures the resin or 'mix', exothermically (by heat). Throughout the book 'Resin Mix' or 'Mix' denotes a portion of catalysed resin.

N.B. Most resins for boat construction, or fitting out, are supplied pre-accelerated thereby doing away with the need for another constituent, i.e. the accelerator. Ensure any resin purchased is marine grade and pre-accelerated.

Glassfibre Mat (E Glass): This is exactly what it says — fibres of glass in mat form. By laying up the glassfibre in the resin solution, the relatively low strength resin and high strength glassfibres result in a material possessing an excellent strength to weight ratio, high impact strength, dimensional stability as well as good weathering and chemical resistance properties.

Glassfibre for boatwork is usually supplied as Chopped Strand Mat (CSM). Other types of mat include Woven Rovings, Cloth and Tissue. Note: $300g/m^2 = 1oz/ft^2$; $450g/m^2 = 1\frac{1}{2}oz/ft^2$; $600g/m^2 = 2oz/ft^2$; $900g/m^2 = 3oz/ft^2$.

Acetone:	The usual and most easily available liquid for cleaning, wiping down surfaces prior to applying a laminate and for washing out brushes and other GRP applicators such as paddle rollers. 'Reclaimed' acetone is often sold as 'brush cleaner' and is significantly cheaper than refined acetone.
Resin putty:	Polyester resin in a putty or paste form which, when mixed with a paste hardener, 'sets off' fairly rapidly. This putty acts as an excellent filler and bedding compound.
Gelcoat:	A resin formulated in such a way as to give a water impervious, hard, shiny surface up against the waxed mould and which becomes the exterior or outside surface. The internal or exposed side of the coating, which should be ideally about 0.4mm $(\frac{1}{64}")$ thick, will be of a tacky, rubbery nature.
Bucket life:	The period of time in which a (catalysed) resin mix can be used.
Cure time:	The period of time taken for a lay-up (of resin and glassfibre) to cure and set off.
Laminate:	Throughout the book 'To Laminate', 'Laminating' or 'Glassing In' means to apply a lay-up of 'Resin Mix' and glassfibre whilst 'A Laminate' refers to one layer of resin and glassfibre.
Useful fact:	$450g/m^2$ ($1\frac{1}{2}$ oz/ft²) CSM, with a resin to glass ratio of $2\frac{1}{2}$ to 1, gives a thickness of about '40 thou' i.e. 6 layers equals about 6.35mm ($\frac{1}{4}"$).

Tools of the Trade (Illus. 9) include:

Cheap polythene buckets in which to mix the resin and catalyst and contain it for application.

Cheap paint or GRP brushes for stippling the resin.

Lambswool and paddle or washer rollers to consolidate the resin and glass laminate.

Trimming knife and spare blades.

Catalyst dispenser.

A large pair of scissors to pre-cut the mat to the approximate size.

A small set of hand scales to weigh the resin (in the bucket).

An electric fan heater.

A decorator's wallpaper-type table on which to measure and cut mat to size.

For the application of small quantities of resin mix, plastic lemonade bottles and vinegar shakers with the tops cut off are very useful but do not use glass containers.

Hints on Application of GRP Laminate

The average ratio of resin to chopped strand mat is 2 to $2\frac{1}{2}$ parts of resin to one part of mat. Usually resin is purchased pre-accelerated and only requires the addition of a carefully measured quantity of catalyst.

The amount of catalyst controls the cure time of the lay-up, but an average measure is 4cc to 0.4536 kg (1lb) of resin. This gives an average bucket life of 20 minutes and the process cannot be held up or reversed. But note that the percentage of catalyst to be added is very dependent on prevailing weather conditions. The warmer the day, the less catalyst is required and, conversely, the colder the day, the more catalyst is needed. As the catalyst is an exothermic activator (that is it produces heat), the more catalyst used, the 'hotter' the mix and the 'faster' the cure.

A further, often forgotten fact is that the humidity must not be too high and damp days are likely to result in humidity being an adverse condition. The only way of coping with this problem, outside of a factory controlled situation, is to heat up the surrounding air, thus reducing the humidity and, incidentally, aiding the laminates to set off more quickly. An electric fan heater is ideal for the purpose. Make sure it's an old one as somehow it will end up covered with resin and mat — a fact not welcomed by the 'soulmate' when he or she wishes to warm up the guest bedroom!

It is a good idea to test a sample mix in order to check the ratio is correct. Enquire of the GRP supplier for further back up information, if required.

Points to Remember

1. Always rough up the area to which the laminate is to be applied with very coarse sandpaper, an old file, hand wire brush, rotary wire brush or grindette. Then clean with acetone, bearing in mind later

strictures. If in doubt apply a proprietary, recommended GRP Yacht Cleaner.

2. Employ polythene buckets to mix the resin, and have two or three available. Rotate them, as 'hot-bedding' a new mix into a recently used bucket can result in it being activated too quickly by the residue of the now fast curing left overs.

3. Do not mix more than 0.9-1.8 kg (2-4 lb) of resin. The bucket life must not be exceeded and once the solution goes rubbery it should be left to go off. An unused resin mix sets in a solid block and can be knocked out of the bucket and dustbinned.

4. To 'wet out' or impregnate the mat use a piece of hardboard (or similar), apply some catalysed resin to the board, lay the mat (cut to the approximate size) on the resin coat and apply more resin to the top of the mat, pulling it through by stippling with a hard brush. Then coat the surface to be laminated with some resin, apply the already wetted out mat and stipple again.

Apart from brushes to stipple out the wetted mat there are a variety of lambswool and paddle washer rollers. Lambswool rollers are used for initially applying resin, whilst brushes and washer rollers pull the resin through the layer of mat being applied and ensure an air free lay-up. Do not over-roll

Illustration 9   Tools of the (GRP) Trade

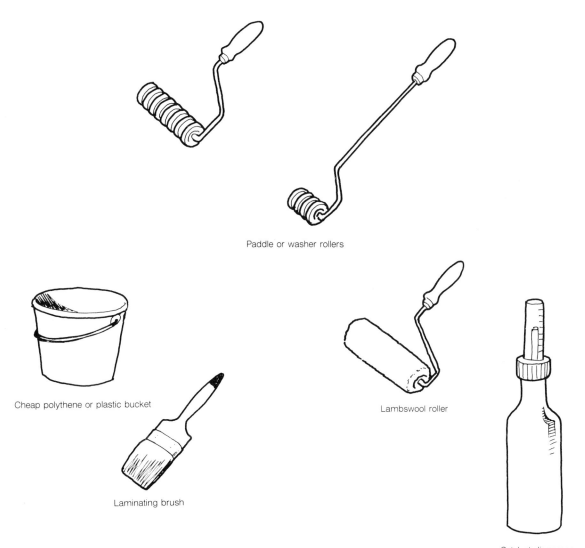

Paddle or washer rollers

Cheap polythene or plastic bucket

Laminating brush

Lambswool roller

Catalyst dispenser

otherwise the laminate just spreads out further and further and further . . . .

5. Do not apply more than two layers of mat at a time as the heat developed can, for instance, ignite nearby woodwork and cause distortion of existing laminates.

6. Trim when the laminate is just going off.

7. Put some acetone in two containers, one in which to place dirty laminating tools after use and another with which to remove any excess resin mix, including drips or runs on existing laminates. When the 'duty' container becomes too 'gungy' throw the sludgy solution away and start a new pot.

8. Where bulkheads and interior mouldings are being laminated in position it is best to mask up the surrounding area, thus ensuring a clean edge as well as protection for the surfaces of the bulkheads or other woodwork (See Illus 38). Brown packing paper held on and edged with masking tape is the usual method where laminating above a vertical surface or simply masking tape when laying up to a pre-determined edge.

9. Resin and CSM can cause severe skin irritation, if not dermatitis. Prior to going into action, apply barrier cream to the hands and lower arms and, whilst actually laminating, wear rubber 'washing up' gloves. When the job is completed clean up with acetone, which results in a sticky feeling, scrub with soap and finish off with plenty of handcream.

10. Be very, very careful when using or storing catalyst as it can cause severe injuries to the eyes if splashed around and is highly volatile. Even when carefully stoppered, catalyst must be stored well away from other materials.

11. Whilst laminating large areas, styrene fumes are released which can, under certain circumstances, such as lack of adequate ventilation, cause severe headaches or light-headedness.

12. Do not smoke when working with GRP and ask long suffering friends who have been cajoled into viewing one's handiwork to resist 'lighting up'.

Buying

Purchase resin in 25kg (55lb) drums with sufficient catalyst. Liquid catalyst is the easiest to measure and mix in the correct quantities, but, as it is highly volatile, must be kept well away from resin drums and out of reach of 'tiny' fingers, dogs, neighbours and so on.

Chopped strand mat (CSM) is purchased by weight (grammes per sq metre (ounces per sq foot)) and a 30kg roll of 450gm (1½oz) will not go amiss. To save storage problems it is best to only stock this weight of glassfibre as it conveniently gives the necessary laminate weights required in multiples of 450 gm (1½oz). Other weights available include 300 gm (1oz), 600 gm (2oz) and 900 gm (3oz) and alternative types of glassfibre available, but rarely used for fitting out, include Woven Rovings,

Cloth and Tissue. Remember to keep the roll of mat dry, preferably leaving it wrapped in the polythene bag in which it was originally packed.

Acetone should be purchased in 20-25 litre (4½-5gall) cans. If clean containers can be obtained, a number of reputable boat manufacturers will supply bulk resin and acetone at fairly advantageous prices. Ensure the moulder of the hull and deck 'throws in' free a few jars of the relevant gelcoats used, remembering white is a colour. With some gelcoat to hand, any scratches or chips that occur during the building programme can be repaired without having colour matching problems at a later date. An owner of a new set of mouldings is certainly in the fortunate position of being able, at the outset and before any damage is done, to take immediate steps to effectively counter the scourge of osmosis — the AIDS of the glass reinforced plastic boat world. Osmosis, for which 'boat pox' is a slang expression, is a word borrowed from more scientific pastures to describe the phenomenon associated with GRP craft, wherein water is absorbed through the outer skin. Initially, small pockets of vinegar-smelling water form behind the gelcoat, as evidenced by blisters measuring from 1½ mm ($\frac{1}{16}$") to 3mm (⅛") in diameter. If left un-checked, the pockets of water, and thus the blisters, expand in size to some 9mm (⅜") and at the same time the liquid diffuses into the surrounding laminates causing separation of the resin and the mat, the whole lay-up eventually going soggy.

It is suggested that the faults encouraging the malaise are often built in by the manufacturers. It would appear that the reasons for osmosis are as widespread as the use of dirty resins; undermixed pigment and/or over pigmented gelcoat; resin to which too much catalyst has been added; damp and or emulsion bound mat; out-of-date catalyst; 'over enthusiastic' use of acetone and etching materials and the application of only one (thin) gelcoat, instead of the two recommended. Tell-tale signs indicating poor manufacturing materials and/or techniques (other than craters, blisters or pinholes) include extensive star crazing, minute cracks and fibres poking through the gelcoat. This latter fault allows 'wicking' or the capillary ingress of water. Perhaps the oddest and most puzzling fact is that boatbuilders with a positive pedigree are not immune from producing craft that 'suffer' from the disease. Conversely, some backstairs, railway-arch builders, moulding craft in technically unacceptable conditions, avoid the scourge — but that's life.

Undoubtedly, it is best for new GRP boats to be treated with a gelcoat protection system, prior to antifouling, such as that produced by the Yacht Division of International Paints. Incidentally, it is important not to forget that water can also permeate from the inside so it is vital to apply an internal finish, as it were. Chapter Sixteen details the necessary procedures.

MAJOR DIFFERENCES IN FITTING OUT STEEL, FERROCEMENT & ALUMINIUM SHELLS

It is possible to achieve a satisfactory GRP bond to both steel and aluminium but careful surface preparation is necessary. The respective plates must be roughed up and clean but, due to the difficulties that can occur, I have omitted to consider it as an option. On the other hand, bonding GRP to ferrocement is a much easier proposition and the descriptions for GRP craft can be followed by owners of ferrocement boats except where otherwise indicated.

STEEL HULLS & DECKS

Steel is an appealingly simple material to fit out. If 'grounds' are required then simply weld them in position. If a structural member is unwanted or in the way then 'flame it' out (Illus. 10). Furthermore, due to the almost inexhaustible number of 'experts' with 'the knowledge' and the equipment (until wanted do I hear!), it is hardly worthwhile an owner learning the skills or buying the tools of the trade (Illus. 11).

Unlike other hull and deck materials, fittings can be welded to the deck. In fact, it may well be an advantage to have a number of the more structural items fabricated and welded in position, more especially the bow roller, fore and aft mooring cleats, main bollards and stanchion bases. After which, I prefer to approach a steel hull and deck as any other shell and thru' bolt the remaining (galvanised) deck fittings. I can already hear the squeaks of protest about drilling holes and possible galvanic action, but unless the job of having fabricated and welded fittings is handled with a feeling for style and appearance, the boat may resemble one of those Tate Gallery exhibits — all bits and pieces similar to a broken bicycle.

Not only do welded deck fittings often appear rather Heath Robinson when fabricated by the 'enthusiastic' amateur, but they tend to incur 'hidden' corrosion between the weld and the shell plate. It is very difficult to completely clean out the crevices of the weld during winter maintenance which can result in, at best, embarrassing and, at the worst, dangerous if not life-costing deck fittings failure. Possible examples include

Illustration 10   Welding In and Flaming Out

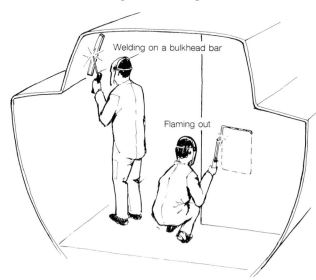

Welding on a bulkhead bar

Flaming out

Illustration 11   Tools of the Welding Trade

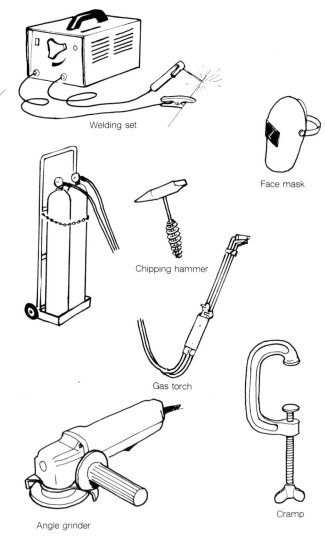

Welding set

Face mask

Chipping hammer

Gas torch

Cramp

Angle grinder

stanchion bases and deck mounted rigging eyes suddenly separating from the deck without warning!

On the other hand, thru' bolted fittings require careful attention to avoid galvanic action and naturally nowhere more so than below the water-line. The golden rules are to insulate dissimilar fittings* such as thru' hull bronze seacocks with gaskets, sleeves, pads and washers and then deluge in sealant (Illus. 12). Despite being fastened to steel, deck fittings require adequate backing pads to spread the load, just as does any other hull and deck material (See Illus. 26b).

Structural bulkheads that are not steel must be bedded to the shell on a resin putty (See Illus. 36) and bolted to an internal frame or bulkhead bar at say 15mm (6″) intervals (Illus. 13a). If frames do not 'fall to hand' and the bulkhead is not essential to the stiffening of the shell, then it is only necessary to weld spaced lugs in the requisite position. Incidentally, it makes the job easier if the lugs are pre-drilled due to the proximity to the shell and the difficulty of getting a drill into position after the lugs are fitted.

Berth framing may require lugs where internal stringers have not been welded at the requisite height and position (Illus. 13b). To aid fixing internal linings, grounds can be welded into position to which soffit blocks may be screwed with self-tapping screws (Illus. 13c).

If the deck edge requires a toe-rail, Illustration 13d details possible solutions.

Foaming Out
Once all the welding work is finished, shot blast and 'foam' out the inside of the hull with a two-pack polyurethane foam. Where applied to an unenclosed

Measured on the Nobility Scale that is

— See Chapter Eighteen

area, it must be sprayed, for on the mixing of the two constituents a very fast chemical reaction takes place, the liquids foaming, expanding and forming multiple, closed plastic cells (which resemble the inside of 'Maltesers'). The resultant layer performs a number of functions for the price of one! It insulates in respect of both temperature and sound, provides buoyancy and acts as the perfect corrosion inhibiter. And don't worry, there is no way it will peel off for it sticks like . . . to a blanket.

Admittedly, the buoyancy attribute is minimal, unless very large areas are treated, but the sound deadening property is an absolute bonus. Engine noise and deck clangs are greatly magnified in steel craft where no provision has been made to attend to the problem.

Incidentally, when foaming out an enclosed space, the two-pack liquids may be poured into the void and the resultant mixture 'left to get on with its own thing'. But beware, the rate and amount of expansion is phenomenal. I have seen the foredeck literally pushed off a plywood dinghy where foam was being introduced as a buoyancy aid. Little and often is the better way to apply the liquids, and a 'breather' hole other than the filler is advisable to allow for even expansion. Once set, the foam can be shaped and cut with a trimming knife.

Illustration 12   Steel Hull Thru' Bolted Skin Fittings

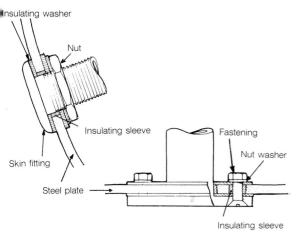

Illustration 13   Fitting Internals and a Toe-rail to a Steel Shell
13a   Bulkhead fastenings to a steel craft

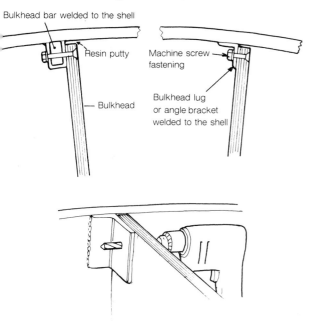

Due to the size of the lug it will not be possible to get in position to drill thru' square

Pre-drill the lug or bracket for the fastening prior to welding to the shell . . . otherwise the body of the drill will be obstructed by the steel plate

13b   Berth framing lugs

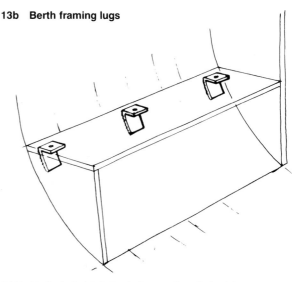

Welded to the hull plate to locate the mounting of a bunk top

13c   Soffit block lugs

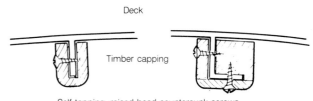

Self tapping, raised head countersunk screws

Internal deck stiffeners & frames timber capped for beauty & safety

13d   Steel deck wooden toe rails & cappings

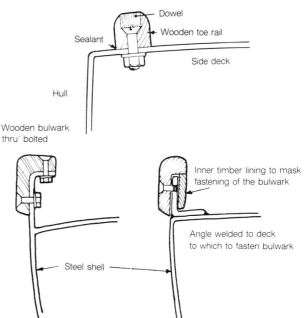

FERROCEMENT HULLS

If webs and the other grounds were not fitted in the hull when it was constructed, then lugs should be fitted to which to thru' bolt the bulkheads (Illus. 14a). On the other hand, bulkheads can be bedded on to an epoxy resin polysulphide adhesive and fixed in position with glassfibre tape bonded to both the hull and the bulkheads. It is important to ensure the ferro surfaces are clean as well as dust and grease free by applying tetrachloride liquid. Utilise a minimum of 15 cm (6") wide tape after which proceed as for a GRP hull bulkhead, using at least 3 layers of tape. Heavy duty bulkheads fixed to ferro webs on larger craft may require to be doubled up with an infill and timber frames (Illus. 14b).

Decks

Very rarely are the topsides of a ferrocement craft constructed from materials other than plywood, alloy, steel or GRP and the treatment for fittings and materials is as for that material.

ALUMINIUM HULL & DECKS

Whereas home constructors of steel craft will hardly find it worthwhile to 'attack' the skills and acquire the equipment necessary to carry out structural additions and alterations, owners of 'ally' boats would be best advised to steer clear of welding aluminium for entirely different reasons. It is a specialist skill and the best results are achieved with specialist equipment. Enough said?

Fitting out requires the same mix of pads, stiffeners, flanges, stringers and lugs as detailed for steel craft — as long as they are aluminium! As aluminium is very prone to electrolytic action, thru' bolted fittings must receive the most careful attention. Fortunately for home completion builders, the problems associated with below water-line skin fittings and seacocks are not so

Illustration 14
Ferrocement Grounds

14a Ferro lugs

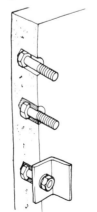

Counterbore drill into the shell, sink the head of the fastening into the hole & epoxy resin in position to give a hull fixing for angle lugs

14b ... & bulkheads

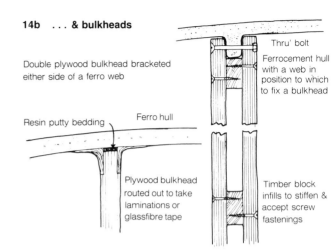

Double plywood bulkhead bracketed either side of a ferro web

Resin putty bedding

Ferro hull

Plywood bulkhead routed out to take laminations or glassfibre tape

Thru' bolt

Ferrocement hull with a web in position to which to fix a bulkhead

Timber block infills to stiffen & accept screw fastenings

great as they once were due to the synthetic items now available. If it is unavoidable to use brass, bronze or gunmetal fittings, it is necessary to apply a mix of the following precautions:-

1. Insulate the fitting and fastenings from the aluminium hull with backing pads, gaskets and sleeves (Illus. 15).
   Suitable insulating materials include delrin, neoprene and tufnol. Nylon itself has the unfortunate physical property of taking up and retaining moisture, especially salt water! This is known as being hygroscopic and is not to be encouraged below the water-line when attempting to insulate two dissimilar metals!
2. Use sealants to which has been added some zinc chromate paste and/or zinc chromate paints.
3. Fit zinc sacrificial anodes alongside each thru' hull fitting.
4. Employ aluminium fastenings where practical and
5. Apply copious quantities of sealant and paint as bedding and covering materials.

NOTE. Always ensure that a manufacturer and or supplier warrants that a product is suitable for the particular purpose to which it is intended to put it to use.

Bulkheads must be set on a zinc based bedding compound and fastened to aluminium angles or bulkhead bars.

Illustration 15 Fastening Thru' and To Aluminium

Gasket washer

Tufnol spacer

Thru' hull skin fitting

Gasket sleeve and plenty of suitable sealant

Nut & washer

Non aluminium fastening sleeve for fastening

Gasket washer

Gasket sleeve

Fitting washer & nut

Hull

ASSEMBLY SCHEDULE, TOOLS & EQUIPMENT

ASSEMBLY SCHEDULE

Below is a 'sample' schedule of assembly for a 8-9m (26/28ft) GRP sailing craft. Naturally the agenda for a motor boat should be adjusted by deleting those items fitted in order to wind power a yacht.

1. Level up the craft fore and aft and side to side; weather-tight the hatches, cockpit locker lids and fit the cockpit drains. Mark out, drill and fix the deck fittings including:-

   the bow roller/forestay, bow mooring cleats, bow bollard, pulpit, stanchion feet, chain plates/rigging fixings, jib sheet thru' deck eyes/track, genoa sheet track, aft deck mooring cleats, main sheet track/main sheet eye, pushpit, mast heel as well as the water and fuel deck fillers. All must be bedded on sealant and thru' fastened on to backing pads. Sealant bed and fix the gunwales, drilling and thru' fastening in such a way that the bolts assist in fastening the hull and superstructure together. Laminate in the holding nuts. Temporarily fix the main hatch runners, main hatch and dropboard frames.

2. Using temporary cabin access steps, position, fix and tack the:-

   a) various 'in hull' stringers/blocks (as per the General Arrangement drawings) — including the chain anchor plate, hull strengtheners, blocks, shelf and bunk stringers.

   b) chain locker bulkhead.

   c) forebunk athwartship bearers on the chain locker bulkhead.

3. Laminate in the above where appropriate.

4. Frame and fit the forebunk then position and fix the:-

   a) main bulkheads, sole bearers, mast support framing, including the hull and deckhead groundings, sub-bulkheads and engine beds.

   b) athwartship bunk bearers on the positioned bulkheads.

   c) main cabin berths framework.

   d) engine fuel pipe track and waterlock silencer hull pad.

5. Laminate in the above, where appropriate.
6. Fit the engine on the engine beds; fit the engine cooling water seacock, fuel tank straps, engine sub-bulkhead and engine fuel pipes.
7. Fit the engine side cheeks and fit the sterngear inboard gland 'T' piece.
8. Run the main electrical cables to the fused switch panel, from whence route to the various required positions, including the watertight deck plugs for the masthead, navigation and stern deck lights.
9. Cut out the rudder thru' hull position.
10. Laminate in the sterngear inboard gland 'T' piece, rudder gland, engine side cheeks and any cockpit locker sub-bulkheads.
11. Clad the berth framing.
12. Cut out the window apertures.
13. Fit the interior lining to the superstructure as well as the visible hull sides and install the windows.
14. Position the water bag or tanks.
15. Fit the thru' hull skin fittings (including those for the toilet and galley sinks, bilge pumps and the toilet), bedding them on mastic and nutting up on to pads.
16. Fit the main cabin table hull mounted block.
17. Fit and fix the main cabin, toilet, wardrobe and forecabin soles.
18. Fit the shelves to the shelf stringers.
19. Finish the galley area including any cupboards and lockers.
20. Finish the toilet area including fitting the WC plinth, the sea-toilet and the toilet vanitory unit. Fix and hang the toilet door.
21. Finish the main cabin area including lockers, engine box cover, main cabin steps, table and the bulkhead trims.
22. Finish the hanging locker, including hanging rails, fore and aft fashion pieces, and fix the forecabin bulkhead trims.
23. Complete all the beadings, edgings, fiddles to the shelves and bulkhead trims.
24. Plumb in the water pipe runs including the connection from the water filler to the water bag or tank inlet and the outlet to the toilet and galley sink pumps. Double up the stainless steel pipe clips, where possible, and use non-toxic hose throughout.
    Connect the toilet inlet seacock to the sea-toilet and the toilet outlet to the outlet seacock. Use reinforced hose and double stainless steel clips.
25. Complete the engine wiring, install the instrument panel and fix the battery in its box.
26. Fit the hull mounted bilge pump and pipe up to the thru' hull skin fitting, via a non-return valve.
27. Fit support bulkheads under the cockpit locker seats, where required.
28. Fit the cockpit locker soles (if called for).
29. Finally, fit the main hatch runners, dropboard frame and bottom dropboard, main hatch and dropboards.

30. Fit the gas bottle, regulator, gas locker drain pipe and bottle strap.
31. Prime the woodwork for finishing coats of varnish and/or paint. Degrease and prime the deck for deck paint. Degrease and prime the hull for antifouling.
32. Paint throughout.
33. Commission the engine, water and bottled gas systems. WHILST THE CRAFT IS OUT OF WATER do not run the engine without ensuring an adequate water supply to the engine cooling water intake; do not run the engine in gear, due to possible damage to the sterngear and do not test for bottled gas leaks with a naked flame!
34. Prior to launching ensure all seacocks and gate valves are closed and that the sterntube is well packed with grease.

Tools & Equipment (Illus. 16)
Before leaving this chapter, a swift run through the tools required in the coming months (and years?) may be of assistance. They include:-
An extension lead connected to a block of fused 3 pin plugs and a lead light.
A neon tube wired up to a length of cable and a 13 amp plug.
A ripsaw.
An electric jigsaw capable of taking wood, metal and GRP jigsaw blades.
A 13mm (½″) chuck, two speed drill with a dovetail jig and morticing attachment.
A flexible sanding disc, for use with an electric drill.
An orbital sander.
A hand drill and full set of high speed drills up to 13mm (½″)
A brace and full set of bits.
A couple of dowel plug cutters, screw countersink bores and a set of hole saws.
Saws including a panel, tenon, pad and coping saw.
A set of bevel edged chisels.
Wood planes, including both metal and wooden bodied planes, a block and combination plane and a Surform or two.
An assortment of screwdrivers, including a Yankee or pump driver.
A set of open ended metric spanners.
A mole wrench.
A hacksaw complete with a number of high speed hacksaw blades (18 & 24 TPI).
Pliers including a pair of wire strippers and insulated handled pliers.
Several hammers including claw and ball peen ends.
A wire brush.
A Stanley knife.
A plumb bob.
A builder's level.

Illustration 16   Necessary Tools and Equipment

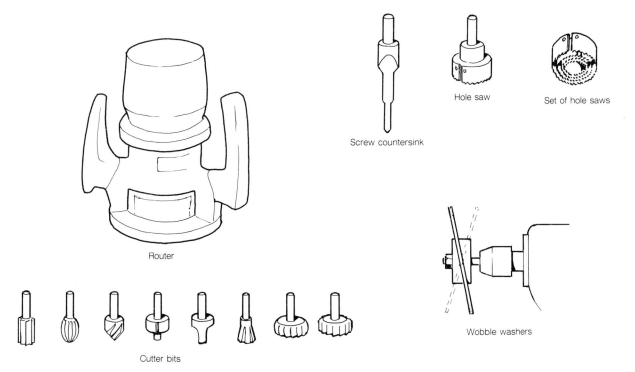

Screw countersink

Hole saw

Set of hole saws

Router

Wobble washers

Cutter bits

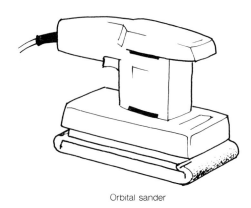

Orbital sander

15cm (6″) rubber flexible and abrasive disc

A large square.
A marking gauge.
A mitre-block.
A boxwood folding rule and steel tape.
As many G-cramps, rack-cramps and clamps as possible.
On board, a Black & Decker Workmate is almost indispensable and 'on shore' a stout, woodworking bench, with an engineer's vice fitted.

NOTE: When working in places where it is possible to grasp a live power tool and step in the 'hoggin' ('solid blocks' of water) at the same time, then it is mandatory to use a transformer and 110 volt power tools. It seems only a few years ago that a world famous yachtsman was maintaining his craft on a slipway when he inadvertently managed to make a link between the sea and the mains with fatal results.

Incidentally, it is preferable to purchase good quality equipment and tools — they will last a lifetime. Certainly, there can be no doubt that it is a false economy to buy inferior, electric power tools. For instance, the cost of two or three cheap jigsaws would, in total, purchase a decent, heavy duty one which would go on and on and on . . . .

For the amount of use they will be put to on the boat, certain items, such as a grindette and router, may be best hired when required, on a daily or weekly basis from a local tool hire company.

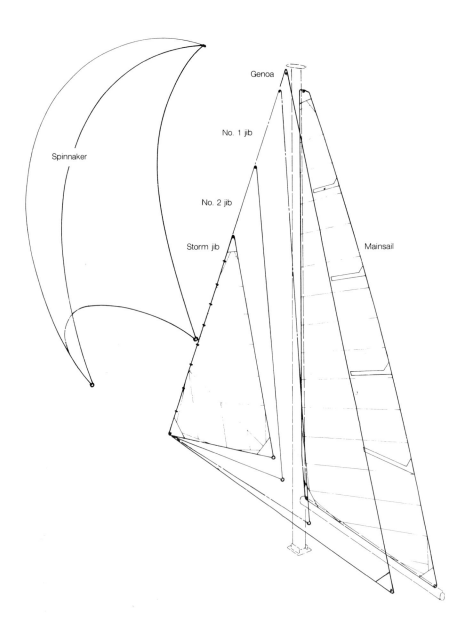

Spinnaker

Genoa

No. 1 jib

No. 2 jib

Storm jib

Mainsail

Sails

TIMBER PROPERTIES, ADHESIVES, SEALANTS, JOINTS, FASTENINGS, BALLAST, STABILITY & BUOYANCY

TIMBER

Hardwood timbers derive from deciduous trees and softwoods from coniferous trees. Very broadly speaking, hardwoods are more resistant to rot, are harder and more expensive than softwoods. Generally, hardwoods are used for structural members, lipping, edging and cover pieces; softwoods for grounds, bearers and battens. Remember when ordering timber to state the requirements clearly and concisely.

Cut timber is sawn in nominal plank sizes of 13mm (½″), 16mm (⅝″), 19mm (¾″), 25mm (1″), 32mm (1¼″), 44mm (1¾″) and 50mm (2″).

and bought:-
1. a) Rough sawn — straight off the saw bench and nominal size.
   b) Prepared or planed — the rough sawn board is planed on both sides losing some 3mm in thickness — 1.5mm per side.
   c) Finished size — where the prepared board

thickness required is stated. It may be that a finished size of 38mm will have had to be machined from a 44mm (1¾″) sawn board.
2. a) Square edged — where the bark and sapwood have been machined off and the edges squared up.
   b) Waney edged — where the sapwood is left *in situ.* The sapwood, which is lighter in colour, really should be removed as it can cause rot to set in.

Hardwood timber
Purchased as:-
1. 'Through and Through' or 'Quarter Sawn' boards or planks. Although through and through is cheaper to purchase as it is more economical for the timber merchant to cut, quarter sawn is the better buy, being less likely to warp (Illus. 17).
2. a) Air dried — when buying hardwoods, air dried is the best purchase as the 'seasoning' has taken place naturally, over a number of years.
   b) Kiln dried — due to the high cost of the air dried option, usually only kiln dried timber is available.

Illustration 17 Timber Cuts

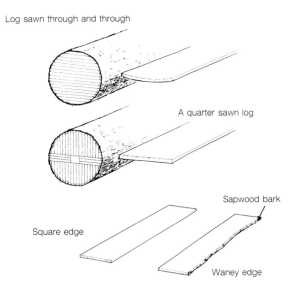

Log sawn through and through

A quarter sawn log

Sapwood bark

Square edge

Waney edge

This process involves the excess moisture being removed in an oven or kiln. Care must be taken not to allow kiln dried timber to soak up excess moisture by leaving it lying about outside or in very damp conditions. It may, amongst other things, cause warping.

Basic faults in hardwoods include thunder or compression shake, which show up as hairline cracks running across the grain, and end shake, which are narrowing splits at the plank ends. Both must be cut out.

Timber options
include:-

Afromosia	From the Congo region. Oily texture, close grained, can be difficult to plane and discolours darkly.
Ash	From the U.K. Long grained and shapes easily, making splendid tiller handles.
Mahogany	Sapele and utile, from America and Africa.
Parana pine	Originates in S. America. Long and straight grained liable to twist and split. Only suitable for interior work such as shelves.
Teak	From India and Burma. Oily, long, even grain. Tough and hard to work.
Iroko	Central Africa. Yellower than teak, for which it can be mistaken. The grain reverses though and it can be difficult to work.
Keruing	Heavy, coarse grained, resinous and only suitable for bearers.

Afromosia, mahogany and teak are generally used for coamings, rubbing strakes, frames, trims and rebated hardwood sections.

Hardwood timber is sold by the cubic metre as 'short' or 'longs'. To complicate matters a 1.5m (5') run of teak is a 'long' and anything over 3-3½m (10-12') is nearly unobtainable whilst mahogany can be purchased in lengths of between 2½-3m (8-10') and considerably longer planks can be found with no difficulty.

Softwood timber
White or soft woods, sold by the metre, are used mainly for 'out of sight' framing, bearers and battening. The usual timbers are fir, deal or pine and to ensure reasonably knot free supplies request 'joinery grade'. Avoid wet and knotty softwood.

Plywoods
Plywood, which is a composite board or sheet made up of cross laminations of timber bonded together, is available in 2440mm x 1220mm (8' x 4') or 3050mm x 1525mm (10' x 5') sheets. The boards are manufactured in 3mm (⅛"), 6mm (¼"), 9mm (⅜"), 12mm (½"), 15mm (⅝"), 18mm (¾") and 25mm (1") thickness.

Plywood Uses
Generally plywoods are used for bulkheads, soles, cladding, bunk fronts and tops, table tops, and linings and shelves.

Linings employ 3 & 6mm (⅛" & ¼") thick plywood; sub-bulkheads and cabin soles 9 & 12mm (⅜" & ½"); general bulkheads 15mm (⅝") and main bulkheads 18mm (¾").

Plywood Grades
Plywood comes in various grades depending upon the type of lamination and bonding used.

Marine grade — to 1088 specification. Usually constructed of mahogany laminations, resin bonded and the most expensive of the plywoods. Must be used for all external plywood requirements and cabin soles.

WPB grade — waterproof and boilproof. Often produced with a face veneer or plastic laminate finish and can be utilised for bulkheads.

Exterior grade — not to be used and suitable only for it's designed use as shuttering ply.

Lining ply — constructed of birch, gaboon or luan laminations of 3mm (⅛") and 6mm (¼") thickness. Very suitable for material covered linings.

Incidentally, there are marine grade plywoods and marine grade plywoods — if you see what I mean. Not all 1088 Kite stamped ply is what it may seem. The Dutch Brunzeel and British Thames Marine products represent quality. A nod is as good as a lamination!

Where bulkheads are placed four-square on to full width cabin soles, builders of Inland Waterway craft can chance the use of the less expensive composite boards such as block and chipboard. It is a risky gamble as any ingress of water will result in this type of board almost literally exploding. Where composite boards must be used, fit and glue them into slotted hardwood grounds, thus sealing the edges which helps counter the dangers of ruination due to excess bilge-water (Illus. 18). Otherwise composite and exterior grade ply boards must be considered a no, no due to their total unsuitability for marine use.

ADHESIVES

The subject and range of glues is a sticky minefield (sorry!) and a little knowledge can be dangerous, so the advice and details given are categorical and without supportive dissertation.

Resorcinol formaldehyde: The best timber to timber glue, browny red in colour and requires a setting temperature of about 10°C (50°F).

Urea formaldehyde: Provides a good timber to timber

Illustration 18   'Grounds' For Composite Board

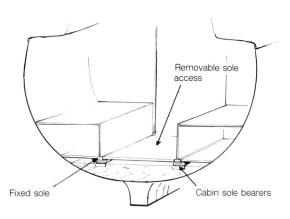

Removable sole access

Fixed sole

Cabin sole bearers

'Grounds' rebated to effectively fix & seal the bulkhead edges & mounted on the fixed portion of the cabin sole

adhesion as long as the timbers are well clamped. Sets clear or pale white in colour and requires a setting temperature of about 5°C (40°F)

Epoxies: The best all round adhesive for wood to GRP, ferrocement and metal adhesion but sets slowly at low temperatures. Beware of very fast setting brands.

Impact: These are the adhesives best suited for sticking plastic laminates to plywood, vinyls, foam-backed headlinings and composition deck coverings to timber and GRP. Strong pressure is required to keep the surfaces together and to stop 'bubbling'. Impact adhesives are petroleum based and give off fumes which can be hazardous in confined spaces.

To be economical with the adhesives, and to keep mess to a minimum, it is best to place them in an old washing up liquid container with the nozzle opened out to facilitate easy flow.

SEALANTS

Except where otherwise detailed, for general purpose 'bedding' use a gungrade, silicone sealant. This will give a long life, flexible, gasket type joint which helps protect surfaces from sustaining hard spots created when deck and thru' hull skin fittings are bolted up tight against the shell.

JOINTS

Illustration 19 details the more common joints which are glued and pinned, screwed and dowelled, slip tongued or screwed as necessary.

Waterproof timber glues are normally based on urea formaldehyde whilst the more oily hardwoods, such as teak and iroko, are best glued with resorcinol based glues.

Dowels should be backed off at the bottom end and have a slight nick along the edge. This ensures that trapped air and glue does not stop them being driven securely home (Illus. 20).

FASTENINGS

Check that brass hinges purchased have brass pins, not steel ones; woodscrews are brass or stainless steel, not chromed steel; other fastenings are stainless steel, but not below the water-line*, and pins or nails are copper or brass. An exception to these dictums can be exercised when, say, fitting a wooden gunwale to an overlapped hull and deck joint. Galvanised 'gutter bolts' may be used as fastenings as long as the heads are well counter-bored and dowelled (See Illus. 24). A useful substitute for screws, especially in the construction of berth units where a ply skin must be fastened at frequent intervals to the framing, are 'Gripfast' ring barbed nails made of silicon bronze.

*Apart from considerations of galvanic corrosion, fastening a gunmetal or manganese bronze thru' hull skin fitting with stainless steel below the water-line,in sea water,will cause problems. Stainless steel, perhaps surprisingly, is prone to penetration and crevice corrosion in underwater conditions.

Illustration 19 Timber Joints

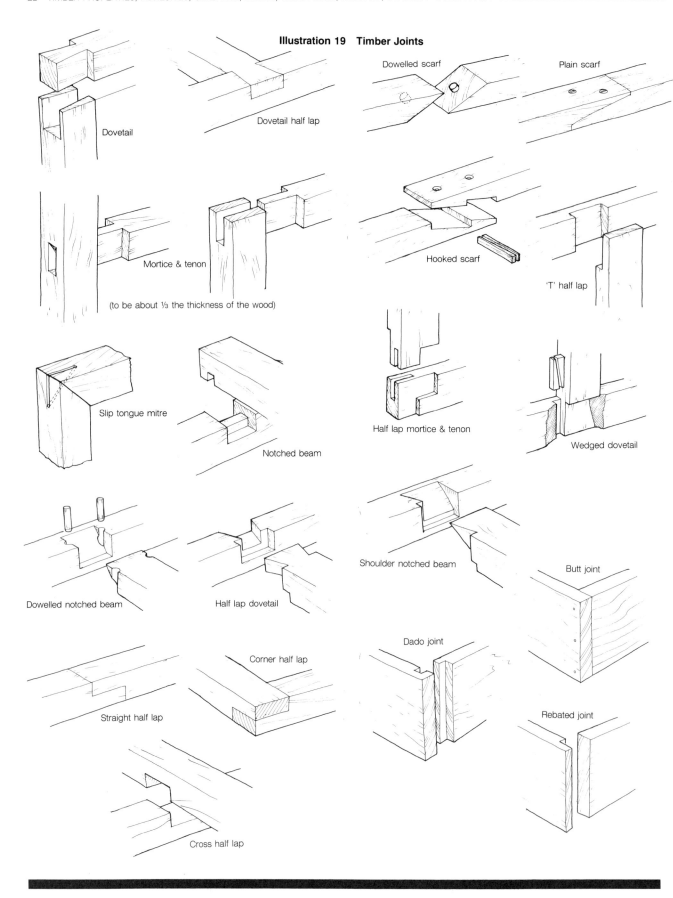

Dovetail

Dovetail half lap

Dowelled scarf

Plain scarf

Mortice & tenon

(to be about ⅓ the thickness of the wood)

Hooked scarf

'T' half lap

Slip tongue mitre

Notched beam

Half lap mortice & tenon

Wedged dovetail

Dowelled notched beam

Half lap dovetail

Shoulder notched beam

Butt joint

Dado joint

Straight half lap

Corner half lap

Rebated joint

Cross half lap

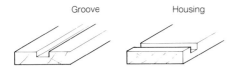

Groove   Housing

'Stopped' groove, rebate & housing

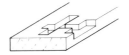

Rebate

Stopped housing joint to give concealed shelf fitting

Top rail

Stile

Mullion

Bottom rail

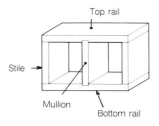

Head

Head

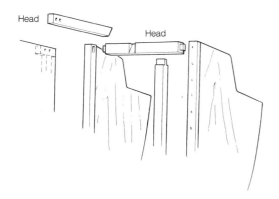

Certain basic fastenings are used in boat construction which include:-
brass and chromed brass, countersunk head woodscrews; stainless steel, self tapping screws with pan, raised or countersunk heads; copper panel pins; 'Gripfast' barbed ring nails and stainless steel, countersunk head, machine screws complete with nuts and washers. Obtaining the required fastenings can be surprisingly difficult, so it is best to track down a reliable source of supply very early on in the project.

Builders of Inland Waterways craft can forget the strictures in respect of stainless steel fastenings below the water-line — as long as anodic protection is fitted. They may be of the opinion that this obsession with the quality of materials is so much 'yellow-wellied' claptrap but it is only necessary to have a look round the average marina or boatyard's hardstanding to observe far too many mouldering hulks — mouldering due to the use of incorrect material and once someone's dream. *See* Chapter Eight for more contentious, material moralising in respect of fresh water boats!

BALLAST

The matter of the craft's ballasting must be dealt with somewhere so why not towards the beginning of the book?

Where the craft has externally fitted, cast iron keels it is of little advantage not to have them fitted by the manufacturer. Leaving a fin keel off until the end of the day has some benefit in terms of lowering the height of the shell to be fitted out. On the other hand, cast iron keels are cumbersome, heavy items to move around with limited equipment and their fitting is really best left to the experts.

Encapsulated keels, where the ballast is internally let into the hull, are a different matter. Quite often ballasting materials other than lead or cast iron are used by amateur boatbuilders but experience has shown that ball bearings, tin plate punchings and similar

Illustration 20   Dowels

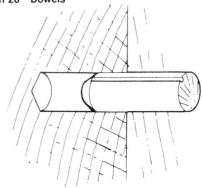

Dowel — backed off at the bottom end & grooved

'extravaganza' are to be treated with extreme caution. The major problem in using them is that they are usually not as dense as the conventional materials and thus the designed ballast weight may well not be achieved, with possibly bad effects on the craft's stability.

Furthermore, these substitute materials are often prone to oxidisation or, to you and I, rust. If an interaction commences, due to the ingress of water and air, then a disastrous chain of events can take place. This is especially so in respect of GRP vessels where the keel moulding may split, spilling out the ballast materials. To help reduce this possibility it is essential to ensure that, whatever medium is used for ballast, it is completely encased in sufficient resin mix, which of course pushes up the cost of the job. Incidentally, the catalysed resin should be carefully introduced otherwise excessive heat and subsequent swelling occurs, which in itself may well distort or burst the keels. Additionally, if the ballast materials are not completely dry before use, this may well stop the resin mix from setting, with similarly dire consequences.

There is available a specially formulated system, based on cast iron shot and a cold curing, resinous paste which gives excellent results. This material is suitable for inclusion in GRP, steel, wooden and ferrocement hulls.

At this stage some understanding of stability and buoyancy may well be of great assistance to the amateur boatbuilder.

Stability
A boat is said to be stable if, when inclined at an angle from its normal floating position, it tends to return to that position.

Buoyancy
When floating normally at rest, that is, virtually upright, a boat is subject to the following conditions:
1. The force of buoyancy acts upwards and equals the weight of the boat.
2. The 'Centre of Gravity' (CG) and the 'Centre of Buoyancy' (CB) must be in the same vertical plane (Illus. 21a)
3. The 'Centre of Buoyancy' (CB) is the 'Centre of Gravity' (CG) of the water displaced by the boat.

When a craft, subject to wind and or a wave motion, is inclined at an angle to the vertical, the centre of buoyancy moves. As long as the centre of gravity is not too high, a righting couple will be formed (Illus. 21b).

If the centre of gravity is too high an overtuning couple is formed and the unstable boat capsizes (Illus. 21c).

It will be seen that it is essential to keep the centre of gravity as low as possible when building or completing a craft, commensurate with the use to which the craft is to be put and the cruising waters it is intended to use.

Illustration 21   Stability, Buoyancy and Centre of Gravity

21a
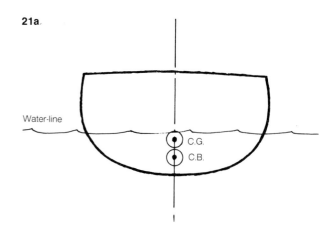

21b
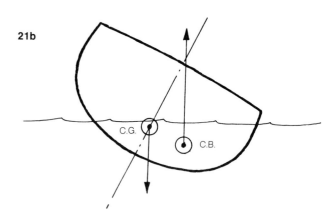

21c
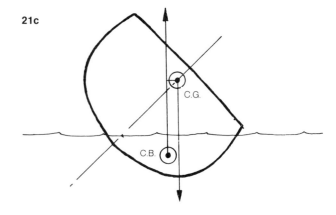

6

'SEALING UP'

The sequence of fitting out a hull and deck is subject to a certain amount of debate and choice but a suggested schedule is outlined in Chapter Four.

GRP

Assuming the craft is located in the open, as are most home completion projects, certainly the foremost task is to 'seal up' the hull deck. It is to be hoped that the shell was purchased complete with deck hatches, main hatch (and garage) and cockpit locker lids. If so, these are best fitted first off. GRP hatches and cockpit locker lids usually only require the reverse flanges cut or trimmed back to size, hinges fitted and the whole checked for binding. Prior to completion of a boat, stick down rings of sponge rubber on to which the locker lids can close, a task best left until the end of the job is in sight, as this type of refinement tends to 'suffer' in the months to come.

The main hatch, runners and slides require detailed fitting but the internal cover strips and trims should be left until the last 'knockings' (Illus. 22a & b). Place a temporary piece of plywood in the main hatchway leaving the fastening of the main hatch frames or keeps and dropboards until lining out the craft.

External Surfaces
Another task to be attended to at an early stage is the protection of the external surfaces, more especially the cockpit coamings, locker lids and sole, as well as the side and foredecks. For general covering of the decks and other surfaces, a plastic coating can be painted on. Areas that will experience the constant traffic of dirty boots should be covered with spare headlining materials or old carpeting, taped down.

Cockpit Drains
It is advisable to fit at least one cockpit drain otherwise, in wet weather, an owner may well face something resembling a small swimming pool every time he (or she) attempts to cross the cockpit (Illus. 23a). Motor sailers with moulded bulwarks will also incur side-decks awash

and the appropriate drains must be fitted (Illus. 23b).

One of the difficulties in fitting cockpit drains early on in the proceedings is that the position of the cockpit drain thru' hull skin fittings are influenced, or more correctly interfered with, by the engine and its attendant paraphernalia. It may well be that the engine and gearbox unit is only a twinkle in an owner's eye at this stage, so temporary steps must be taken to cope with

Illustration 22 Fitting the Main Hatch

22a GRP sliding main hatch

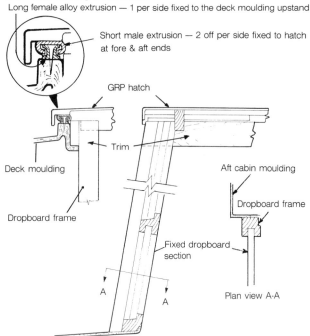

Long female alloy extrusion — 1 per side fixed to the deck moulding upstand

Short male extrusion — 2 off per side fixed to hatch at fore & aft ends

GRP hatch

Trim

Deck moulding

Dropboard frame

Aft cabin moulding

Dropboard frame

Fixed dropboard section

Plan view A-A

Section through main cabin entrance dropboard frame

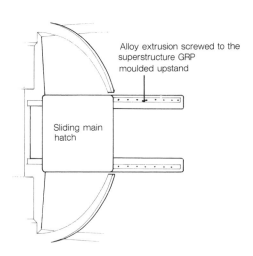

Alloy extrusion screwed to the superstructure GRP moulded upstand

Sliding main hatch

Plan view in way of main hatch

22b Wooden main hatch assembly

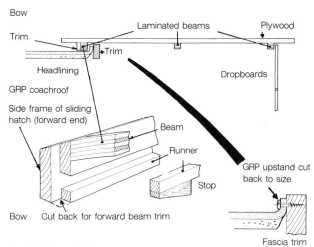

Bow

Trim

Laminated beams

Plywood

Trim

Headlining

Dropboards

GRP coachroof

Side frame of sliding hatch (forward end)

Beam

Runner

Stop

GRP upstand cut back to size

Bow   Cut back for forward beam trim

Fascia trim

Section through hatch on centre line

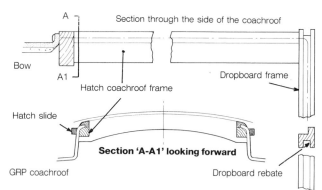

A

Section through the side of the coachroof

Bow

A1

Hatch coachroof frame

Dropboard frame

Hatch slide

Section 'A-A1' looking forward

GRP coachroof

Dropboard rebate

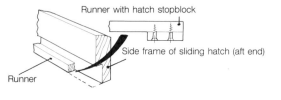

Runner with hatch stopblock

Side frame of sliding hatch (aft end)

Runner

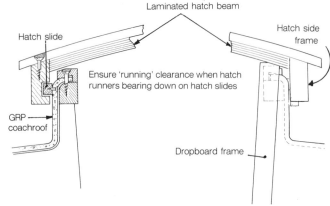

Laminated hatch beam

Hatch side frame

Hatch slide

Ensure 'running' clearance when hatch runners bearing down on hatch slides

GRP coachroof

Dropboard frame

Temporarily assemble to position hatch slides

Illustration 23   Cockpit and Scupper Drains

23a   Cockpit drains

23b   Scupper drains

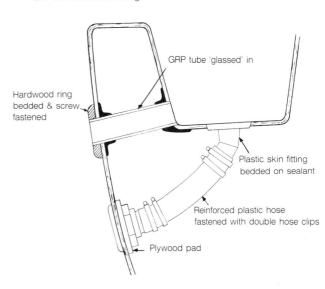

GRP hull & deck moulding

GRP tube 'glassed' in

Hardwood ring
bedded & screw
fastened

Plastic skin fitting
bedded on sealant

Reinforced plastic hose
fastened with double hose clips

Plywood pad

Ensure the backing pads are as large as is practical & bedded on sealant

Illustration 24   Hull to Deck Joints
24a   Flush deck flange joint

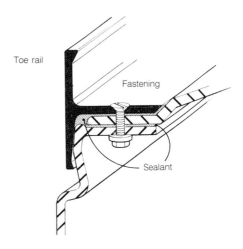

Toe rail

Fastening

Sealant

the situation. The cockpit sole position of the drains is often indicated by the deck being indented in the manufacture, so it is difficult to go wrong here but at the hull end. . . . A good wheeze is to drill out the rudder stock or sterntube thru' hull hole, attach a temporary pipe to the cockpit sole skin fitting and exit it through one of the two points.

Hull to Deck Joints
Hopefully, the shell is now reasonably watertight, but if an owner did not purchase the hull and deck mouldings bonded together this is the very first task to carry out. Where the craft is a flush deck model the usual practice is to bed the deck to hull flange on sealant and bolt right through an aluminium toe-rail and the flange joint (Illus. 24a).

If the hull to deck joint is a 'Top Hat' the two flanges should be bedded on sealant, thru' bolted at regular intervals — say every 15cm (6") — and laminated internally. 'Top Hat's' are usually capped with a rubber extrusion (Illus. 24b).

Where the deck overlaps the hull (Illus. 24c) — the most usual type of joint — fasten the two together with widely spaced 'big head' pop rivets. If there are any nasty gaps between the hull and deck,after pop riveting the two together, fill them with a resin putty mix or sealant. After which the type and style of external 'rubber' or gunwale capping must be considered. There are a number of options which include one of the proprietary aluminium tracks bedded on sealant and bolted thru' the deck and hull. A rubber insert is pushed into the track when it is in position. The task is made infinitely easier if a liquid detergent is applied to the rubber (Illus. 24c). A timber gunwale is more difficult to achieve but results in a very satisfying contribution to the craft's overall appearance (Illus. 24d). Don't forget to rebate the bottom inside edge, in order to seal the hull and deck overlap joint, and to scarf the timber run, as it is impracticable to machine lengths any longer than about 1¾-2½m (6-8ft.) Start at the bows and ease the gunwale gently round but if it is too sharp a 'turn' at the bows, halve the thickness and laminate inner and outer timber sections which may be fixed to each other 'on the job'. Ensure the fastenings, which can be roofing or gutter bolts, are countersunk and dowel finished. As elsewhere, bed the timber gunwale on sealant.

The transom gunwale of an overlap jointed hull and deck usually presents problems, if it is planned to fit a timber capping, as quite often there is a downward and inward sweep in this area (Illus. 24e). A 'former' must be made and the necessary section laminated (*See* Mast Beams & Illustration 42, Chapter Seven).

Motor sailer decks are often moulded in the shape of a vertical 'Top Hat' (Illus. 24f) or a bulwark, the timber cappings for which require some detailed work. This

24c   Overlap joint . . . with aluminium track gunwale rubber

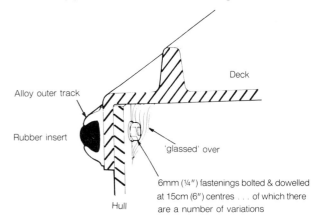

24d   . . . with timber gunwale

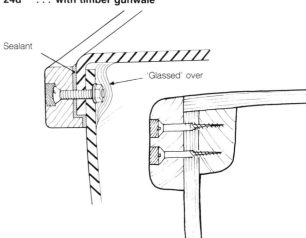

24e   Transom gunwale

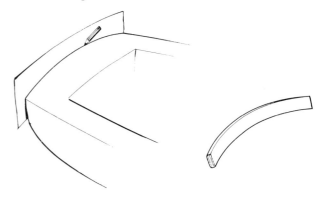

Temporarily screw a thin piece of plywood to the transom & scribe the outline thus enabling both the inward and downward sweep to be 'described'. Cut out the shapes from timber up to 6mm (¼") thick, gluing up & temporarily screwing onto the transom until 'set'. Then remove, clean , round off, bed on mastic & thru' bolt.

24b   Top hat hull to deck joint

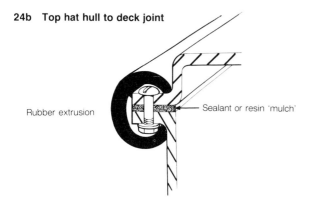

is especially so in the area of the bows where the cladding should be made up of a number of 1-2m (3-6ft) lengths shaped and scarfed together, bedded on sealant, thru' bolted in counter bored holes and dowelled (Illus. 24g).

After the gunwales are finally fitted and bolted in position, apply a resin mix to the internal nut heads and laminate over them and the inside of the hull to deck join with up to 4 layers of CSM.

Chain Plates & Rigging Eyes

Chain plates and rigging eyes come in various shapes, sizes and types. The name chain plate originated from the fact that standing rigging, in days of yore, ended in chain and were fastened to the hull with a plate! By their very configuration chain plates are usually fastened to the hull of a yacht. But this results in high windage and detrimentally affects the windward performance, so standing rigging moved inboard and rigging eyes came into being (Illus. 25a). Where possible, the 'pull' on the rigging fixings must be transferred to the internal bulkheads and the hull and deck (Illustration 25b).

Variations on the theme have come about in respect of, for instance, flush decked yachts where bulkheads may not be conveniently to hand and the load of the lower shrouds is transferred directly, via straining bars, to the hull (Illus. 25c).

Now, back to the question of the sequence of fitting out.

Deck Fittings

Observation reveals that owners often concentrate on the internals, leaving the deck fittings to a later day. But as most deck fittings must be thru' bolted, are often very close to the gunwale and/or aggravatingly coincide with positioned bulkheads, it makes life considerably easier to fit the major deck fittings whilst still having an uncluttered interior. This leaves ample room to arrange backing pads, tighten up the fastening nuts and, where necessary, file or bolt crop off overlong bolts. The deck fittings referred to include the stemhead bow roller, pulpit, bow and aft mooring cleats/bollards and fairleads as well as stanchion feet, genoa tracks and chain plates/rigging eyes.

If the vessel is a yacht and there is no precise indication of the position of the deck tracks and sheet leads, refer to Chapter Nine.

Deck fittings must have as large a base as possible, thus avoiding a 'punching effect' (Illus. 26a), and be drilled out for countersunk head fastenings of at least M6 (¼") diameter. I have heard it suggested that it can add to the effectiveness of fastening deck fittings if the holes are not drilled out 'size' or even clearance but are drilled for, say, a 75% tap thread. The fastening is then screwed down through the shell resulting in a partial thread in the skin. I cannot recommend this practice, for although in ideal conditions it would be laudatory,

24f Bulwark vertical top hat

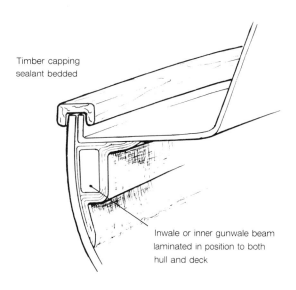

Timber capping
sealant bedded

Inwale or inner gunwale beam
laminated in position to both
hull and deck

24g Bulwark gunwales

Bed the gunwale on sealant, fasten with 6mm (¼") stainless steel countersunk head machine screws & dowel

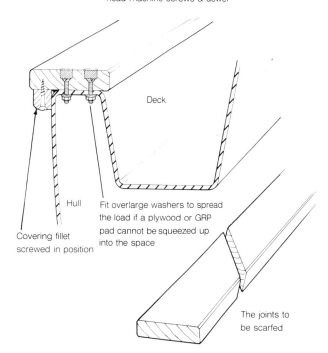

Deck

Hull

Covering fillet
screwed in position

Fit overlarge washers to spread
the load if a plywood or GRP
pad cannot be squeezed up
into the space

The joints to
be scarfed

Illustration 25   Chain Plates and Rigging Eyes

25a Chain plates

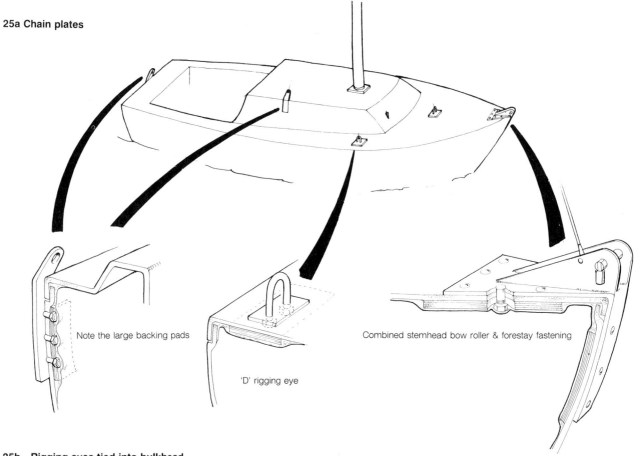

Note the large backing pads

'D' rigging eye

Combined stemhead bow roller & forestay fastening

25b   Rigging eyes tied into bulkhead
Deck rigging eye thru' fastened to a bulkhead. If no bulkhead is to hand fasten
to a fillet laminated 'in the way' of the rigging eye or treat as in Illustration 25c

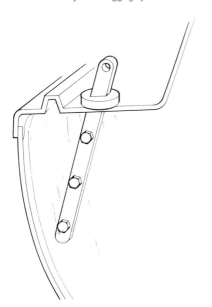

the chances of perfectly lining up four or more drillings and then tapping the threads absolutely square to the surface, and to each other, are too remote for safety's sake. It is more likely to result in damage to the shell and/or the fastenings.

There are some excellent, matched, anodised aluminium deck fittings on the market, combining attractive styling and adequate engineering. They are pre-drilled and countersunk for sufficient fastenings of a requisite diameter to ensure the fittings do not tear out of the deck under extreme loads. To further secure the fastness of the deck fittings, they must be bedded on sealant and thru' bolted using an internal backing pad on which to tighten the holding nuts and washers. And don't forget to bed the backing pad on mastic (Illus. 26b). The choice and method of fitting backing pads depends on their location in the craft and the shell material (Illus. 26c). The various cut-outs from the main hatch and window areas are quite adequate to use as pads as long as they are covered by inner linings. This is because they are not particularly sightly. On the other

25c Flushdeck

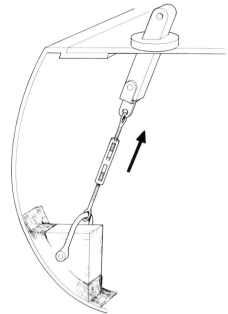

Deck rigging eye strain transferred to the hull via a straining bar or rigging screw. The hull pad/block must be large enough to transfer the forces over a wide area.

Illustration 26   Fastening Deck Fittings

26a   An inadequately sized/fastened deck fitting acting as a punch

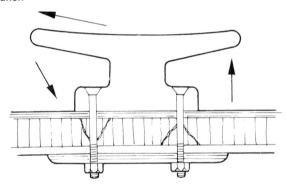

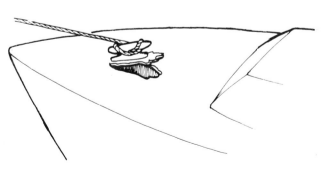

Avoid over large fittings with undersized bases & or unpadded fastenings.

26b   A well 'bedded' fitting

Use countersunk head machine screws unless the plate of the fitting is insufficiently thick enough to accept a countersink. In this case fit roundhead bolts.

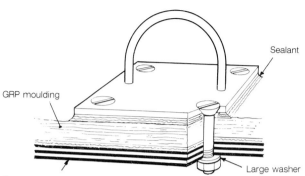

Backing pad of marine ply or GRP cut-outs

hand, marine ply offcuts make a very good pad, whether hidden or in sight and the mechanical properties of marine ply ensures it will not split, as might a mahogany or teak hardwood pad. A sufficiently thick piece of plywood allows the fastening nuts to be countersunk but do use the largest washers possible, preferably of the 'penny' type. On odd occasions a feature may have to be made of a backing pad where it cannot be covered or hidden.

Often the cabin deckhead and decks will have been 'manufactured' with an end grain balsawood sandwich let into the lay-up. This is incorporated for a variety of reasons, one of which is to ensure the large, flat areas do not flex and creak when being pounded across by innumerable yellow wellied feet. On the other hand, balsa does cause a problem in that it does not cope very well with small area compression loads, such as those of a small base deck fitting (Illus. 27a). Where there is not sufficient headroom to allow a backing pad to be positioned over the sandwich construction, then it is best to neatly cut away the balsawood in the localised area and 'let in' a plywood pad. Ensure the exposed balsa sandwich and pad is laminated in and, if at all possible, fit a sealant bedded, thin plywood pad over the whole area (Illus. 27b).

Toe-Rails

Side-deck toe-rails are often moulded into a GRP deck and the manufacturer may have filled the resultant 'nib' with sawdust or 'micro balloons', laminated in position (Illus. 28a). Obviously pads must be fitted where thru' fastening rigging eyes and genoa sheet tracks in these areas. If no infill has been provided, shape, fit and laminate hardwood blocks into the recess prior to fastening down deck fittings (Illus. 28b). Incidentally, it is bad news if the indent has been filled up with near neat resin, which has very poor mechanical qualities (Illus. 28c). In these cases it is best to carefully rout out the excess resin and proceed as above.

26c   Deck fitting fastenings & doublers

Bed the fitting on a suitable sealant

For suitable sealants *See* the
relevant paragraph in Chapters Five & Six

Countersunk to take a dowel

Handrails matched inside & out,
sealant bedded &
thru' bolted

GRP deck
Plywood or GRP pad (which should
be as large as is practically possible) bedded
on sealant or epoxy resin

Plywood/timber deck
As for GRP deck

Ferrocement deck
As for GRP deck

Steel deck
As for alloy deck except substitute steel for alloy pad

Aluminium deck
Doubler pad or plate welded in place — or a pad of alloy, sealant bedded

Chafe Plates

Deck surfaces, bulwarks or gunwales that might experience undue wear and tear should be fitted with shaped, stainless steel chafe plates, although 'sacrificial' pads will suffice equally as well. Craft with bulwarks are particularly prone to damage in the area of the fairleads, where mooring ropes can cause damage as can the anchor chain on its 'journey' from a foredeck mounted chain pipe to the anchor chain roller (Illus. 29).

Illustration 27   Thru' Bolting a Balsa Core

27a   Fastenings thru' 'untreated' balsawood & the possible weakness

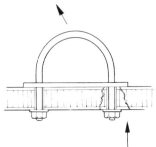

27b   Balsa backing pads

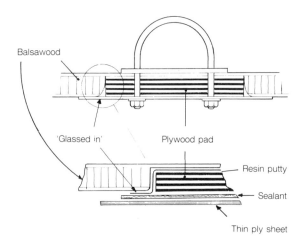

Balsawood

'Glassed in'

Plywood pad

Resin putty

Sealant

Thin ply sheet

Illustration 28   Moulded Toe Rails

28a

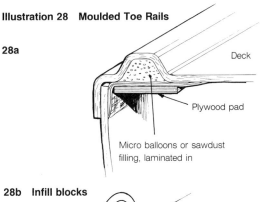

Deck

Plywood pad

Micro balloons or sawdust filling, laminated in

28b   Infill blocks

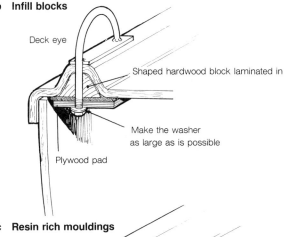

Deck eye

Shaped hardwood block laminated in

Make the washer as large as is possible

Plywood pad

28c   Resin rich mouldings

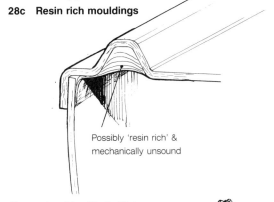

Possibly 'resin rich' & mechanically unsound

Illustration 29   Chafe Plates

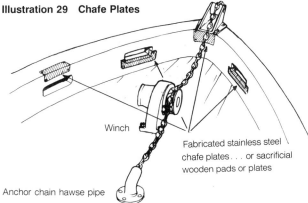

Winch

Fabricated stainless steel chafe plates . . . or sacrificial wooden pads or plates

Anchor chain hawse pipe

No, No's

External fittings must not be fastened with screws or pop rivets, and do not forget that wherever nuts are used — so must be washers.

STEEL, PLYWOOD, FERROCEMENT & ALUMINIUM

The preceding description for GRP hull and decks, combined with the comments in Chapter Three in respect of the differences in fitting out the various shells, takes in most variations on the theme.

One point to bear in mind is that whatever the material, deck fittings must have internal pads to spread the load of both the fitting and the fastenings (*See* Illus. 26c). Steel and aluminium decks may well have the doublers welded in position but otherwise the differences may be minimal, even to the type of gunwales. On the other hand, the hull to deck joints of differing shell materials present the builder with a number of alternative options but they usually make little difference to the amateur boatbuilder (Illus. 30).

Illustration 30   Other Material Hull to Deck Joints

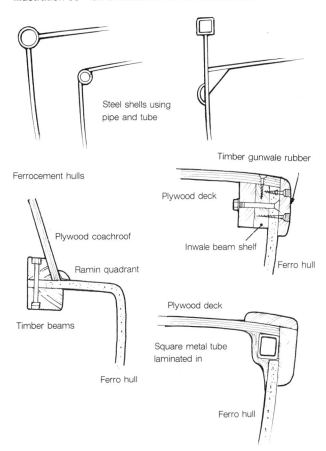

Steel shells using pipe and tube

Timber gunwale rubber

Ferrocement hulls

Plywood deck

Plywood coachroof

Inwale beam shelf

Ramin quadrant

Ferro hull

Timber beams

Plywood deck

Ferro hull

Square metal tube laminated in

Ferro hull

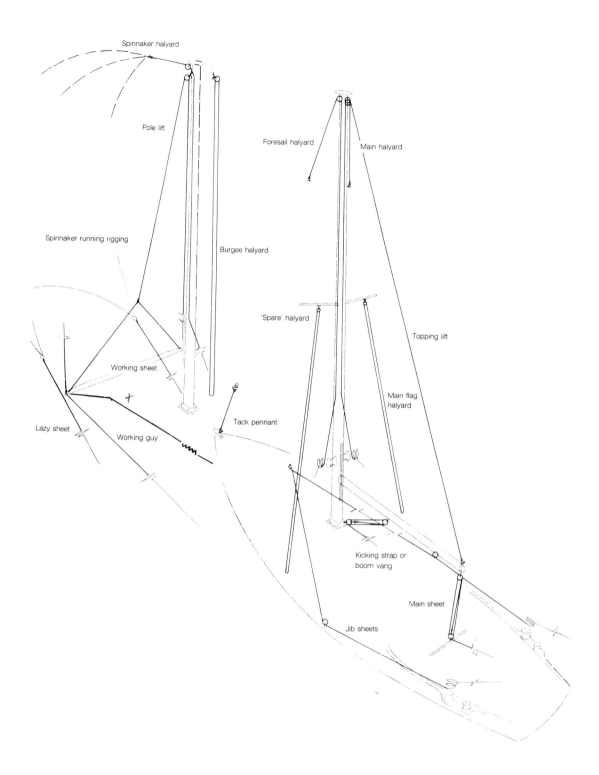

Spinnaker halyard

Pole lift

Spinnaker running rigging

Working sheet

Lazy sheet

Working guy

Burgee halyard

Tack pennant

Foresail halyard

Main halyard

'Spare' halyard

Topping lift

Main flag halyard

Kicking strap or boom vang

Main sheet

Jib sheets

Running Rigging

THE MAIN INTERNALS

Now at last the stage that most builders of home completion craft usually consider the point at which matters are really getting underway — fitting some bulkheads.

Well . . . just a minute, not yet!

INTERNAL DATUM POINT

It is normal to work from one internal datum point for all measurements. This is often the anchor or chain locker bulkhead which must be very carefully fitted in the correct position. Prior to locating any other bulkheads, mark on the hull interior, with a chinograph pencil, the various major bulkhead positions measured from the chosen datum point (Illus. 31). Check that the layout of the forecabin, galley, toilet compartment, main cabin, quarter berth, as well as the berth lengths, all appear satisfactory. Builders of Inland Waterways craft may measure from either or both of the main cabin/cockpit bulkhead and the forward cabin bulkhead (Illus. 32).

Do not forget:-

1. To allow for the bulkhead thickness when extending the measurements from the face of the datum point.
2. That a toilet compartment minimum width should be about 0.75m (2'6"), but 0.9m (3') is preferable.
3. That the forecabin berths can allow for crossover of the toes and here a minimum length of about 1.75m (5'9") is acceptable.
4. That a satisfactory galley length is 0.9m (3ft) plus.
5. That main berths should not be less than 1.83 (6ft) long, but 2m (6'6") is preferable.
6. Shoulder to hips require 0.53m (1'9") and foot clearance 0.33m (1'1").
7. The wasting of a berth from shoulder/hips to foot clearance can take place over about the last 0.76m (2'6")
8. To check the craft is level relative to its water-line otherwise the bulkheads will be out of square.
9. To allow comfortable, full standing headroom requires 6'2".
10. The minimum:-
    Door width is   0.47m (1'6½")

Seat height above any sole* is 0.46m (1'6")
Minimum seat width is 0.53m (1'9")
Minimum single berth width is 0.61m (2'0")
Minimum double berth width is 1.07m (3'6")
'Small of back' height when
seated is 0.23m (9")
Shoulder height when seated is 0.58m (1'11")
Eye height above seat is 0.74m (2'5")
Eye height standing is 1.65m (5'5")
Headroom when seated is 0.97m (3'2")
Tiller hand height is 0.74m (2'5")
Back to 'ball' of extended foot
when seated is 1.08m (3'6"'
NOTE: These measurements are average indicatio

BULKHEAD TEMPLATES

The main bulkheads of a craft of between 8m and 8.5m (26-28ft) are the: (a) chain locker, (b) forecabin and (c) main cabin forward bulkheads (Illus. 31).

The fore and main cabin bulkheads often form the toilet compartment to one side and a hanging locker on the other side. On a yacht they are usually positioned so that one of them is conveniently in the way of, and forms part of,the framework necessary to support the deck stepped mast. Motorboats are not constricted by the necessity to prop up any spars, which many would regard as a jolly good thing, and are thus not constrained by the 'unreasonable' demands that sail power imposes.

Galley, quarter berth and engine compartment divisions normally make up the major sub-bulkheads.

The main bulkheads, usually of 18mm (¾") ply, constitute a major expense and it is important to obtain the maximum amount of bulkhead from the minimum amount of 2440mm x 1220mm (8' x 4' or 32sqft) sheets. Note that 3050mm x 1525mm (10' x 5') panels are also available and these larger boards may help minimise the amount of waste. This concentration on keeping off-cuts to a minimum requires accurate bulkhead patterns or templates so that the plywood sheets can be marked off to obtain the most economical cutting procedure. The manufacturers of the craft may allow templates to be taken from their own patterns, if they are in the business of finishing the particular boat, but Murphy's Law says not, or perhaps that an alternative layout is required.

Although it may at first sight appear a waste of time and money, it is imperative to obtain accurate templates if costly materials are to be used to the best advantage.

*A good friend who originally read one of the innumerable draft copies of a forerunner to this book, pointed out that I had not detailed 'cushion squash'. Obviously when calculating seat heights, the cushion thickness must be taken into account as must the average bodyweight compression of the cushion — thus the dear boy's 'cushion squash factor'.

There are three methods, or a mixture of each, suitable for the amateur boatbuilder. Incidentally, use hardboard or lining ply to make the templates.

METHODS OF TEMPLATING (Illus. 33a, b & c):

Method 1.
Firmly fix in position a vertical upright, of say 50mm x

Illustration 31   Major Bulkhead Positions

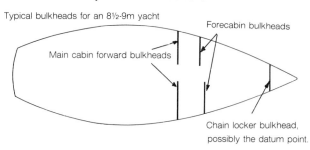

Typical bulkheads for an 8½-9m yacht

Also required will be another 2 sheets of 18mm (¾") faced plywood

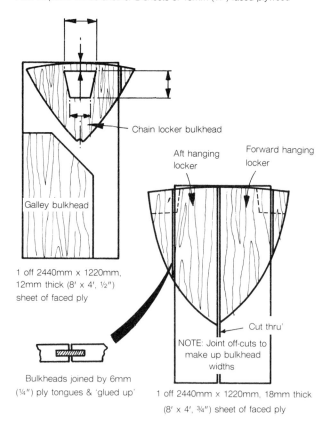

1 off 2440mm x 1220mm, 12mm thick (8' x 4', ½") sheet of faced ply

Bulkheads joined by 6mm (¼") ply tongues & 'glued up'

1 off 2440mm x 1220mm, 18mm thick (8' x 4', ¾") sheet of faced ply

NOTE: Joint off-cuts to make up bulkhead widths

25mm (2" x 1") whitewood, outboard of the eventual inside edge of the bulkhead and mark off in millimetres (or inches). Place a large set square against the upright. Rest on top of the horizontal of the square a rigid wooden rule and then record the horizontal lengths at various vertical heights. The turn of the bilge, due to

Illustration 32   .... and Inland Waterway Datum Points

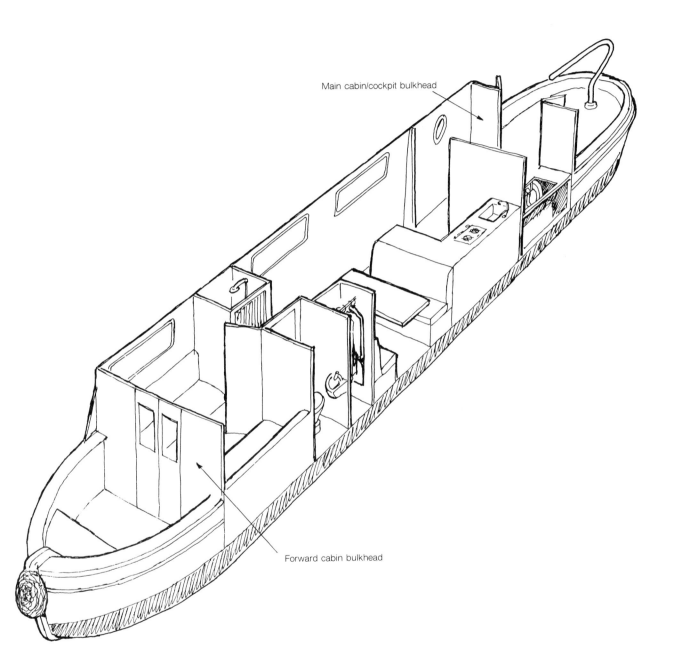

Main cabin/cockpit bulkhead

Forward cabin bulkhead

the usually fast decrease in width for a very small decrease in height, requires a horizontal measure to be fixed to the hull and the vertical upright at the greatest width, again marked off in millimetres. Using a plumb bob, record the heights at various horizontal widths. Mark on the template the vertical and horizontals, which determines the maximum dimensions, and the various recorded distances, adding up to 13mm (½″) to allow for final fitting. Cut out the resultant outline with a jigsaw and try for size.

The point will be covered in this chapter, but for the moment take note that the bulkhead need not, in fact should not, be an exact fit and gaps or clearance of between 3mm (⅛″) and 6mm (¼″) around the sides of the mouldings are acceptable. The resultant template will touch in places and have gaps in others.* Don't worry, all will be made plain.

Method 2. Lightly wedge at least two spaced battens near to the vertical and two to three spaced horizontally or near to the horizontal. To these frames, pieces of thin ply or hardboard are fixed once they have been individually fitted to the particular portion of the shell. To obtain the correct shape on the individual template pieces, the method used is very much the same as for marking out or scribing in a shaped vinyl floor covering. Using a block of wood shaped to an arrow point, and with a hole at about 25mm (1″) centre to take a pencil, keep the pointer vertical to the hull side, and scribe round the interior of the hull. The resultant pencil line describes accurately the shape and outline on to the relevant template. Cut out final fit to the interior and fasten to the battens in the correct position. If this is executed all the way around the inside of the hull and deck in the way of the intended bulkhead, a complete skeleton template is created. Prior to removing the template, check that the frame battens are secure and, if necessary, screw a diagonal batten on each side.

Lastly-

Method 3. Starting with a sheet of template material nudged up against the cabin side, roughly cut it away until the furthest portion of the hull is reached. By making a scribing block, as used in Method 2 but with the pencil hole at about 50mm (2″) centre, the internal shape of the shell can be accurately marked on the template.

Do not leave too much bulkhead to be finally planed from the vertical inboard face as these edges should be trimmed with a hardboard capping, at a later stage.

---

* The above applies equally to GRP, steel, ferrocement and aluminium shells. In the case of plywood and timber hull and decks, where the internal finish will be both smooth and gently contoured, the bulkhead fit to the internal shape of the shell should be as snug as is possible.

Illustration 33   Making Bulkhead Templates

33a   Method 1

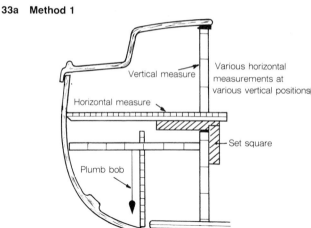

Various height measurements at various horizontal distances

33b   Method 2

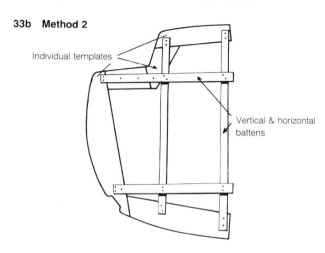

33c   Method 3

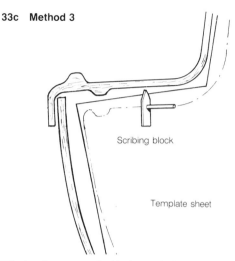

Difficult as it may seem the block must be kept vertical or the bulkhead will be undersize on the hull edge

CHAIN LOCKER BULKHEAD

To obtain the most economical use of plywood for the chain locker bulkhead, it may be necessary to joint two pieces of ply. There is no magic in this. The join should be in the vertical plane and it may be best to add two 'cheeks' to a central piece of ply, more especially if a chain locker access hatch is to be fitted in the bulkhead. To join the 'cheeks' use a power-saw to cut a slot in the ply edge, do the same to the cheek pieces and plane down a hardwood slat or ply tongue to fit the slot and glue (Illus. 34).

STRINGERS & BEARERS

Before attaching the bulkheads, any hull stiffening stipulated on the drawings must be fitted. Quite often the designer details longitudinal stringers and hull mounted bearers for the bunk tops and shelves. Even if they are not itemised they should be fitted but, prior to being able to secure them in position, the height of the cabin sole must be determined, so that the bunk height can be set and thus the position of the berth and shelf stringers. It is to be hoped that the craft's drawings portray the various positions!

Of course there are other pads, beams and blocks to be fitted to the inside of the shell to aid the fixing of various shelves and units. As any longitudinal stringers are best tied into the main and sub-bulkheads, by cutting the bulkheads around the glassed in member, their fitting must be taken into account at this stage.

Under no circumstances must any item be screwed directly into the shell.

Illustration 34   Cheeks

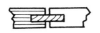

6mm (¼") hardwood slat
or plywood tongue
prior to 'gluing up'

For stringers, bearers and blocks use rough sawn 50mm x 25mm (2" x 1") battens with the edges planed off. If necessary coffin cut to persuade them round the curve of the hull, for instance in the way of the bows. Bed the timbers on resin putty and laminate in position with a minimum of 3 layers of 450g/m² (1½oz) CSM. The hull stringers may well have to be wedged in position while the resin putty sets. A couple of athwart planks, 'G' cramped together, help sort this out (Illus. 35). Feather the laminates against the shell sides because they may well show up and at some stage will have to be covered or masked. Rough sawn timber is used because it gives a better bond with the laminate and the

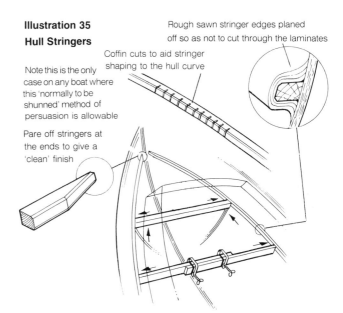

Illustration 35
Hull Stringers

Rough sawn stringer edges planed off so as not to cut through the laminates

Coffin cuts to aid stringer shaping to the hull curve

Note this is the only case on any boat where this 'normally to be shunned' method of persuasion is allowable

Pare off stringers at the ends to give a 'clean' finish

Employ wedges or athwartship planks to hold stringers in position whilst evenly spaced 'bandages' of laminate are applied. This fixes the stringers prior to 'glassing in' over the whole length

sharp edges are removed so they don't knife through the laminates as they are stippled down.

It may be remembered that earlier I referred to the fact that a snug or tight bulkhead fit to the shell is not required — in fact it is detrimental. The reason is that even if a bulkhead could be made a perfect fit to the interior of the comparatively bumpy inside of a GRP shell, which is unlikely, it is undesirable as the 'raw' bulkhead bearing on the inside of the hull and deck is bound to form 'hard' spots. In practice these become visible, especially after unflagging use of a craft. More worryingly stress points may well occur. Fortunately, to a large extent, bedding any wooden member on resin putty does away with both the hard spots and stress points. It not only allows the joint to be mechanically perfect but acts as a glue, thus enabling them to be laminated in position without untoward movement, and the use of seven or so assorted helpers.

Don't forget that whatever is being laminated to the interior of a GRP craft, or ferrocement shell for that matter, the area must be roughed up and then cleaned with acetone to ensure a satisfactory bond.

At last! Now to fit the bulkheads. Well, not just yet!

BULKHEAD MATERIALS

Cost is always a major consideration and nowhere more so than when choosing the material from which to make the bulkheads. Experience has proved the most cost effective is plywood. Suitable plywoods are, not surprisingly, marine grade, usually stamped '1088', and the less expensive WBP, which stands for waterproof and boilproof. The problem with the choice is that the

Illustration 36   Routing Out the Bulkhead Edges

The laminating rebate must be up to 5mm ($\frac{3}{16}$″) deep (on an 18mm bulkhead) & 76mm (3″) wide routed out parallel to the outer shell edge

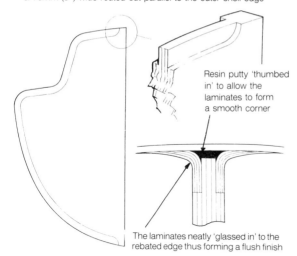

Resin putty 'thumbed in' to allow the laminates to form a smooth corner

The laminates neatly 'glassed in' to the rebated edge thus forming a flush finish

'average 1088' plywood is not much better than a well manufactured WBP board. Suffice to say most manufacturers of seagoing craft use WBP ply for main and sub-bulkheads, where the edges are laminated in position, and marine ply for cabin, toilet compartment and hanging locker soles as well as external uses. DO NOT USE External grade ply, blockboard or chipboard, for the decision will probably be regretted, bearing in mind the (imprecise) truism 'fix in haste, repent at leisure!'. To be more precise, these latter materials cannot cope with damp conditions, let alone a positively wet environment and literally explode if they get a good soaking. Need I say more?

When considering thickness, major bulkheads should be cut from at least 18mm (¾″) whilst sub-bulkheads may be fabricated from 12mm (½″) ply. For ease of finishing off, plywood faces that 'show' can be purchased with a decorative veneer face.

If the plywood bulkheads were laminated into the GRP shell without any further preparatory work, the bond between the plywood and the overlaid laminate might well be of a poor quality, due to the shiny and, sometimes oily, finish of the plywood. Furthermore, this join is very much 'in the eye'. To ensure a good bond and a neat finish it is preferable that the edges of the bulkheads to be laminated are routed out for a depth of approximately 5mm (3/16″) and a width up to 76mm (3″), parallel to the outline of the shell (Illus. 36). This gives the laminate a rougher surface to which to adhere and allows the completed laminates to finish almost flush with the bulkhead surface, thus aiding the neat fitting of cover strips later on in the building process.

Where the reverse side of a bulkhead is to be the face of a hanging locker or toilet compartment, it is general practice to use either a plywood veneered on both sides

or a board with one veneered face and the other covered in a plastic laminate balancer. Gluing a 'balancer' in position is best carried out prior to fitting a bulkhead. To attach a 'balancer', lay the ply down on trestles in a horizontal plane and use the correct impact adhesive, following the instructions to the letter. Do resist the temptation to put the two faces in contact before the stipulated time, and place a number of weights on the plastic laminate during the setting time in order to stop the surface bubbling (Illus. 37).

Illustration 37   Gluing On A Balancer

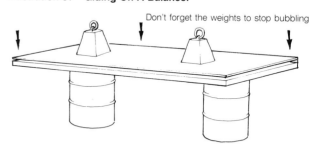

Don't forget the weights to stop bubbling

FIXING & SQUARING UP

Now, at last, offer the bulkhead to its 'in hull position' and bed on resin putty. Prior to laminating in, mask up the plywood faces with strong brown paper and masking tape to save resin runs spoiling the finish of the bulkhead face (Illus. 38).

Illustration 38   Masking Up the Bulkheads

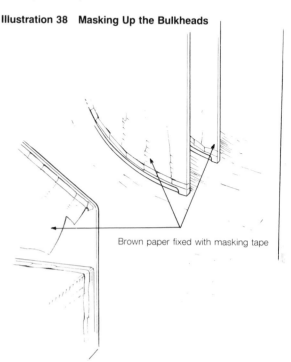

Brown paper fixed with masking tape

To aid holding the bulkheads in position, temporarily drive shallow wedges between the shell and the bulkhead and 'G' cramp butt straps to the bulkheads (Illus. 39). The butt straps may, if necessary, be replaced by temporary athwartship beams tapped downwards into position, the ends jamming into the narrowing hull shape, and laminated in for the time necessary to complete the bulkhead bonding.

Ensure all bulkheads are vertical, with a builder's level and plumb bob, as well as being at right angles to the centre line of the craft. Use either a large set square, as employed for marking out the corners of say a tennis court, or by measurement applying 'Pythagoras'. He, a citizen of Samos island, proposed that the square on the hypotenuse of a right angle triangle is equal to the sum of the squares of the other two sides and to date this has not been disputed (Illus. 40)!

Illustration 39   Cramping A Bulkhead In Position

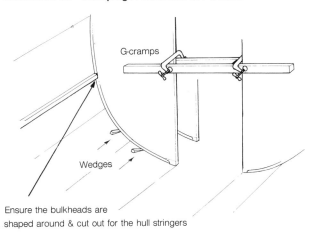

Ensure the bulkheads are shaped around & cut out for the hull stringers

All bulkheads must be laminated on both sides with 4 layers of 450gms/m² (1½oz) or 3 x 600gms/m² (2oz) but prior to glassing in, 'thumb' resin putty into the join to give a rounded surface on which to stipple the laminates (*See* Illus. 36). Do not forget to feather off the laminates against the shell and to trim the edges on the bulkhead side with a sharp knife whilst the laminates are still just wet or rubbery. Too soon, and it drags the laminates about. Too late, and my goodness it is a tough job. One way to neaten cured laminations is to include a grindette in the boat building kit. This powerful electric tool takes a 10cm (4") sanding disc and can be used to grind down excess laminate as well as unsightly bumps.

The laminated hull stringers and bulkheads effectively become an integral part of the shell and are usually relied upon by the designer and manufacturer to give the necessary stiffening to the monocoque construction of a GRP hull and deck.

Two other structural members, the cabin sole bearers and the mast beam frames, should now be laminated in position, thus completing the internal strengthening and fitting of the major or primary internal members.

CABIN SOLE BEARERS

The athwartship cabin sole bearers can be cut from softwood and should be a minimum of 38mm (1½") thick. Those fitted to either side of the main bulkheads must be screwed or thru' bolted to them, prior to laminating in position, thus not only forming a fixing for the edges of the various cabin soles (or floorboards) but giving the bulkhead as heavy and wide a 'marriage' to

Illustration 40   Pythagoras and Squaring Up

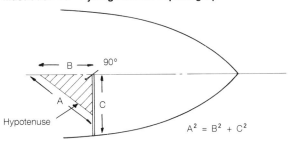

$$A^2 = B^2 + C^2$$

So if B = 50cms & C = 70cms then 50 x 50 + 70 x 70 = A. Thus A = 86cms give or take a millimetre!

the hull as possible. Do not reduce the number of bearers, it only results in an undulating sole. Dry fit and then bed them on resin putty, after which, laminate in position with up to four well overlapped layers of mat, remembering to leave the limber (drainage) holes unobstructed. Line the limber holes with halved cardboard tubes, cutting them off flush when trimming the feathery edges of the laminate (Illus. 41).

In the days of timber ships a chain was threaded through the limber holes, fixed loosely at either end, and when the chain was joggled any rubbish clogging the waterways was dislodged — clever these Chinese!

At this stage consider, if fitting a hull mounted bilge pump, where it will be located.

MAST BEAM FRAMES

Assuming the vessel is a yacht and the mast is deck stepped, the other main structural item is an athwartship, internal deckhead mast beam frame. It may well have to be laminated to the required shape, if a suitable 'tree' is not available, which fortunately results in a stronger and more economical article than cutting one out of a solid piece timber. The finished beam for a 8.5m (28ft), high aspect rigged yacht, should measure approximately 635mm x 760mm (2½" x 3"). The individual timber laminates may be hardwood or plywood of between 8mm & 9mm ($\frac{5}{16}$" & ⅜") thickness.

Illustration 41   Cabin Sole Bearers

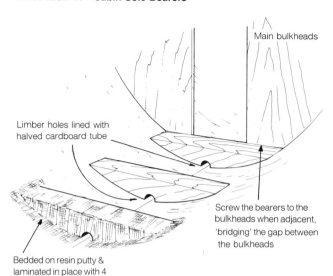

Main bulkheads

Limber holes lined with
halved cardboard tube

Screw the bearers to the
bulkheads when adjacent,
'bridging' the gap between
the bulkheads

Bedded on resin putty &
laminated in place with 4
layers of 450g/m^2 (1½ oz) mat

Use a convenient board for the jig or former with the deckhead shape transferred and wooden chocks or pegs describing the outline of the required beam. The strips of timber or plywood are then slipped into the jig, pre-glued with a resorcinol formaldehyde adhesive and wedged firmly into position. Wipe off excess glue and leave to set. Do not stir. To aid releasing the beam from the board when it is completed, brown paper the face of the jig or make up the beam on thin timber battens (Illus. 42).

Laminating the completed beam in position would probably result in an untidy finish. It is preferable to bed it on resin putty to the deckhead and glue and bolt the beam through the main bulkheads. Where possible ensure that the beam extends to the cabin sides. An added stiffening and strengthening is provided by fitting

Illustration 42   Beam Lamination

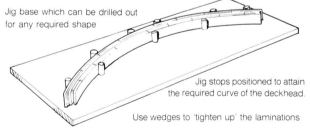

Jig base which can be drilled out
for any required shape

Jig stops positioned to attain
the required curve of the deckhead.

Use wedges to 'tighten up' the laminations

vertical jambs, either side of the inboard edge of the main bulkheads, from the underside of the deckhead mounted beam down to cabin sole bearers, if possible, or to plywood plates glassed to the hull. These plates are important as a 50mm x 50mm (2″ x 2″) jamb acts as a punch if mounted directly on to the inside of the hull. The ideal arrangement is to form a complete framework

in the area of both the hull and deckhead with not only an athwartship beam but fore and aft frames and sole bearers (Illus. 43 & 44).

These suggestions ensure that the main bulkheads have sole bearers screwed and laminated to their hull end, a mast beam attached to the top or deckhead as well as mast beam jambs either side of the bulkhead passageway. By fixing in position fore and aft sole and deckhead beams, the whole creates a box shaped framework in the way of the mast loading.

Illustration 43   Mast Deckhead Beams

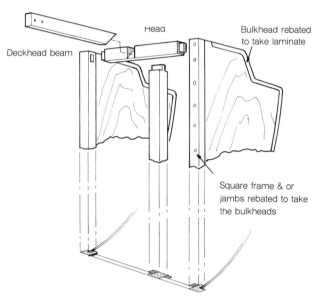

Head

Bulkhead rebated
to take laminate

Deckhead beam

Square frame & or
jambs rebated to take
the bulkheads

Frames & heads stub morticed tenoned but beware of cutting away too much timber!

Illustration 44   . . . and the Framework

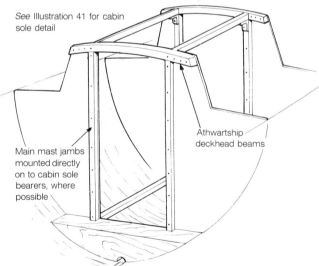

See Illustration 41 for cabin
sole detail

Main mast jambs
mounted directly
on to cabin sole
bearers, where
possible

Athwartship
deckhead beams

Fore & aft heads & sole bearers bolted & glued to the 'return' bulkheads. Support the head beams with knees

If the main bulkheads cannot be fiddled into position almost directly beneath the mast heel, then a tube with welded flanges, top and bottom, should be fitted *in situ*. The pillar tube may be of stainless steel up to about 38mm (1½") diameter. In excess of that diameter and it is best to use steel and have it sheradised — a shiny, metal peened finish. Do not forget to mount the pillar flanges on hull and deckhead plates and that an unsupported tube's resistance to compression halves if it deflects overmuch — so support the tube where possible, by tying it into a, hopefully, fairly adjacent bulkhead (Illus. 45).

STEEL, FERROCEMENT & ALUMINIUM CRAFT

For essential differences in fitting the 'Main Internals' refer to Chapter Three.

Illustration 45   Mast Support Tubes

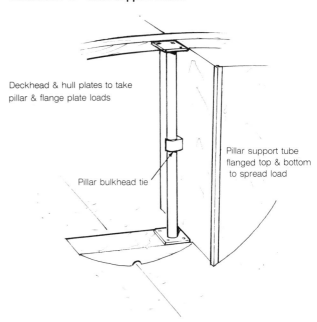

Deckhead & hull plates to take pillar & flange plate loads

Pillar support tube flanged top & bottom to spread load

Pillar bulkhead tie

Small craft dinette berth layout

A galley unit made up of GRP internal mouldings with a two part sink to the left (one of the pumps is the sea water supply) & cold storage locker to the right of the cooker.

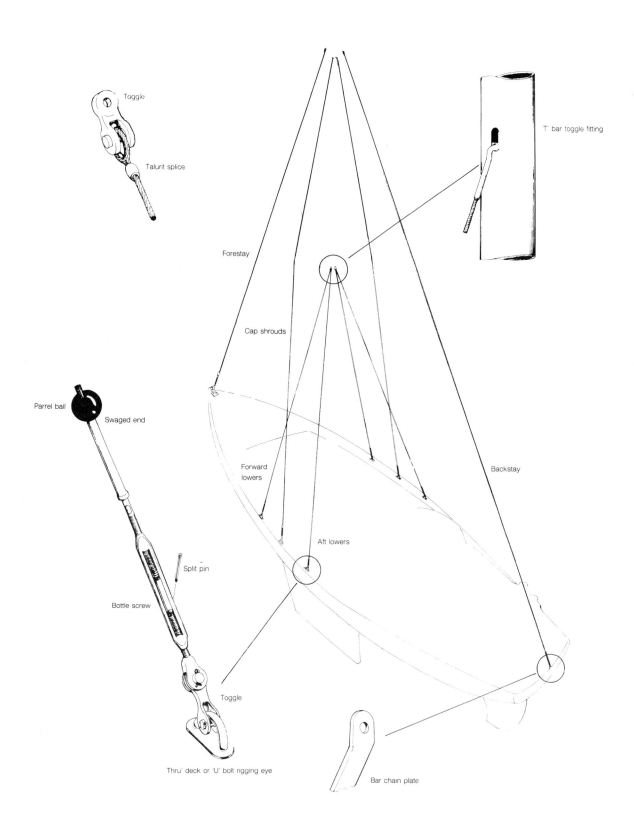

Toggle

Talurit splice

'T' bar toggle fitting

Forestay

Cap shrouds

Parrel ball

Swaged end

Forward lowers

Backstay

Split pin

Bottle screw

Aft lowers

Toggle

Thru' deck or 'U' bolt rigging eye

Bar chain plate

Standing Rigging

FRESH OR INLAND WATERWAY CRAFT

Due to differing requirements and elements, craft built for the Inland Waterways are entitled to separate treatment. The methods of building detailed elsewhere in the book are based on standards and requirements enforced by the sometimes awesomely destructive power of the sea. It is accepted that it is hardly likely that a 9m (30ft) narrow boat, or for that matter a Thames or a Broads cabin cruiser, will be bodily lifted up and slammed down on its side in house high, rolling waves. It is also accepted that it is no more likely that a seagoing craft is liable to encounter the hazard of its propeller becoming entangled with a submerged supermarket trolley cunningly positioned in an unavoidable bridge hole. These differing, disparate prerequisites are, quite rightly, met by different solutions resulting in quite diversely shaped and constructed boats.

Assuming the shell is of an adequate construction, vessels designed for the inland waters require less emphasis to be placed on the role of bulkheads, hull stringers and berth units forming fully integrated, unitary construction with the hull and deck. Conversely, more attention must be paid to, say, external protection to contend with lock walls and towpath coping stones. Heavy gunwales, bow timber snubbers, stern quarter cladding and hull mid section rubbing bands are all methods used to protect the shell. These claddings must be adequately fastened and the use of wood or self tapping screws is to be decried. Properly thru' bolted fastenings with adequate backing pads should be fitted (Illus. 46).

Moreover, where a 'seakindly' shape is not paramount, and less, if any, emphasis has to be placed on ballast ratios and righting moments, greater accent can be placed on internal dimensions, including adequate headroom. The chines may be squared up, resulting in improved storage space beneath berth units and behind the galley fascia, roomy toilet compartments in which the units do not have to climb the hull side, and hanging lockers that can comfortably accommodate dresses and suits without their becoming creased and crushed. Accommodation is more easily planned, as there are no deck mounted mast loadings to consider with the resultant necessity for strategically positioned bulkheads.

GRP shells, which dominate river and Broads craft, still retain a 'boat shape' but steel rules the canal system where naturally, and sensibly, the outlines emulate those of their worthy predecessors, the working boats, being straight sided and square bottomed.

Debatedly, standards of construction can be varied. (Dare I use the word reduced?) An example of this is best illustrated in connection with the bulkheads. Whereas the detail to date has insisted on all bulkheads being good quality plywood of sufficient thickness,

Illustration 46   Cladding on an Inland Waterway Boat

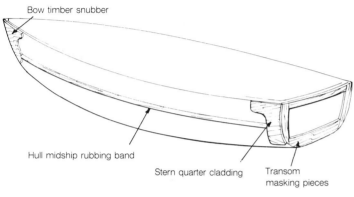

Bow timber snubber

Hull midship rubbing band

Stern quarter cladding

Transom masking pieces

Illustration 47   Fresh water Craft Bulkheads

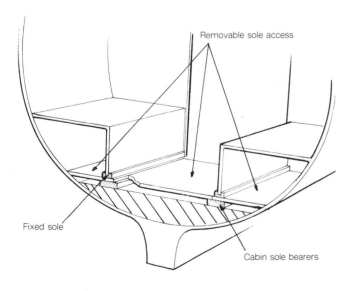

Removable sole access

Fixed sole

Cabin sole bearers

'Grounds' rebated to effectively locate & seal the bulkhead edges mounted on the fixed portion of the cabin sole

routed out around the edges to facilitate laminating in, bedded on resin putty and tied into longitudinal stringers, inland waterway craft may be fitted with poorer quality plywood, a size down, or even faced chipboards as long as the edges are well sealed. (I write 'may' but cannot wholeheartedly advocate these lessening of standards). Moreover, the method of internal fitting out can be varied by first laying down the cabin sole right across the internal area of the craft and 'bulkheading' down to it, rather than to the shell (Illus. 47 & *See* Illus. 18). Whilst this squared up cabin sole makes fitting out very much easier, do not fall into the trap of leaving the sole in one piece. It will then be impossible to lift sections in the event of requiring to gain access to the hull. Nothing like having to remove all the internal units to take a peek at a teeny-weeny hull leak!

Builders of canal craft are even more fortunate in that the square sided hulls and the relatively kindly environment allows suitable, 'bought in' cupboard and galley units to be fitted. Windows need not be as substantial as those fitted to seagoing craft and thus louvred units can be deployed, which go a long way to solving cabin ventilation problems (Illus. 48a). Again, although I am not an advocate of the practice, perspex or glass can be fitted into rubber surrounds fixed into window cut-outs (Illus. 48b).

The sophistication of the domestic equipment and fittings may be greatly increased. It is to be admitted that these refinements are energy consuming but, at the worst, a flat battery adjacent to Goring Lock towpath is one thing, whilst the same situation approaching Alderney Race with adverse wind and tide conditions and the need for the engine to start quickly, very quickly, is another ball game altogether!

Whilst discussing matters domestic, there is a school of thought that favours fitting calorifiers for heating domestic water. Briefly, a calorifier utilises the exhaust gases or engine cooling water to heat the water. This is achieved by either jacketing the exhaust pipe in a cylinder through which domestic water circulates or by passing the hot engine cooling water through a domestic water tank in a series of coils. I am not a champion of these systems as the engine must be run for a sufficient time, daily, to allow the water to be heated. I still prefer the use of a bottled gas 'powered' water heater, more especially now that some of the equipment available is so excellent and reliable (*See* Chapter Fourteen).

This wider freedom of choice of fitting out is balanced by the wide ranging regulations appertaining to all aspects of a cruiser and its equipment. The Thames River Authorities, amongst other Waterway Boards, have enforced strict standards for a number of years covering engine, fuel and gas installations, as well as effluent and waste disposal. Once upon a time, anything went on the canal system but the regulations insisted upon by the British Waterways Board are now probably

Illustration 48   Inland Waterway Windows

48a   Louvred windows   or   Hopper windows

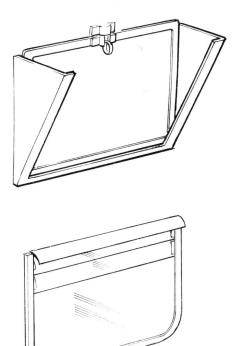

48b   Fixed glass or perspex windows

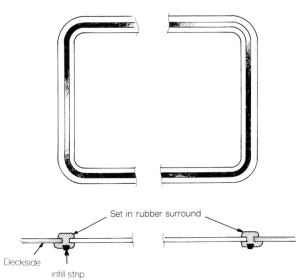

Set in rubber surround

Deckside

infill strip

the most rigorous of all the inland water regulatory bodies. I have passingly referred to some of the requirements but do not apologise for reproducing a sample of the BWB standards, at the end of the chapter.

Outboard motors are very popular for propelling craft up to about 7½-8m (25-26ft) in length. Installation is much easier as the outboard motor is a self-contained unit designed to be removed from the craft, when necessary. Instead of fixed engine beds, the boat is (or should be) fitted with an adequate self-draining outboard well, so designed as not to allow water to slop into the cockpit (Illus. 49). But before purchasing an engine, do establish whether the craft's transom is designed for a short or long shaft motor.

Inboard engine installations and their associated gear are substantially the same as for their seagoing cousins. The most marked difference may be the 'plumbing' of the engine cooling system, assuming of course, that the power unit is water cooled! They are usually closed circuit, often routed via pipes or tubes (keel cooling) laid alongside the keel and through which the water is pumped, prior to being led back to the engine (Illus. 50a).

Illustration 49   Outboard Motor Wells

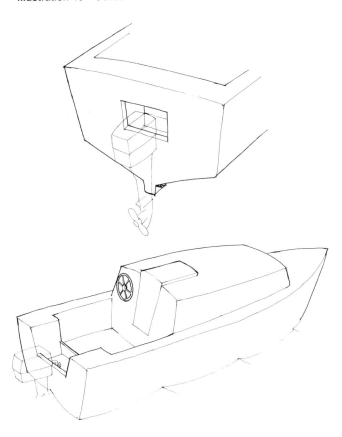

Illustration 50 Keel Cooling and Swim Tanks

50a Keel cooling

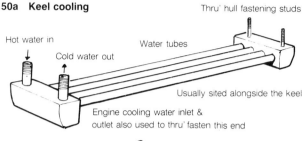

Thru' hull fastening studs

Hot water in

Cold water out

Water tubes

Usually sited alongside the keel

Engine cooling water inlet &
outlet also used to thru' fasten this end

50b Swim tank

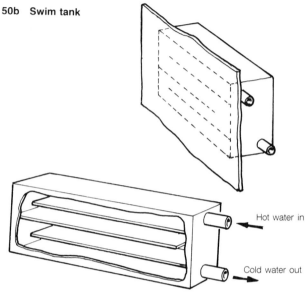

Hot water in

Cold water out

Only practical in conjunction with a steel craft where the hull side of the tank
can be welded directly to the hull

Note for both systems the engine manufacturer must be contacted to advise
on the relevant specification required for this or that engine horsepower

Illustration 51 Weed Traps

A hatch at least gives hand & arm access to the externals

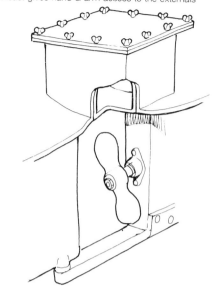

An inspection/weed hatch or an outboard motor trunking & plug

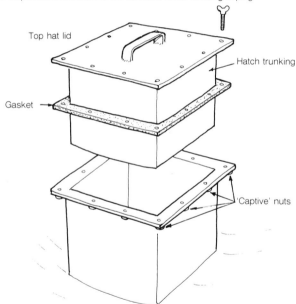

Top hat lid

Hatch trunking

Gasket

'Captive' nuts

The trunking infill is to stop cavitation & turbulence that could occur where the
trunking is not 'filled'. The gasket & holding down nuts & bolts must be in good
condition

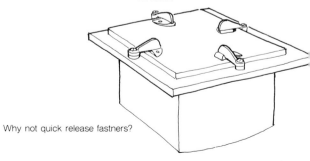

Why not quick release fastners?

The other increasingly popular option is a swim tank
welded against the hull, beneath the water-line. The
water is pumped around the tank along a series of water
courses (similar to a penny slot machine) in order to
increase the length and time that the coolant benefits
from the interface with the hull side and thus the chilling
effect of the surrounding water (Illus. 50b).

Weed traps are a useful and necessary fitment to canal
craft in order to give easy and constant access to the
outboard gland, propeller and rudder (Illus. 51).

Apart from traditional canal cruisers with their stern
mounted rudder and tiller (Illus. 52a), steering is usually
by dash/bulkhead mounted wheel, drum, wire and
pulleys (Illus. 52b) or wheel and cable (Illus. 52c).

In closing, the question of cost and the depth of an
owner's pocket, as always, influences the choice of
building materials. The temptation must be ever present
to penny-pinch on the price and thus the quality of, say,

A weed hatch (or mud box) might be considered as an engine water coolant draw off point

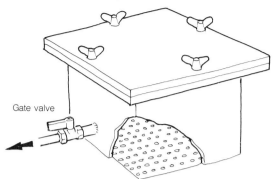

Gate valve

It is necessary to have a minimum of 25/30 x 9mm holes or 50/60 x 6mm drillings

Illustration 52   Steering Options

52a   Tiller Steering

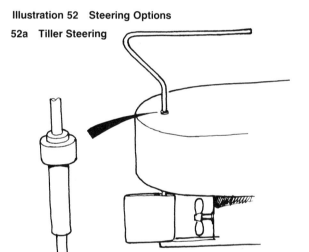

52b   Outboard Motor Steering Layout

Spring tensioners

Self-aligning pulleys

Wire & drum

The spring tensioners allow the cable length to alter as the wire is wound round the drum, without exerting undue strain on the pulleys

the plywood and fastenings. I can only reiterate that my personal opinion — bias do I hear? — is that no less than WBP (waterproof and boilproof) grade plywood should be used for main bulkheads; that the cabin soles should be marine grade ply and that all fastenings should be marine quality. I can hear the wails of derision but, to reinforce my advice, wander around any inland boatyard and view the sad, neglected, rotting vessels that were once the 'apple of someone's eye'. Take a good look at the number of occasions that poor quality plywood or chipboard has been used and has disintegrated and note the zinc plated screws or what is left of them! Just consider if all the time and money spent in completing any boat deserves a similar fate!

A SAMPLE OF BRITISH WATERWAYS BOARDS STANDARDS

(Illus. 53a, b & c & *See* Illus. 32).
Reprinted by kind permission of the British Waterways Board.
Please note: These are extracts relevant to this book's coverage, therefore the numbers are not sequential and are as listed in the original BWB publication, which is due for reissue in 1987/8, possibly subject to various sections being enforceable by local bye-laws.

CONSTRUCTION & EQUIPMENT

Life-saving Equipment
A4   At least one lifebuoy of British Standards Institution (BSI) or Department of Trade (DOT) approved pattern shall be stowed on each boat in a position readily accessible from the steering position.
A5   All cabin boats shall have means of escape of at least 0.2 square metres in area forward and aft in each cabin.

Equipment: General

A7 Boats which are to navigate river waterways or commercial waterways shall be provided with an anchor and anchor chain or anchor warp or both and proper means of securing the chain or warp on board, adequate to provide safe holding power when anchored on those waterways.

A9 At least three mooring positions shall be provided, one at the bow and one at each side of the stern. Fittings shall be cleats, bollards, samson posts or rings, strongly fitted and of appropriate size.

A10 A weed hatch, if fitted, shall have a cover at least 150mm above the normal laden water-line and shall be watertight when secured.

A11 A suitable bilge pump and/or bailer shall be carried in each boat.

A12 Handrails of adequate strength shall be fitted where applicable for the full length of all cabin tops.

A13 Every boat shall have ready for immediate use proper fenders of suitable material including a bow fender affixed in a position to prevent damage on impact with other vessels or structures and, in the case of boats fitted with a rudder which extends longitudinally aft of the hull, a stern fender secured to prevent the rudder being trapped between the mitres of lock gates.

A14 Powered boats shall be furnished with a suitable whistle or horn which can be operated from the steering position.
Note: A bell is not a suitable substitute.

A15 Every boat to be navigated between sunset and sunrise or in restricted visibility, shall have navigation lights installed to comply with the Merchant Shipping (Distress Signals & Prevention of Collision) Regulations 1983 so far as is practicable.
Note: Although the range of visibility and height of the lights required by this standard may be departed from because of the physical limitations of the navigation, their number and character must be adhered to.

A16 An adequate fixed white light showing a flat beam dead ahead to a beam on both sides shall be fitted for use when navigating through tunnels.

A17 Every opening in the hull of a boat above the normal water-line (including those used as intakes or outlets for air for engine cooling purposes) shall be so positioned that its lowest point is not less than 250mm above the normal laden water-line of the boat, unless such openings are securely connected to ducts or pipes which are watertight up to that level.

A18 Every opening in the hull of a boat below the normal water-line provided for use as an intake for water shall be fitted with an adequate valve or cock adjacent to it, so positioned as to be readily

52c   Cable Steering

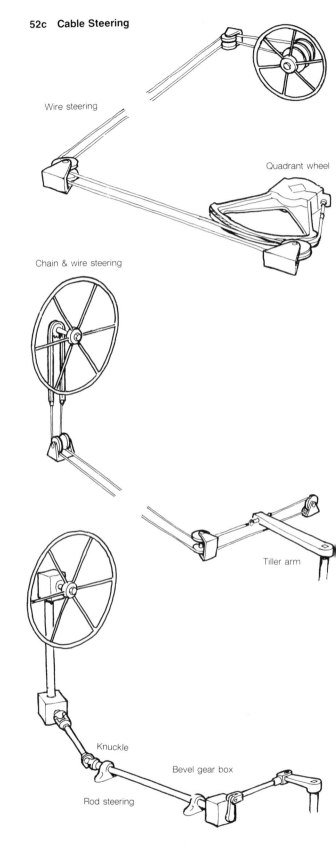

Wire steering

Quadrant wheel

Chain & wire steering

Tiller arm

Knuckle

Bevel gear box

Rod steering

Illustration 53   British Waterways Board Standards*

53a   External Equipment

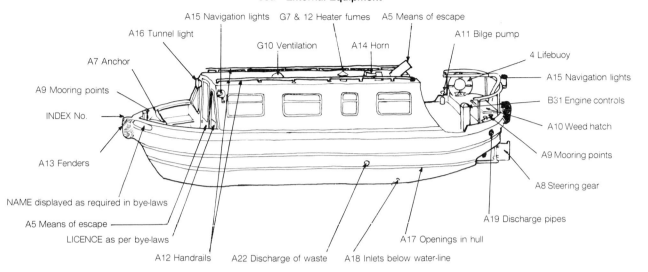

A15 Navigation lights
A16 Tunnel light
G7 & 12 Heater fumes
A5 Means of escape
G10 Ventilation
A14 Horn
A11 Bilge pump
A7 Anchor
4 Lifebuoy
A9 Mooring points
A15 Navigation lights
INDEX No.
B31 Engine controls
A10 Weed hatch
A13 Fenders
A9 Mooring points
A8 Steering gear
NAME displayed as required in bye-laws
A5 Means of escape
LICENCE as per bye-laws
A19 Discharge pipes
A17 Openings in hull
A12 Handrails
A22 Discharge of waste
A18 Inlets below water-line

* With acknowledgements to The British Waterways Board

53b   Sections B & C: Engines (inboard) & Electrical

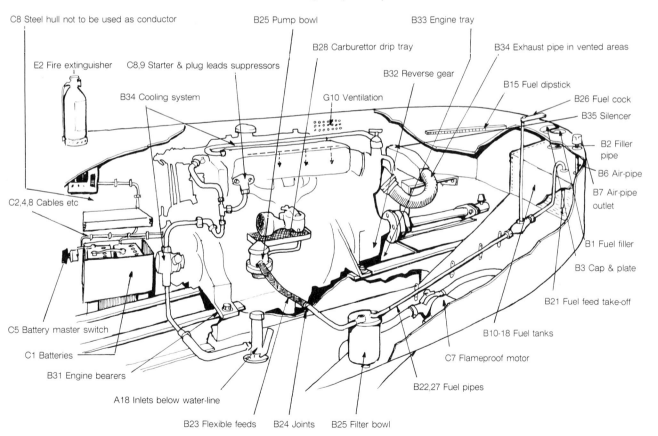

C8 Steel hull not to be used as conductor
B25 Pump bowl
B33 Engine tray
E2 Fire extinguisher
C8,9 Starter & plug leads suppressors
B28 Carburettor drip tray
B34 Exhaust pipe in vented areas
B32 Reverse gear
B34 Cooling system
B15 Fuel dipstick
G10 Ventilation
B26 Fuel cock
B35 Silencer
B2 Filler pipe
B6 Air-pipe
B7 Air-pipe outlet
C2,4,8 Cables etc
B1 Fuel filler
B3 Cap & plate
B21 Fuel feed take-off
C5 Battery master switch
B10-18 Fuel tanks
C1 Batteries
C7 Flameproof motor
B31 Engine bearers
B22,27 Fuel pipes
A18 Inlets below water-line
B23 Flexible feeds
B24 Joints
B25 Filter bowl

accessible for immediate use.

A19 Every pipe for overboard discharge installed in a boat shall be permanently connected to the hull so as to be watertight to a level 250mm above the normal laden water-line.

A23 Connections for fresh water filling, fuel filling and toilet pump-out shall be situated not less than 250mm apart and shall be marked with clearly visible, engraved, stamped or cast labels on the deck fittings or immediately beside them indicating the purpose of each connection.

Prevention of pollution

A22 No sanitary appliance capable of discharging polluting matter overboard shall be fitted in any boat. All waste from sanitary appliances other than from a sink, washbasin, bath or shower shall be contained aboard the boat either in an approved chemical system or in a properly constructed holding tank ventilated to the external air, to be discharged ashore.

ENGINES

The following standards apply to all boats fitted with inboard engines unless specifically exempted.

Fuel filling pipes

B1 Filling pipes shall be taken to deck level or so arranged as to ensure that any fuel overflowing will not be discharged into the bilge or other part of the boat.

B2 The filling pipe shall have an external diameter of at least 38mm and any flexible hose employed shall be of non-kinking material approved for the fuel used. A deck-fitting is to be either brazed, welded or fastened into the deck to make a watertight seal.

B3 Screwed or other gas-tight caps shall be located at the deck filling positions and an engraved, stamped or cast label indicating the type of fuel shall be located on the deck fittings or immediately beside them.
Note: Labels stating 'Fuel' shall not be used.

Fuel tank air pipes

B6 An air pipe shall be fitted at the end of each tank opposite to that at which the filling pipe enters the tank and/or at the highest point of the tank. The material used shall be non-kinking and approved for use with the fuel concerned. Each air pipe shall be of an internal diameter of not less than 12mm and in no case less than twice the internal diameter of the fuel feed pipe to the engine.

B7 The open end of each air pipe shall be situated at least 100mm above the top of the tank and in a position where no danger will be incurred from escaping fuel or vapour when the tank is being filled, and each opening shall be furnished with a wire gauze diaphragm flame trap of incorrodible material which can be readily removed for cleaning or renewal. The total area of the clear openings of the gauze shall not be less than the cross-sectional area required for the air pipe.

Fuel tanks

B10 Petrol tanks shall be made of stainless steel, mild steel (hot dip galvanised after making up), copper or brass. Interior painting is not allowed.

B11 Diesel fuel tanks shall be made of mild steel or glassfibre reinforced plastic to the requirements of the current British Standard Specification (BSS) No. 476 Parts 6 and 7.
Note: BSS476: Part 6 relates to a fire propagation test and BSS476: Part 7 relates to a surface spread of flame test.

B12 Materials shall be of adequate thickness for the capacity of the tank which shall be capable of withstanding an internal pressure of $0.25kg/cm^2$.

B13 All joints and seams of metal tanks shall be efficiently welded, brazed or close riveted.

B14 Fuel tanks shall be securely fixed on bearers (unless they form an integral part of the hull) and installed as far as is reasonably practicable from the engine. No petrol or paraffin tank of more than 2.5 litres shall be installed within 1 metre of any engine or heating appliance unless it is insulated and protected by an efficient baffle.

B15 Sight glass fuel gauges shall not be used. Dipsticks, when fitted, shall be calibrated and only be used via gas-tight fittings and must not be able to strike the bottom of the tank. Fuel level indicators, if fitted, shall be of a type which does not allow escape of fuel or vapour in the event of damage to the indicator.

B16 Tanks and all connections shall be readily accessible for inspection.

B17 Tanks shall be effectively bonded by low impedance metallic conductors to their deck filling connections, and in the case of a non-conducting deck or hull, tanks shall also be efficiently bonded to an earth point in direct electrical contact with the surrounding water, for the discharge of static electricity.

B18 Tanks may be emptied only by means of a suitable drain valve, arranged so that it cannot be left open inadvertently.

Fuel pipework: General

B21 The fuel supply shall be drawn through the top of the tank by means of an internal pipe extending to near the bottom of the tank. In the case only of gravity feed systems a feed from a cock or valve

53c Fire Precautions, Gas & Appliances

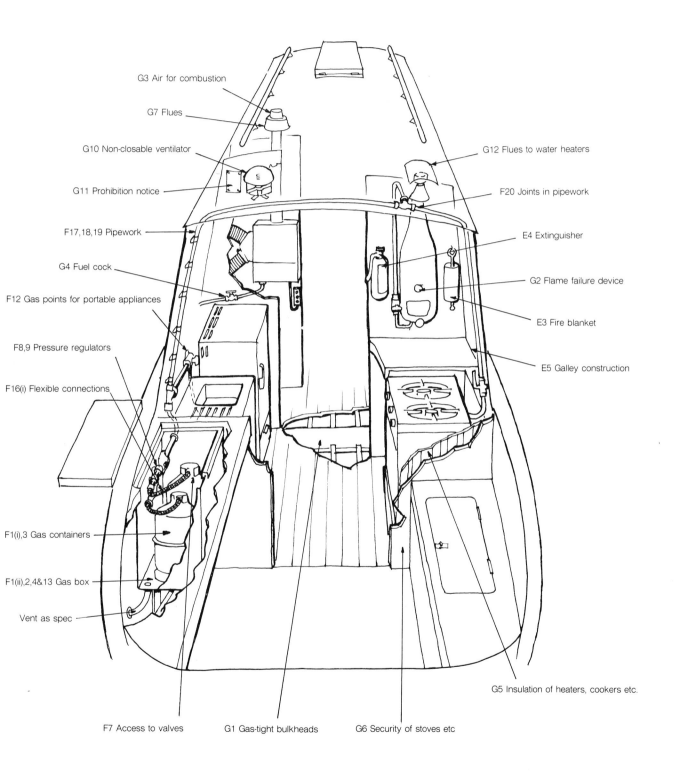

G3 Air for combustion

G7 Flues

G10 Non-closable ventilator

G11 Prohibition notice

F17,18,19 Pipework

G4 Fuel cock

F12 Gas points for portable appliances

F8,9 Pressure regulators

F16(i) Flexible connections

F1(i),3 Gas containers

F1(ii),2,4&13 Gas box

Vent as spec

G12 Flues to water heaters

F20 Joints in pipework

E4 Extinguisher

G2 Flame failure device

E3 Fire blanket

E5 Galley construction

G5 Insulation of heaters, cookers etc.

F7 Access to valves

G1 Gas-tight bulkheads

G6 Security of stoves etc

directly screwed in near the bottom of the tank will be permitted.

B22 All fuel feeds and pipes permanently charged with fuel shall be made of softened copper, stainless steel, aluminium alloy, or (for diesel installations only) mild steel of suitable size, fixed clear of exhaust systems and heating apparatus and adequately supported to minimise vibration and strain.

B23 Flexible tubing shall be used only in the engine compartment. It shall be of minimum practicable length, be reinforced and have an internal diameter of not more than half its external diameter; and shall have a fire-resisting quality similar to that specified in BSS 3212.

B24 All connections shall be made with efficient screwed compression, cone or brazed joints. Soft soldered joints shall not be used.

B25 Glass or plastic bowl filters shall not be used.

B26 A cock or valve shall be fitted in the fuel feed pipe as near as possible to the fuel tank in a position where it can be easily operated. If it is not visible the position shall be clearly marked. In all petrol engine installations where the steering position is remote from the fuel tank a second cock or means of operating the main cock on valve close to the tank shall be fitted immediately accessible from the steering position.

B27 Fuel pipes shall not be run in the bilge water area.

B28 Carburettors (other than of the downdraught type) shall be fitted so as to allow any overflow therefrom to drain into a spirit-tight metal drip-tray, the top of which shall be covered with copper or brass gauze of flame-resisting mesh soldered to the tray all round. The tray shall be removable or be fitted with a cock for emptying.

Engine Installation

B31 The engine shall be suitably installed and bolted to engine bearers designed to distribute the load. All controls shall be operable from the steering position.

B32 Every boat shall have effective means of reversing.

B33 An oil-tight tray made of metal shall be fitted between the engine bearers. It shall be longer than the combined length of the engine and reverse-reduction gearbox unit, and shall be constructed so as to prevent leakage of oil into any part of the boat. In the case of a metal or glassfibre hull, a tray is not required if structural members form an oil-tight box section constructed to meet the requirements set out above.

B34 The cylinders and exhaust system shall be effectively cooled. In the case of air-cooled engines or where water is not passed through the exhaust pipe the exhaust pipe shall be effectively lagged. Exhaust pipes shall not pass through unventilated compartments.

B35 Exhaust pipes shall be effectively suppressed by a silencer and no form of exhaust cut-out shall be used.

Electrical Installation

The following standards apply to all boats having electrical equipment installed.

C1 All batteries shall be securely installed so as to prevent movement and damage. All battery compartments shall be satisfactorily ventilated and provided with covers of insulating and non-corrosive material. No battery may be fitted beneath or adjacent to any petrol tank, cock, pipe or filter.

C2 Cables shall be of adequate current-carrying capacity and of approved construction and grade. They shall be insulated and sheathed so as to be impervious to attack by fuel or water. They shall be clipped at not more than 300mm intervals or run in suitable conduit.

C3 Main circuits shall be installed above bilge water level, and all except starter circuits shall be protected by circuit breakers or fuses of a design suitable for marine usage.

C4 All cables shall be installed as high as is practicable in the boats, and they shall be run clear of all sources of heat such as exhaust pipes. They shall not be run adjacent to fuel or gas pipes.

C5 A master battery switch capable of carrying the maximum current of the system (including starter circuits) shall be installed in an accessible position as close to the battery as possible. Electric bilge pumps, security alarms and fire pumps when fitted may have circuits which bypass the master switch but only if separately protected by fuses or circuit breakers.
Note: A battery isolating switch must not be used to open-circuit a running alternator except in an emergency when damage to the alternator could be acceptable.

C6 Main starter motor leads subject to high current shall have soldered or pressure crimped lugs. Sparking plug leads shall be supported clear of the engine block and cylinder head.

C7 Electric motors other than intrinsically safe flameproof motors shall not be fitted in any petrol engine, gas or fuel compartment.

C8 A steel hull shall not be used as a conductor in an electrical circuit.

C9 The spark ignition and generating systems of engines and all electrical equipment on the boat shall be effectively suppressed against causing radio and television interference.

Outboard Engines

The following standards apply to all boats using or carrying outboard engines.

Fuel tanks

D1 Fuel tanks shall comply with Standards B10 to B13 inclusive and they and all associated pipework, cocks, etc. shall be suitably protected against external impact.

D2 Fuel tanks of the standard outboard portable type shall be located securely.

Note: Petrol not carried in fitted tanks shall be stowed in metal containers each with a maximum capacity of 5 litres and of a type manufactured in accordance with the Petroleum Spirit Motor Vehicles Regulations SRO 1929 No. 952 or the Petroleum Spirit (Plastic Containers) Regulations SI 1982 No. 630.

Fuel pipework: General

D5 A cock shall be fitted in the fuel pipe from the tank in the case of a gravity feed system.

Engine Installation

D8 Outboard engines shall be securely fitted in accordance with the manufacturer's recommendations and instructions.

D9 Exhaust noise shall be effectively suppressed.

FIRE PREVENTION & EXTINGUISHING EQUIPMENT

E1 Boats shall carry not less than the number of extinguishers detailed below which shall be of a type and capacity approved by the BSI or Fire Offices Committee.

When no cooking, heating or fuel-burning appliances are installed, the number of extinguishers carried may be reduced by one 1.0kg Halon or equivalent extinguisher.

Note:

1. It is recommended that a combination of extinguishers is carried so as to allow use of the most effective extinguishing medium for different fires. For example, foam extinguishers are most suitable for liquid fires, but must not be used on live electrical equipment, and halon extinguishers may give off dangerous fumes in a confined space.

2. Fire buckets, if provided, shall be in addition to the equipment specified in Standards E1 to E4 in this section.

E2 In boats with a separate engine room or compartment one fire extinguisher of approved type shall always be kept in the engine room or in a position readily accessible to any enclosed engine space.

E3 In boats fitted with cooking facilities, a fire blanket ready for immediate use shall be kept nearby.

E4 A fire extinguisher of approved type shall always be kept on a bracket fixed in the galley or space where cooking facilities are installed.

E5 In boats with hulls constructed of glassfibre reinforced plastic (GRP) those areas of high fire risk, such as an engine room, fuel compartment or galley, shall have any GRP structure coated with suitable, fire-retardant material.

BOTTLED GAS INSTALLATIONS

The following standards shall apply to all boats with bottled gas installations.

Bottled gas containers

F1 Every container (whether in use or not) shall be either

a. secured on deck away from hatches and other opening so that any escaping gas is dispersed overboard; or

b. placed in a separate compartment or box above the water-line, with gas-proof and flame-retarding sides and bottom, and with a lid. Such a compartment or box shall be of sufficient depth to contain the height of the cylinder(s), cylinder valve(s), and regulator(s). Such a compartment or box shall have provision for allowing any escaping gas to be vented overboard by means of a metal pipe or opening direct through the side of the boat as near as is practicable to the bottom of the compartment

Length of boat	Min number of extinguishers	Alternative types of extinguisher & min. total capacity		
		Dry powder or Halon	CO2	Foam
Below 9m	2	2.5	4.5kg	18 litres
9m to 12m	2	3.5kg	6.0kg	18 litres
Over 12m	3	6.0kg	9.5kg36 litres	
		Min. size of each extinguisher		
		1.0kg	1.25kg	9 litres

or box. The pipe or opening shall have a minimum internal diameter of 12mm for a cylinder of up to 15kg capacity and shall be enlarged in cross-sectional area proportionately for additional gas storage.

F2 Any compartment or box as specified under Standard F1 (b) shall be constructed of sheet metal of 1mm minimum thickness with joints welded or brazed, or of fire-retarding glassfibre reinforced plastic of adequate thickness.

Note: If any gas cylinder is stowed in a well, it is to be treated as under F1 (b).

F3 All containers shall be installed in an upright position with the valve uppermost and not adjacent to any cooking or heating appliance or in an engine or fuel compartment.

Bottled gas installations:

General

F4 The installations shall comply with the current British Standard Specification No. 5482: 'Domestic Butane and Propane Gas-burning Installations, Part 3: Installations in Boats, Yachts and other Vessels'. Except where they are at variance with these standards, in which case the latter shall apply.

Cylinder valves & regulators

F7 Ready access to the main gas valve(s) shall be provided.

F8 Pressure regulators may be mounted either separately from the cylinder(s) or with a direct connection to the cylinder(s). Pressure regulators not directly connected to cylinders shall be securely fixed within the compartment specified in Standard F1 (ii). In both cases a flexible connection to the current BSS 3212 shall be fitted to facilitate the replacement of cylinders.

F9 Regulators of the external manual-adjustment type shall not be fitted.

Portable gas appliances

F12 Each point intended for use with a portable appliance shall be provided with a control tap and bayonet or screwed connection.

F13 Where small, self-contained portable gas appliances having the burner screwed direct to the container are used, such appliances if stored in the boat, shall be placed, when not in use, in a compartment or box constructed as set out in Standard F1 (ii).

Note: Such appliances should be used on the boat only when they are attended.

Pipework

F16 Flexible tubing, conforming to the relevant parts of the current BSS 3212, of minimum practical length and of incombustible material not injuriously affected by gas, shall be used:-

(a) for the immediate connections to containers or to regulators directly attached thereto but not extended to the interior of the boat or outside of a vented container housing; and

(b) for the connections between portable appliances and their control points.

F17 All fixed pipework other than that which forms an integral part of gas-burning appliances shall be made of solid drawn copper or stainless steel, and shall conform to the relevant BS Specifications.

F18 All fixed pipework shall be short, and run as high as possible and shall be secured at intervals of not more than 500mm. It shall be adequately protected against mechanical damage and deterioration.

F19 No pipework shall be run through the bilge water area, or adjacent to electric cables or exhaust pipes, or in any other position prejudicial to its safety. It shall not run through engine and/or electrical compartments unless carried in gas-proof conduit admitting jointless pipe only.

F20 Joints in pipework shall be kept to a minimum, and they shall be readily accessible for inspection. A fixing clip shall be provided not more than 150mm on each side of each joint. Joints shall be made with compression fittings.

Note: Copper pipework should be carefully bent wherever practicable in preference to cutting and installing connectors.

Appliances

The following standards apply to all boats fitted with cooking, heating and refrigerating appliances.

Stoves, fires, refrigerators, continuously-burning & pilot light appliances

G1 Gas or paraffin refrigerators in petrol-engined boats shall not be installed in the engine compartment, and shall be completely isolated from it. There shall be a gas-tight bulkhead across any such boat from the bottom of the boat up to the cabin sole level between the engine compartment and the refrigerator.

G2 All appliances of the catalytic type or with pilot lights or having continuously-burning flames shall incorporate a flame failure device to cut off the gas supply to the main and pilot burners.

G3 In petrol-engined boats, air for combustion to such appliances (both for main and pilot light burners) shall be:-

(a) drawn and exhausted through an approved flame trap;

or

(b) piped from a point inside the boat above the

level of the ports, windows or other means of ventilation in the compartment in which the appliance is installed.

G4 Stoves fired by fuel oil shall have fuel storage and pipework which complies with Standards B1 to B27 inclusive and a valve or cock to shut off the fuel supply in a readily accessible position within the same compartment as, but at a safe distance from, the stove.

G5 Woodwork and all other combustible materials adjacent to all appliances shall be suitably insulated against excessive heat or treated with incombustible material.

G6 Domestic cooking or heating appliances (whether using solid, liquid or gaseous fuel) shall be securely fastened down in order to eliminate undue strain on pipework or fittings and to prevent overturning in the event of a collision, and shall not be placed nor used close to fuel containers or engines.

G7 Flues to every fuel-burning appliance shall be of adequate internal diameter, effectively insulated and of suitable material, and shall be satisfactorily maintained to ensure the safe passage of gases to the outside of the boat.

Ventilation

G10 Adequate through ventilation of a type which cannot be shut off must be provided in accordance with the requirements of BS 5482 Part 3 : 1979 in vessels in which bottled gas or liquid fuel appliances are used.

G11 Written instructions shall be prominently displayed on board the boat prohibiting the blocking of ventilators.

G12 Water heaters shall be installed as near to the deckhead as possible while allowing adequate ventilation for their flue outlets.

EXEMPTIONS

Standard A22 shall not apply to:-
(a) boats entering the Board's waterways from seaward for shelter from stress of weather, and
(b) boats which are not registered by the Board as houseboats and which frequently proceed to sea, provided that:-

(i) Such boats are navigated or moored only in the pound immediately above the first lock upstream of the point of entry from seaward into a waterway controlled by the Board and
(ii) no enactment or by-law is in force prohibiting the discharge of polluting matter from boats into that part of the waterway. This exemption shall not apply to the Gloucester and Sharpness Canal north of its junction with Sharpness Dock Basin.

Standard C8 shall not apply, in respect of the starter motor and generator and their respective circuits only, if these form part of the original equipment of the inboard engine installed in any boat licensed as a pleasure boat or commercial vessel, or registered as a houseboat, by the Board prior to 1st January 1980.

H4 Standard B21 shall not apply to any boat licensed as a pleasure boat or commercial vessel, or registered as a houseboat, by the Board prior to 1st January 1980 in respect of any fuel tank the upper plate of which forms part of the deck or is so close beneath it as to render satisfactory alteration impracticable provided that the cock or valve required by Standard B26 is fitted direct to that fuel tank.

H5 Standard D5 shall not apply to any outboard engine which was manufactured with an integral fuel tank and carburettor and with no external pipework or cock or valve in the fuel feed line, provided that the engine was in use on a boat which was licensed as a pleasure boat, or registered as a houseboat, by the Board prior to 1st January 1980.

H7 Any boat formerly used for the commercial carriage of freight or passengers or as a tug or an an icebreaker which has had maintained in it an original engine installation and which is to be licensed for use as a pleasure boat or registered for use as a houseboat unless used for the purposes of hire, shall not be required to comply with Standards A9, B6, B14, B15 and B21.

H8 Standard A13 shall not apply in respect of the stern fender of a butty boat, or other type of vessel where it is not practicable to fit a suitable stern fender.

Here endeth the lesson!

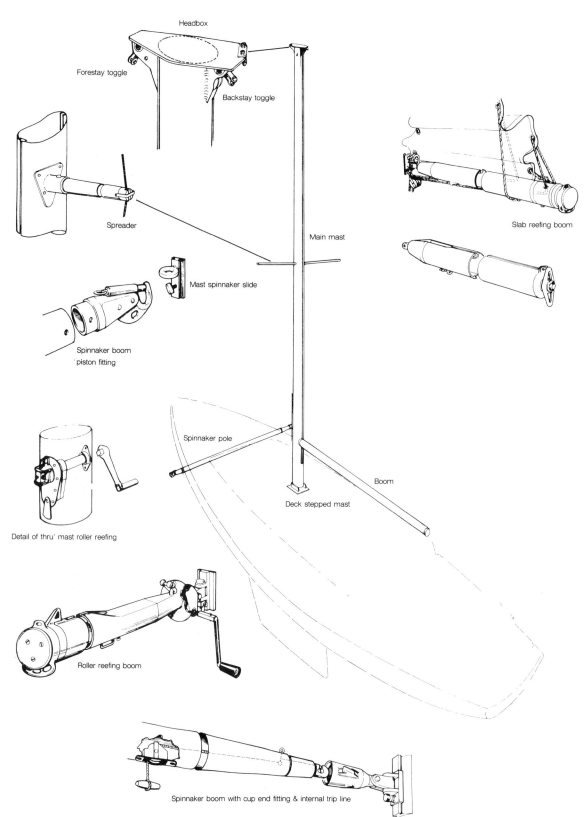

Headbox

Forestay toggle

Backstay toggle

Spreader

Main mast

Mast spinnaker slide

Spinnaker boom
piston fitting

Slab reefing boom

Spinnaker pole

Boom

Detail of thru' mast roller reefing

Deck stepped mast

Roller reefing boom

Spinnaker boom with cup end fitting & internal trip line

Spars

9

'FREE MOTIVE POWER'

SPARS

The style of rig and more especially the type of mast must be more than a 'twinkle in the builder's eye', even at the outset of the job. This is because the requisite mast base and the required standing and running rigging deck fittings should be attached as detailed in Chapter Six. For reasons of both capital outlay and storage, the spars themselves may not yet be needed. On the other hand, once the decision has been made about which manufacturer's product to purchase, they should at this stage, if the reasons are outlined, supply just the heel, pot, T base or tabernacle fitting.

The choice of spars, and for that matter standing and running rigging and sails, can cause a great deal of heartache and research unless dealing with a boatbuilder who is currently completing the particular model. For instance, the sail plan may have been altered due to practical experience proving that alterations to the rig would be beneficial. If in doubt, contact the nominated spar manufacturer to check on the latest specification, not forgetting that changes to the mast may effect the rigging and sail dimensions.

Will slab or roller reefing boom, external or internal halyards be fitted?

There is not only a bewildering array of mast manufacturers, specifications and prices, but there is at least one supplier of kit masts . . . . Who would tackle completing a yacht? When comparing prices, carefully check the detailed specifications, more especially that the navigation lights' wiring requirements are priced in any quotation. If internal halyards are fitted why not dymo label the various exit halyard slots (Illus. 54a)? It does help the smooth running of a yacht with a makeshift crew. Whilst doing so, why not label the mast electric cables as well as the various winches where cockpit winching is planned (Illus. 54b)?

One last point to consider is 'angling' deck and mast mounted winches so preventing overriding. This was standard practice some years ago but seems to have dropped out of sight in recent times (Illus. 55).

Illustration 54   Labelling Internal Halyards, Mast Wiring Cables and Cockpit Winches

54a   Running rigging (& mast cable) identification*

For example:- One digit on each cable

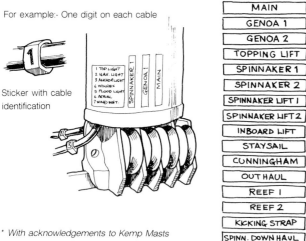

Sticker with cable identification

MAIN
GENOA 1
GENOA 2
TOPPING LIFT
SPINNAKER 1
SPINNAKER 2
SPINNAKER LIFT 1
SPINNAKER LIFT 2
INBOARD LIFT
STAYSAIL
CUNNINGHAM
OUT HAUL
REEF 1
REEF 2
KICKING STRAP
SPINN. DOWN HAUL

* With acknowledgements to Kemp Masts

Running rigging identification stickers make sailing easier, giving safer & more effective sail handling, even with a new crew.

Mast Heels

It has been assumed that the mast is deck mounted as it is comparatively rare now to come across keel stepped masts, except on competition yachts. The mast pot is the simplest of heels but can prove to be a bit of a pig when attempting to step the mast, which must be absolutely upright in order to slide into the pot. The 'T' bar eases the problem considerably and is the more modern fitting, enabling the centre of effort to be adjusted without major alterations (Illus. 56a).

Tabernacles are usually fitted to motor sailers and aid the lowering and raising of the mast without the assistance of 'your expensive' local boatyard. Its main function is to enable a vessel to navigate fixed bridge rivers and continental canals. The tabernacle top pivot point should be tall enough to allow the lowered mast to rest as close to the horizontal as is possible even where a wheelhouse is fitted (Illus. 56b).

SAILS

The selection of a sailmaker is very much a matter of personal choice and price. Ensure that sails are complete with sail bags and ties on the bottom of the bag. Also, why not have head, tack and clew stamped

54b   Labelling cockpit winches

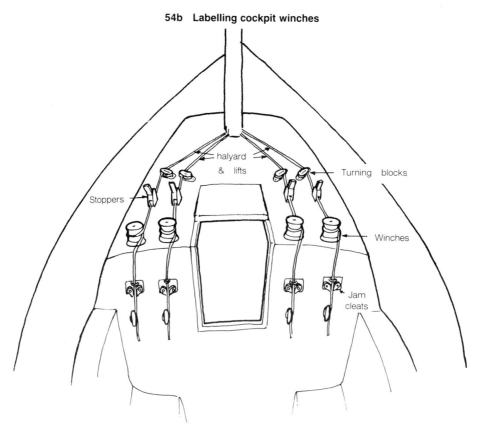

Illustration 55   Angling Winches

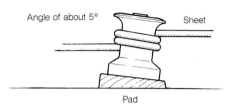

Angle of about 5°   Sheet

Pad

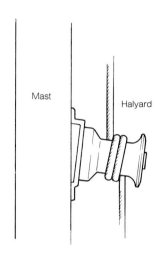

Mast   Halyard

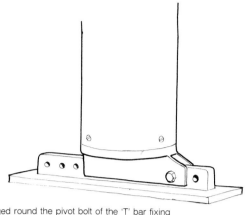

Hinged round the pivot bolt of the 'T' bar fixing

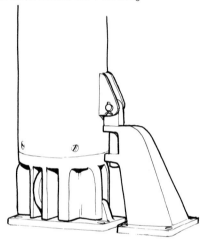

Pivots round the pivot!

Illustration 56   Mast Heels

56a   Deck stepped mast heel fittings

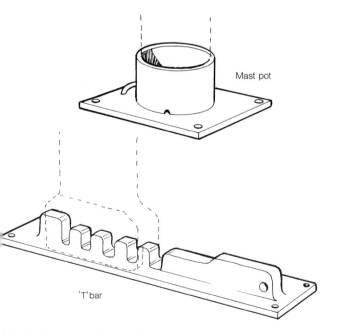

Mast pot

'T' bar

This aluminium casting has a mating section affixed to the mast heel

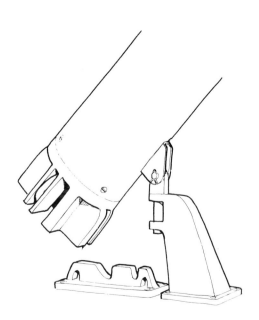

56b   Tabernacles

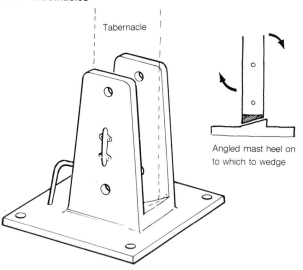

By removing the bottom locating bolt the mast can swivel on the top bolt

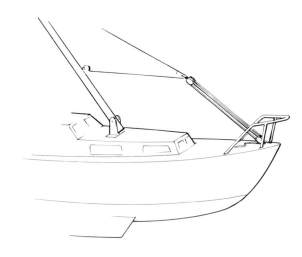

Lowering a tabernacle mounted mast using block & tackle from the foredeck

on the appropriate corner? Most useful when searching for a particular sail point and precariously lodged on a pitching foredeck, as is the tie on the bottom of the bag.

Whether to fit foresail reefing, instead of purchasing a suit of foresails, and mainsail roller or slab reefing — much depends on an owner's intentions. Will it be to cruise or race? Illustration 57 sketches a guide to the spar, sail and rigging details.

It has been pointed out that some manufacturers and, surprisingly, a few designers supply little or sparse detail pertaining to the rig. This may well result in not a little swearing, much thought and some cunning. The formulae listed later in this chapter give some useful information to help make up for any lack of knowledge.

RIGGING

Standing Rigging

As for the mast, so with the rigging. Suppliers' specifications must be examined as closely as their prices. Is a tack pennant included, are toggles fitted, are the bottle screws like for like and are shroud rollers and parrel balls thrown in? If not purchasing rigging from the manufacturer of the craft, it may well be best to have the standing rigging made up at the masthead (or top end), so the mast can be 'dressed', leaving the deck end a foot or so long, for precise fitting when the mast is finally stepped.

Standing rigging should be of 1 x 19 stainless steel wire i.e. one wire rope made up of 19 separate wires. It is usual for each of the main standing rigging wires (cap shrouds, forestay and backstay) to have a breaking strain equal to the displacement of the craft, whilst the lower shrouds, inner forestay and twin backstays can be one wire size down on the main rigging requirements. The rigging screws should be matched to the particular wire size and breaking strain.

Running Rigging

Running rigging can be divided into sheets and halyards. Nowadays halyards are usually wire with rope tails or pre-stretched, 3-strand polyester whilst sheets are more often than not made of plaited polyester.

The running rigging can be completed at any time as the lengths are not so exacting but ensure that tails are spliced into wire halyards with pre-stretched ropes where appropriate.

The use of Lloyds recommended colour coding would not go amiss and is as follows:-
Main halyard, main boom topping lift,
main sheet and general   White
Genoa, jib sheets and halyards   Blue
Spinnaker gear   Red
Other colours available are green, often utilised for topping lifts, and gold, or more accurately yellowy-orange, used for the remaining headsail sheets and halyards.

EMPIRICAL FORMULAE FOR SAIL SIZE & POSITION CALCULATIONS

All the following calculations are arrived at with some resource to generalisation or a common factor or coefficient found to have given the correct answer and are, by their nature, approximations.
Displacement: To calculate the displacement of a craft the following will be of assistance:-

Displacement in Tons =
Length x Maximum Beam x Midship Draft x Coefficient

Illustration 57   Spar, Sail and Rigging Plan and Sketch for an 8½-9m Yacht

Standing Rigging: — ALL 1/19 Stainless Steel

■ Forestay   6mm Bearing to Bearing

■ Backstay   6mm Bearing to Bearing

2 Cap Shrouds   6mm Bearing to Bearing

2 Aft Lower Shrouds   5mm Bearing to Bearing

2 Forward Lower Shrouds   5mm Bearing to Bearing

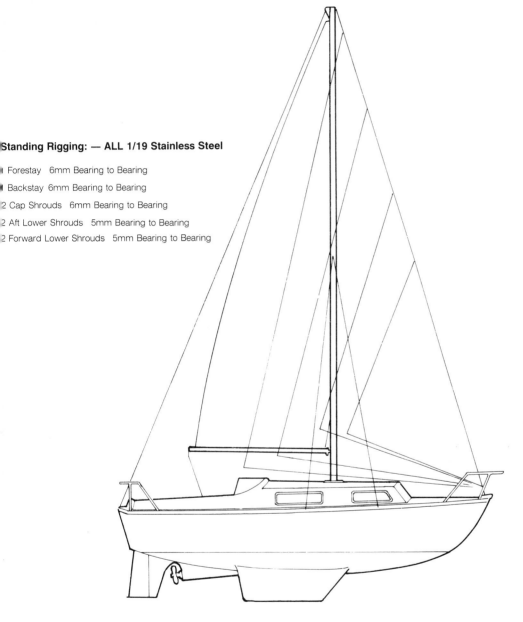

Running Rigging

Jib halyard — 4mm 7/19 s/s with 76mm (3″) (Manganese bronze) snap shackle spliced onto one end & the other end, into — 10mm multifilament polypropylene

Main boom topping lift — 6mm with thimble & $\frac{3}{16}$ 'D' shackle rove thru' swivel block & $\frac{3}{16}$ 'D' shackle

Burgee halyard — 3mm flag line

Signal halyard — 3mm flag line

Jib sheet — 10mm multifilament polypropylene with thimble & $\frac{5}{16}$ 'D' shackle whipped and sewn into centre

Main sheet — 10mm multifilament polypropylene onto fiddle and jamming blocks & swivel block both with ¼ 'D' shackles

Tack pennant — 1 strop — 4mm 7/19 s/s with thimble & 76mm (3″) manganese bronze snap shackle one end & ¼ 'D' shackle other end. 6″ OAL

Kicking Strap — 8mm 3 strand prestretched polyester onto fiddle & jamming & fiddle blocks, both with $\frac{3}{16}$ 'D' shackles

Main halyard — 4mm 7/19 s/s with ¼ long reach 'D' shackle shackled to one end & spliced to the other end into 10mm multifilament polypropylene

Illustration   57 contd

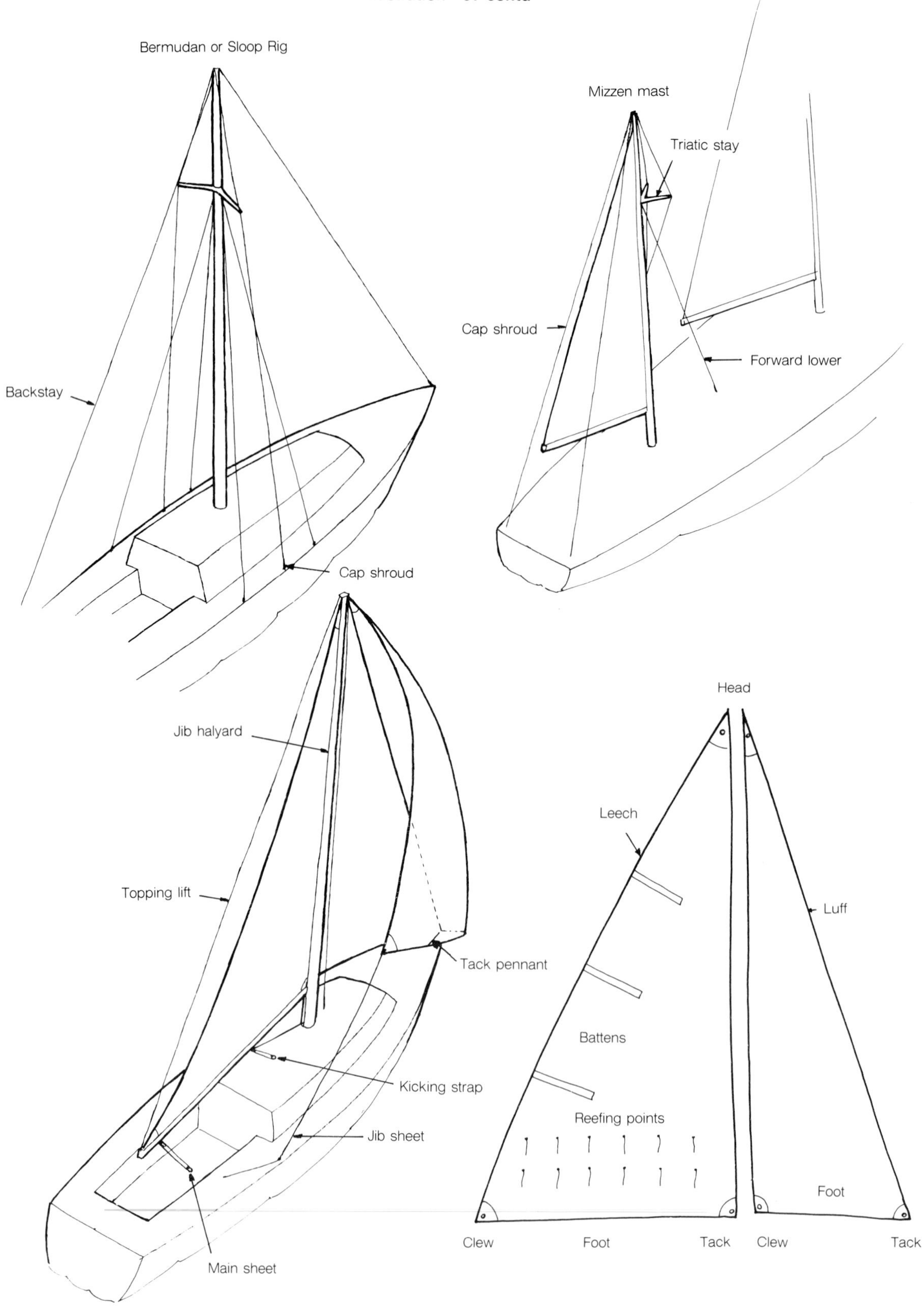

Bermudan or Sloop Rig

Mizzen mast

Triatic stay

Backstay

Cap shroud

Forward lower

Cap shroud

Jib halyard

Head

Leech

Topping lift

Luff

Tack pennant

Battens

Kicking strap

Reefing points

Jib sheet

Foot

Main sheet

Clew   Foot   Tack   Clew   Tack

Illustration 58   The Centre of Lateral Resistance

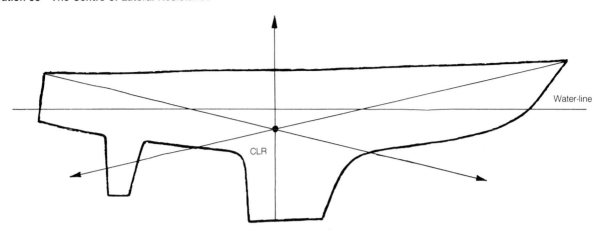

Water-line

CLR

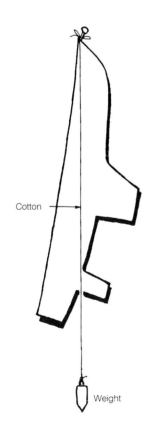

Cotton

Weight

Where length is the water-line length, all dimensions are in feet and the block coefficient, which varies between 0.4 and 0.55, is taken as an average of 0.5

Thames Measurement or Tonnage: Can be calculated as follows:-

$$\frac{\text{Length} - \text{Beam x Beam x } \frac{1}{2} \text{ Beam}}{94}$$

Where length is the distance between the on deck perpendiculars of the foreside of the stem and the after side of the stern post, all measurements being in feet.

Required Sail Area: To calculate the required sail area various assumptions must be made. These include the approximation that at relatively low speeds, skin friction of the craft may be considered in terms of the wetted surface. The formula that results is

$$\text{Sail area in sq ft} = 2 \sqrt{L \times B \times D}$$

Where L is the water-line length, B is the extreme water-line beam and D is the mean draft, all in feet.

Having arrived at the total sail area, it is most important to determine that the centre of effort of the sail plan is correct in relationship to the Centre of Lateral Resistance of the Hull.

The Centre of Lateral Resistance (CLR) of the Hull: An approximation can be made by:-

1. Cutting out an accurate scale profile of the underwater shape of the craft in cardboard and then:-
2. Finding the point where the cut-out is balanced on the head of say a pin,

Or:-

2a. By hanging the cut-out from at least three points, including the bow and transom with a weighted cotton hanging down.

A point will be established which will be the Centre of Lateral Resistance (Illus. 58).

The Centre of Effort of the Sail Plan (CESP): Can be calculated for a Bermudan or sloop rigged craft as follows:-

1. Taking the mainsail, draw a line from the head of the sail to the centre of the foot; draw a line from the clew to the centre of the luff. Where the lines cross is the centre of effort for the mainsail.
2. For the foresail repeat the exercise. Join the two centres of effort.
3. Establish the ratio of the respective sail sizes as a percentage i.e. if the mainsail is twice the size of the foresail then the centre of effort is two-thirds of the way along the line towards the mainsail end (Illus. 59).

It would appear that perfect balance would be achieved by having the Centre of Effort directly above the Centre of Lateral Resistance. Practice shows that this does not achieve the best results and that CESP should be slightly ahead of the CLR. This distance is called the 'lead'. Too much 'lead' results in an undesirable amount of 'weather helm' — a little weather helm being deemed the best

compromise. If the CESP is behind the CLR then 'lee helm' occurs.

The above enables initial calculations to take place and should be used in conjunction with the following:-

Comparisons

Taking the basic craft details, including the hull composition & configuration; overall length; water-line length; overall beam; water-line beam; displacement and the ballast ratio, comparison may be made with similar craft. This allows further guidelines to the type and spar dimensions as well as standing rigging and sail detail. Lastly, but not least, consultations with the chosen mast manufacturer often pays handsome dividends and results in expert advice on both spar and rigging detail.

Tabulating the various results and shaking (not stirring!) should give the required knowledge. Of course this is only a start . . .

SAIL & DECK PLAN

Now fairly accurate sail and deck plans can be drawn (*See* Illus. 57 & 60) starting with any known details of the mast, its deck position and sail outlines. The angle

Illustration 59   The Centre of Effort of the Sail Plan

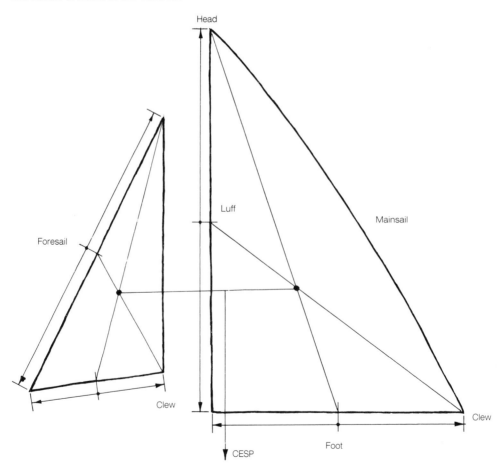

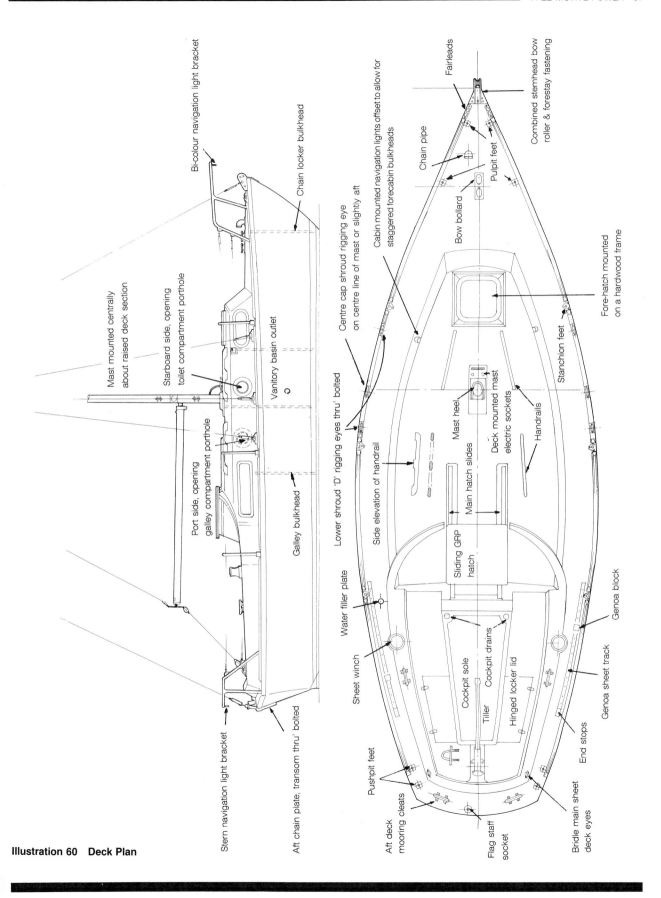

Bi-colour navigation light bracket

Chain locker bulkhead

Fairleads

Combined stemhead bow roller & forestay fastening

Chain pipe

Cabin mounted navigation lights offset to allow for staggered forecabin bulkheads

Centre cap shroud rigging eye on centre line of mast or slightly aft

Pulpit feet

Bow bollard

Mast mounted centrally about raised deck section

Starboard side, opening toilet compartment porthole

Vanitory basin outlet

Fore-hatch mounted on a hardwood frame

Stanchion feet

Lower shroud 'D' rigging eyes thru' bolted

Side elevation of handrail

Mast heel

Deck mounted mast electric sockets

Handrails

Port side, opening galley compartment porthole

Galley bulkhead

Main hatch slides

Sliding GRP hatch

Water filler plate

Genoa block

Sheet winch

Cockpit sole

Cockpit drains

Tiller

Hinged locker lid

Genoa sheet track

Stern navigation light bracket

Aft chain plate, transom thru' bolted

Pushpit feet

Aft deck mooring cleats

Flag staff socket

Bridle main sheet deck eyes

End stops

Illustration 60   Deck Plan

of the bottom of the various foresail triangles at the clew must be equally divided and lines drawn down to the deck (Illus. 61a). These sheet lines give the position and overall length of the foresail and genoa sheet tracks. Taking the No. 1 Jib sheet angle at the deck and an equal angle from the deck indicates the cockpit coaming position of the sheet winches. If this is not easily to hand, the position can be juggled. It may well be that the sheets will have to be led from the foresail lead block to a deck or pushpit mounted snatch block and back to the winch (Illus. 61b). Where an overlong sheet track would result from servicing all the foresail sheet lines, individual thru' deck eyes complete with snatch blocks, can be fitted for, say, the storm jib.

Illustration 61   Sheet and Halyard Leads

61a   Sheet lines

In determining the path of sheets and halyards, consider the 'fall' of the rigging and that the turning blocks, sheaves, deck plates and leads must be allowed to move freely throughout any angle that will be imposed on them.

61b   Cockpit coaming winch positions

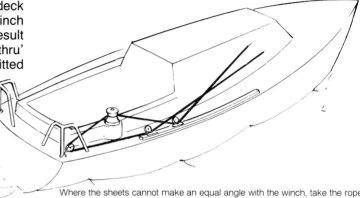

Where the sheets cannot make an equal angle with the winch, take the rope back to a snatch block, fastened to the pushpit base.

If short handed cruising is planned, attention must be given to leading the halyards aft from the bottom of the mast along the deck top, via blocks and leads and jamming cleats to cockpit mounted winches (*See* Illus. 54b).

The main sheet arrangement usually involves a compromise. The modern day habit of sheeting in the mainsail very, very hard often means siting the main sheet track midway along the boom length. On craft over 9m (30ft) in length, this may well entail mounting the track across the main hatch garage (Illus. 62a). On vessels under 9m (30ft) in length, the track might have to be positioned on the bridge deck or an athwartship, cockpit seat mounted track (Illus. 62b). The disadvantage of this arrangement is that access through the main hatch can be 'exciting' and may necessitate fairly speedy movement. (There is nothing like being zapped across the cockpit by a fast travelling main sheet when the craft is going about or when involved in an involuntary gybe!) The boom length may indicate the main sheet being fastened to the cockpit sole. If this is so for goodness sake don't use some ridiculously short piece of track — fit a thru' deck eye as no effective use will result from such a small length of travel (Illus. 62c). The more dated and leisurely positioning involves fastening the main sheet to the boom end and mounting a track across the transom deck or cockpit coaming moulding upstand. On the other hand, why not fit an aft deck rope bridle or a 'sheet horse as not everything old fashioned should be dismissed out of hand (Illus. 62d). An advantage is that a sheet horse doubles up as a most satisfactory mast rest when the spars are stepped, for one reason or another.

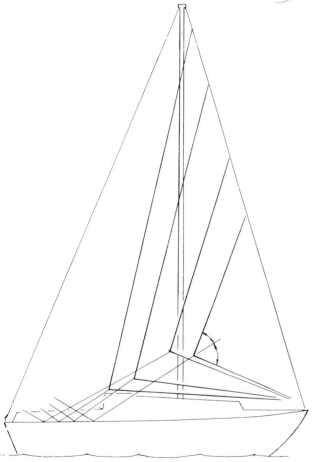

Foresail sheet (rope) line equally bisects the clew (corner) giving ideal point on the deck for the snatch block eye & or genoa lead block to be positioned.

Illustration 62   Main Sheets

62a   Main sheet track, cabin roof mounted

62b   Main sheet track, bridge deck & cockpit seat mounted

62c   Cockpit mounted main sheet eye

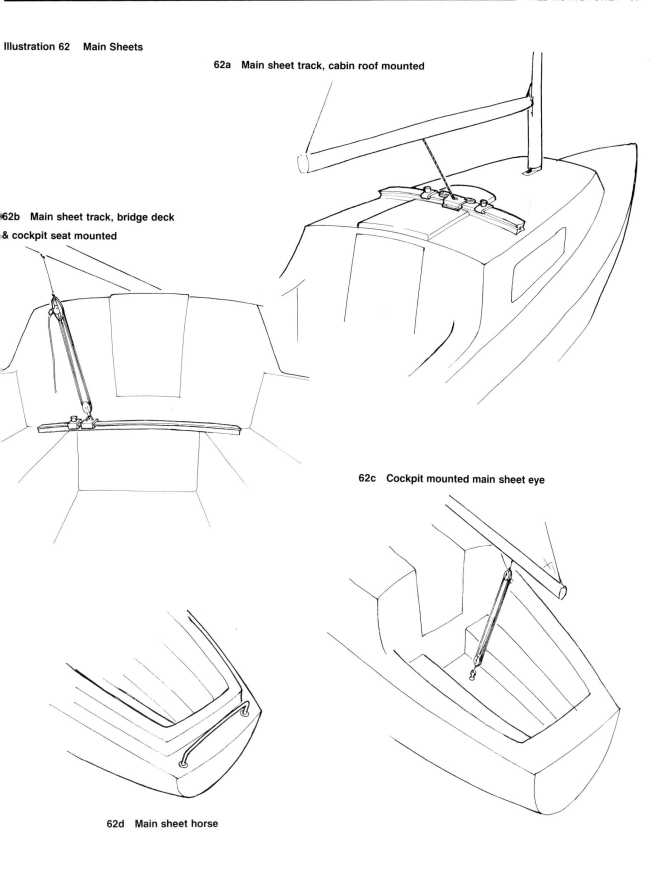

62d   Main sheet horse

Above An aft hanging locker bulkhead, shelf hull stringer & chain plate backing plates in position.

Left The chain locker bulkhead, in position with one of the hull stringers butted up against the bulkhead. The bulkhead & stringer have been bedded on resin putty & are ready to be laminated in position. The routed edge of the bulkhead & the rough sawn, arrised edges of the stringer should be noted.

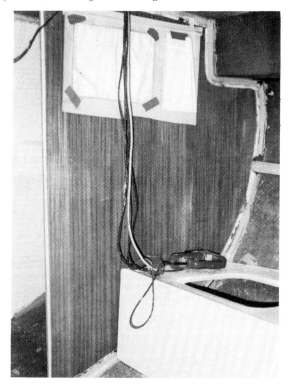

An interior moulding & shelf stringer in position, prior to laminating.

A bulkhead, hull stringer & a berth moulding, all prior to laminating, resin puttied in place.

10

FITTING THE ENGINE ('IRONHORSE, IRON TOPSAIL' . . .)

THE CHOICE OF ENGINE

Generally, the governing factor in selecting the correct engine for a boat must be the maximum design speed of the hull. The lowest horsepower engine which drives the craft close to its top design speed, using about ¾ of the engine's maximum revolutions per minute (RPM) is satisfactory. Obviously, an owner may want to have some power in reserve or, expressed another way, may wish to ensure that the engine can do the job without having to operate at nearly full load for long periods. On the other hand, fitting overpowered engines only creates excessive waves and pushes up the fuel consumption, with very little commensurate increase in speed.

The pitch of a propeller is the distance that it would move a boat forward in one complete revolution, that is if it were turning in a solid substance. As a propeller is driving the boat through water slip occurs, which is expressed as a percentage of efficiency.

Most of the craft about which this book is concerned have 2 or 3 bladed propellers. Usually yachts have two bladed propellers so that when the blades are at rest, they are masked by the skeg, thus reducing drag. Three bladed propellers, which are more efficient in transmitting propulsive thrust, are more often fitted to motor sailers and powered craft.

The following formulae, as well as the charts outlined in Illustration 63, aid in making decisions in respect of engine size, propeller pitch and diameter, bearing in mind the propeller to hull clearance requirements detailed in Illustration 65b.

A displacement craft's maximum speed may be approximated from the formula:

$$\text{Maximum speed in knots} = 1.4 \sqrt{\text{length}}$$

Where length is the water-line length in feet.

For a craft to exceed its hull designed critical speed, it must be capable of planing.

To calculate propeller slip the following formula can be used:

$$\text{Slip per cent} = \frac{100 \text{ Pitch (ft)} \times \text{RPM} - \text{Speed (knots)} \times 101.3}{\text{Pitch} \times \text{RPM}}$$

Usually the propeller is stamped with figures and letters on the boss i.e. 12 x 8LH. This indicates that the overall diameter is 12″, the pitch is 8″ and the propeller is left-hand. (See later notes for an explanation of right and left hand).

To calculate propeller pitch:

$$MPH = \frac{RPM \text{ on shaft x pitch}}{1056}$$

where the MPH is the maximum speed, as calculated above.

To calculate 'RPM on shaft':

$$\frac{Engine \text{ RPM}}{Gearbox \text{ Reduction}} = RPM \text{ on shaft}$$

Unfortunately for the amateur boatbuilder, or the professional for that matter, there is a confusingly wide choice of marine engine manufacturers and marinisers.

Before settling on a particular unit it is necessary to decide on the combustible — diesel or petrol fuel — the engine capacity, reduction gearbox ratios and the method of transmitting the drive to the propeller. Help! Thankfully the options can be reduced to a manageable list, depending on the type of craft and the physical dimensions available.

The following are a random list of some of the matters for consideration.

If at all possible ensure the installation is flexibly mounted, which helps keep noise and vibration to a minimum. Do not be tempted to underpower the craft in order to save a few pounds (sterling), as it will be money 'well thrown away'.

Although the possible sale of the vessel may not be more than a deeply submerged thought, the adverse effect of fitting a petrol engine on the marketability of

Illustration 63   Propeller and Speed Charts

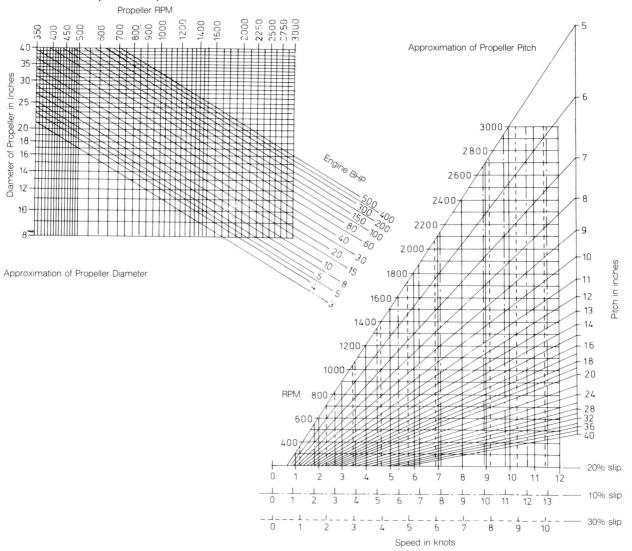

the craft must be borne in mind. Petrol power is, quite simply, a very poor selling point. Another fuel that appeared to be gaining some ground for driving canal craft was low pressure, bottled gas but the concept appears to have faded away. On the other hand, as the possibility of the bottled gas conversion of internal combustion engines has faded away, 'electric' powered boats are slowly, if tentatively making a long but apparently sturdy debut.

It is tempting to obtain a second-hand marine engine. This would appear to ensure a worthwhile saving in costs, if a suitable unit can be found. It is as much a pity that so many supposedly overhauled units, sold by firms engaged in this field, have brought their owners grief as it is a pity that marinisation kits are not more easily available, for a wider variety of engines.

A final word of warning is addressed to the owner planning to purchase a marine engine from one source and sterngear from another. He must ensure that the propeller is the correct 'hand' for the gearbox or reduction box. Nearly all prime units rotate clockwise (facing the front of the engine) which requires a right-hand propeller. However, due to gearbox and reduction box gearings, the required 'hand' may become left. So beware! Incidentally, the hand of a propeller indicates which way the propeller rotates when driving ahead. If, with the craft in ahead, the top of the propeller turns to port, it is a left-handed propeller; if to starboard, a right-handed propeller.

One other 'small' consideration is to ensure the propeller shaft coupling matches the gearbox coupling.

ENGINE INSTALLATION PACKAGE

An example package for a 10-12hp marine diesel engine and the parts that must be included to give a workmanlike installation in, say, an 8m (26/28ft) craft is as follows:-

Exhaust kit	water injection bend	1
	exhaust hose	12ft
	waterlock	1
	skin fitting & gate valve	1
	60° connector sleeve	1
Water inlet	seacock & strainer	1
Electrics	engine loom	1
	instruments	1
Controls	2 lever control box	1
	cable — gearbox) to length	1
	cable — throttle) required	1
	end fitting kits — gearbox	1
	— throttle	1
Ancillaries	flexible mountings	1
	flexible coupling	1
	propeller shaft coupling	1
Fuel kit	filler	1
	fuel tank	1

Sterngear	stainless steel propeller shaft 25mm	1
	sterntube complete with inboard and outboard bearings	1
	propeller* 13 x 9, 3-bladed	1
Ancillary installation	pack of engine compartment insulation;	1
	sterntube remote greaser;	1
	fuel pipe & water coolant pipe, to required length	1
Tools	sump pump	1
	tools	1

the propeller hand is determined by the engine characteristics.

For the purpose of the main body of this Chapter I have made certain assumptions:

1. That the engine is diesel
2. That the engine horsepower is between 8 and, say, 50hp.
3. That the chosen drive system is the conventional, 'in line' installation

and

4. That the shell is GRP (See further on in this Chapter for details of installation in craft manufactured in other materials).

The manufacturers of the craft may be able to save time, and a lot of headwork, if they can advise which marine power units fit more easily than others. Incurable romantics may also believe that the manufacturer will be able to supply engine bed details. Oh, ho, ho! Murphy's law says . . .

To expand on the term 'in line', there are a number of basic types of engine installation including:-

'Z' drive (Illus. 64a): the engine is tucked up to and sometimes mounted on the transom internally, with the drive leg hinged on the transom externally. This type of installation is only suitable for power craft.

'V' drive (Illus. 64b): the engine is mounted facing aft

Illustration 64   Various Engine Drives and Installations

64a 'Z' drive

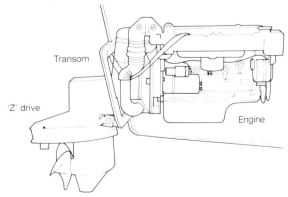

64b 'V' drive

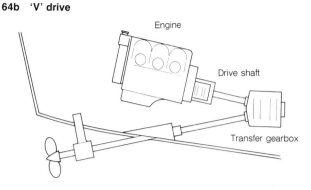

(not forward) and the drive is linked to a conventional propeller shaft by a 'V' drive transmission box. Usually only fitted to power craft and, due to the expense of the gearbox, not really within the scope of this book.

Hydraulic drive (Illus. 64c): the engine can be located 'wherever you will' with the drive transmitted to the propeller shaft by a hydraulic pump and piping.

Hydraulic drive is usually installed in yachts but is more expensive than the conventional sterngear or a:-

Sail/'S' drive (Illus. 64d): a fairly recent innovation where an outboard or inboard powerhead is directly attached to a substantial but short, outboard type drive leg via a composite, flanged engine bed, the whole being fixed directly through the craft's hull. This makes for ease of installation and has become quite popular

Lastly but not least is the:-

In Line Installation (Illus. 64e): still the most popular method is the conventional, inboard power unit and gearbox mounted in line with and coupled directly to a propeller shaft. This system is the one described in detail in this Chapter but most of the basic principles apply to the other installations.

Before settling down to the nitty-gritty there are, naturally enough in such an individualistic pastime, variations on a theme, one of which is the use of pulleys

64c Hydraulic Drive

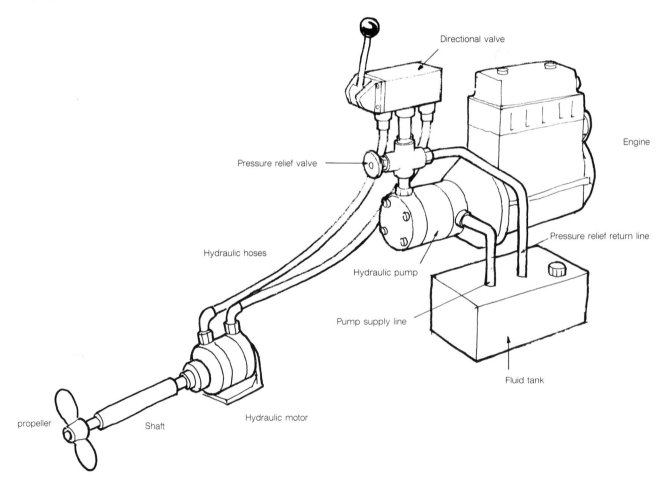

64d Sail drive

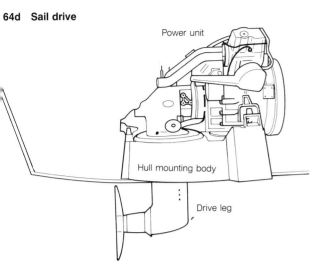

Power unit

Hull mounting body

Drive leg

64e Conventional in line

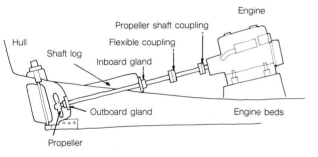

Engine

Propeller shaft coupling

Flexible coupling

Hull

Inboard gland

Shaft log

Outboard gland

Engine beds

Propeller

should be satisfactory as the designer will have allowed for the skeg to be shaped and situated in such a way that the largest propeller size required can be swung without the blades touching the hull or dipping beneath the skeg. Should the matter be in doubt pay attention

64f Belt drive

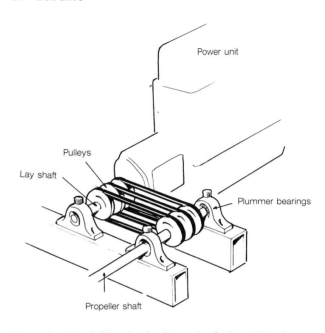

Power unit

Pulleys

Lay shaft

Plummer bearings

Propeller shaft

Illustration 65   Drilling for the Sterntube Outboard Bearing

65a   Outboard gland pilot drilling

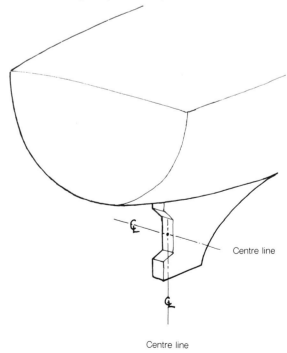

Centre line

Centre line

and belting (Illus. 64f). This allows the engine to be offset and the pulleys can be sized to give further gearing which is not such a Heath Robinson idea as might appear at first sight. Toothed belting is used on modern production car engines for driving overhead camshafts. Just a thought!

It is beneficial to obtain details of the basic dimensions of the proposed power unit and mock up a jig. This should be an outline of the engine, gearbox and reduction gear with blocks of wood and scrap plywood positioning the mounting feet and drive coupling. If it is a modern engine, there is quite likely to be available an installation jig. On the other hand . . . .

Whatever, now is the moment to proceed to the:-

THE LINE UP

Drill thru' the skeg in the way of the sterntube outer bearing, making the hole just large enough to take some string. Now, how does one know exactly where to drill this pilot hole? Well, normally it is in the centre of the skeg, that is on the centre line of the hull, as well as midway in a vertical plane (Illus. 65a). This position

to Illustration 65b which gives the recommended propeller to hull as well as keel and rudder clearances.

To establish the position of the engine beds, stretch the string inboard from the pilot drilling towards the bow of the craft, on the centre line. Each engine manufacturer advises the maximum angle of the particular units' installation, which is very rarely more than 15°, with an average of about 12° or 13°. Usually it is desirable to

65b   Propeller to hull, keel & rudder clearances

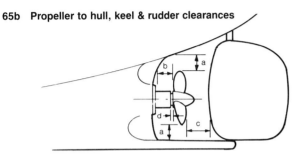

Recommended propeller to hull minimum clearances are as follows:
1. Between the tips of the propeller & the hull a minimum of 50mm (2") — 'a'
2. The distance between the aft end of the propeller & the leading edge of the rudder should not be less than ⅓ of the propeller diameter as should the distance between the leading edge of the propeller & the keel — 'b' and 'c'
3. The distance between the propeller hub & the outboard gland shoulder should be approximately 12-13mm (½") — 'd'

keep the angle as large as is possible within the prescribed limit. This helps to locate the engine as far back in the craft as possible, saving it projecting too far into the main cabin, as well as keeping the length of the propeller shaft as short as is practicable. Various methods of measuring the angle of the string, and thus

Illustration 66   The Angle of Installation

66a

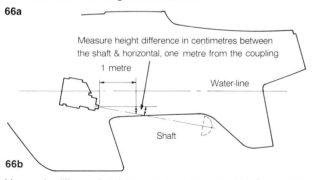

66b

Measure the difference in height over 1 metre, along the shaft. The angle is given by reading off the table:

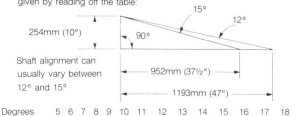

Degrees	5	6	7	8	9	10	11	12	13	14	15	16	17	18	19	20
Centimetres	9	10	12	14	16	18	19	21	23	25	27	29	30	32	34	36

the engine installation, are detailed in Illustrations 66a & b. A protractor with level glass can be used, which saves a great deal of juggling.

FITTING THE ENGINE

Marine engines must be fitted following the manufacturer's instructions to the full stop. The engine mock-up referred to above makes it a fairly simple matter to approximately line up the string and the drive coupling of the jig. Then rough out a plywood profile of 'the to be' engine beds, which may well require quite a lot of 'tooing and fro-ing'. In practice the engine beds are usually up to a 13mm (½") below the centre line of the propeller shaft which allows for laminating in the beds with up to 2700gm (9oz) of CSM as well as 1½mm ($\frac{1}{16}$") for the engine packing pieces or shims.

Experience leads me to advise that a pair of rough, softwood beds should now be cut out and offered up for size. When they appear satisfactory, position them in the hull, re-threading the string through the skeg pilot hole, checking that not only is the angle correct but that

Illustration 67   The Engine Beds

67a

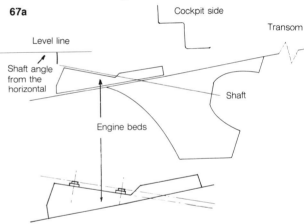

Top of engine beds parallel to & a minimum of 13mm (½") below the angle of the shaft to allow for 'glassing in'

the string is parallel to the top surface of the engine beds. If all is well, place the engine jig or, if necessary, the engine on the beds and re-check the line and angle with the string held to the gearbox or reduction box coupling (Illus. 67a).

After the engine bed patterns are satisfactorily shaped the actual beds can be cut out of hardwood, keruin or iroko. Round off the top edges (for laminating), bed on resin putty, batten together (levelled athwartships) and 'tack' them in position with bandages of laminate (Illus 67b). The skeg must now be drilled out and the sterntube temporarily fitted in place. The inboard end will require wedging approximately in position. Place the engine on the beds, insert the propeller shaft and re-check the shaft

67b   Tacking them in position

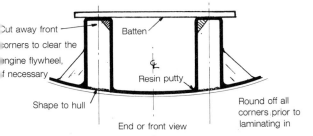

Cut away front corners to clear the engine flywheel, if necessary

Batten

Resin putty

Shape to hull

Round off all corners prior to laminating in

End or front view

Glass in engine beds with between 2400-3000g/m² (8 to 10oz) laminate feathering over the surrounding hull 150mm-230mm (6″ to 9″)

Batten engine beds together level across the tops, fix in position bedded on resin putty & 'glass in'

Laminate into the skeg & hull with a minimum of 3 layers of 600g/m² (2oz) mat

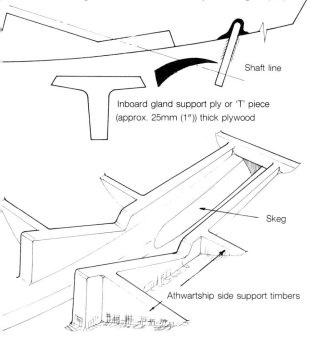

Shaft line

Inboard gland support ply or 'T' piece (approx. 25mm (1″)) thick plywood

Skeg

Athwartship side support timbers

Illustration 68   Block and Tackle or Hoist

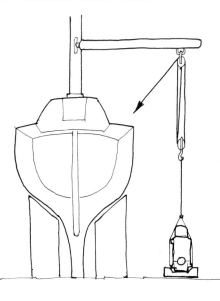

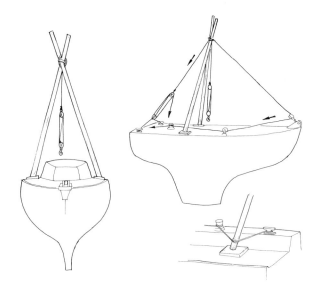

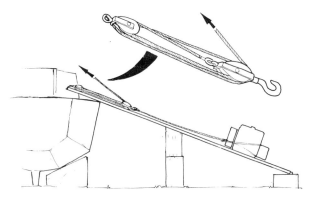

alignment. Should the engine and shaft appear to be spot on, forget the congratulations, remembering that the top face of the beds requires to be lower, as explained above. After making the necessary adjustments, finally glass in the engine beds. And do not forget to fit an engine tray in between the beds or, where possible, simply laminate an athwartship baffle at each end of the beds, thus forming an effective, in situ tray.

I realise that I have been lightly throwing about phrases, such as 'place the engine on the beds' and there you are struggling with an intractable lump of unco-operative and expensive cast iron (rather like those car manuals of the 1950s which used to blithely say 'having removed the crankshaft'). I suggest that a substantial beam is placed across the main hatchway and from this is strung a simple block and tackle, a hoist or similar (Illus. 68).

Sterntubes

The final stage of installation can now take place with the cutting out and fitting of the inboard gland support, which may be a block of wood or a 'T' piece of plywood, laminated into the skeg cavity (See Illus. 67b). The hole for the sterntube must be a tight fit. It may well be, if the information were not to hand at the time, that the sterntube has been ordered overlength. This is satisfactory as long as there is enough thread for the tube to be cut to the correct length and still allow the glands to be screwed on without having to cut more thread (Illus. 69a).

Rather than fiddle about with all these separate tubes, glands and inboard gland blocking, an owner might decide to fit a shaft log (Illus. 69b). If not, bed the outboard

Illustration 69   Sterntubes

69a   Overlong sterntube

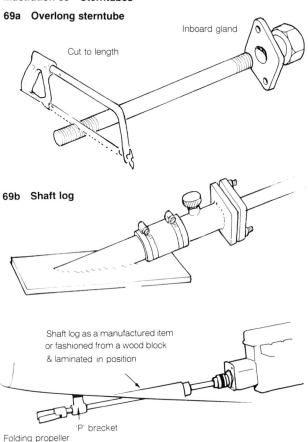

Inboard gland

Cut to length

69b   Shaft log

Shaft log as a manufactured item
or fashioned from a wood block
& laminated in position

'P' bracket

Folding propeller

gland on sealant prior to fastening to the skeg. Where possible a block of wood or a metal plate should be laminated into the skeg to accommodate the fastening bolts. I have reservations about the more usual methods of fixing outboard glands, and for that matter other items, and Illustration 70 sketches a more satisfactory alternative. When the sterntube is finally positioned it should be uniformly and lightly greased and the skeg

cavity filled with two pot polyurethane foam (See Chapter Three, Foaming Out). Don't be too heavy handed as the foam displaces an enormous volume. When the action has ceased it can be cut to shape and laminated over. The basic installation of the engine, beds and sterntube is now complete (Illus. 71).

Illustration 70   A 'Better' Fixing for Sterntube and Engine Fastenings

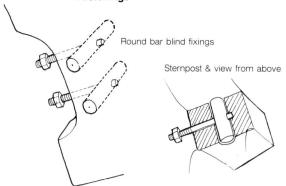

Round bar blind fixings

Sternpost & view from above

Have machined some round bar, preferably of the same material as the fastenings with a drilled & tapped thread through the diameter into which fastenings can be screwed

Drill out the entrance to give a lead to the bolt

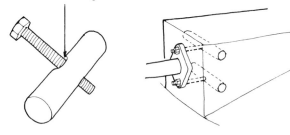

Round bar of a compatible material & sufficient diameter to accept the requisite fastening

It should be long enough to reach each side of the item into which the bar is to be fitted, possibly cut short to allow the drilled hole to be stopped off at both ends

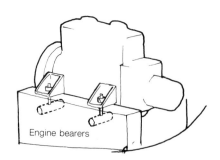

Engine bearers

Illustration 71   The Basic Engine, Beds and Sterntube Installation

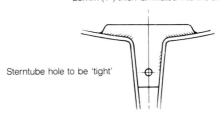

Inboard gland 'T' piece, a minimum
25mm (1″) thick laminated into the skeg

Sterntube hole to be 'tight'

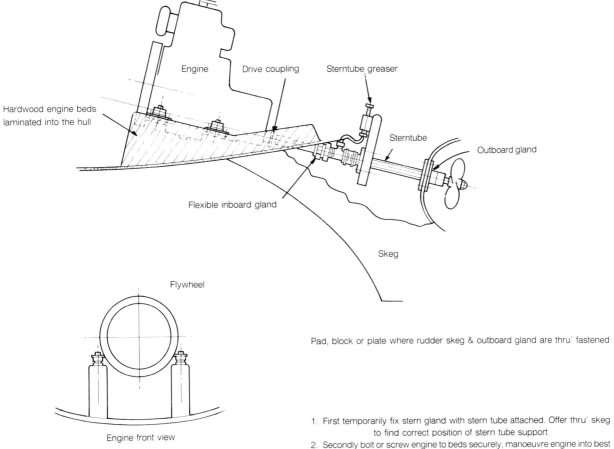

Engine

Drive coupling

Sterntube greaser

Hardwood engine beds
laminated into the hull

Sterntube

Outboard gland

Flexible inboard gland

Skeg

Flywheel

Engine front view

Pad, block or plate where rudder skeg & outboard gland are thru' fastened

1. First temporarily fix stern gland with stern tube attached. Offer thru' skeg
to find correct position of stern tube support
2. Secondly bolt or screw engine to beds securely, manoeuvre engine into best
position to align shaft. It may be advantageous to leave out the packing gland
assembly at this stage in order to better judge the shaft clearance around stern
tube. Finally laminate beds in position.
3. Bolt up coupling temporarily to access alignment (place feeler gauges all
round the coupling).

Propeller Shaft

Similarly to the sterntube, the shaft may have been ordered over-long (at the inboard end) with the propeller end tapered, keywayed and threaded, for the matching propeller and nut. The inboard end can now be cut to size. One of the most neglected and incorrectly executed tasks, even by professional boatbuilders, is the fixing of the shaft to its drive shaft coupling. Some engines come complete with well engineered couplings whilst other manufacturers are rather more casual. Certainly the coupling and shaft must be machined for both a keyway and a pinch bolt or tapered drive pin (Illus. 72). A subsequent paragraph discusses the installation of larger engines, as these instructions are suitable for units up to about 20hp. Over and above that horsepower, although the basic details remain the same, certain items require different treatment.

Illustration 72   Propeller Shaft Fixings

Flexible Couplings & the Final Alignment

Assuming the engine is flexibly mounted, either the inboard gland of the sterntube should be flexibly mounted, as in a shaft log installation (See Illus. 69b) or a flexible coupling must be inserted into the propeller shaft (Illus. 73).

To check the alignment of the engine/gearbox and the propeller shaft initially bring together the shaft and gearbox coupling flange faces. The location shoulder of the one should slide easily into the recess of the other. If they do not, does the engine require moving (Illus. 74) by:-

1. Raising or lowering parallel to the beds.
2. Tilting by raising or lowering one end only.
3. Moving on its axis.

Once the flanges are able to mate (goody!), press them together and rotate the propeller shaft through several revolutions. Place a flat edge across the outside diameter of the couplings and get the line up as true as is possible. After which check the clearance between the flange faces with a set of feeler gauges at a number of opposite points around the flange faces. The maximum difference allowed between the readings should be 0.05mm (0.002") (Illus. 75).

Illustration 73   Flexible Couplings

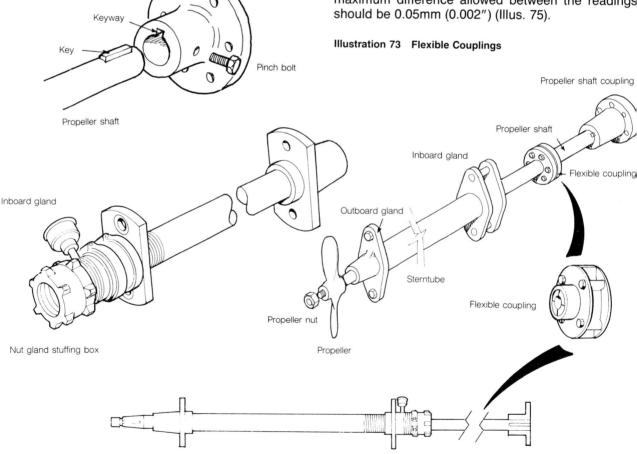

Sterngear assembly comprising flexible inboard bearing gland, sterntube & plain outboard bearing (as distinct from a cutlass bearing)

Ilustration 74 Final Line Up

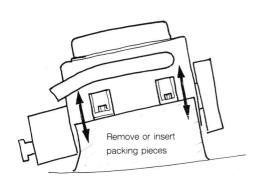

Remove or insert packing pieces

Edge the engine to left or right . . .

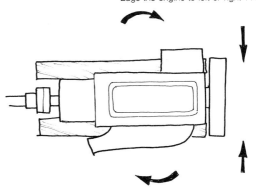

or swing about its axis

Illustration 75 Clocking the Flanges

There should be no more than 0.05mm (2 thou' or 0.002") difference in the two 'A's' reading

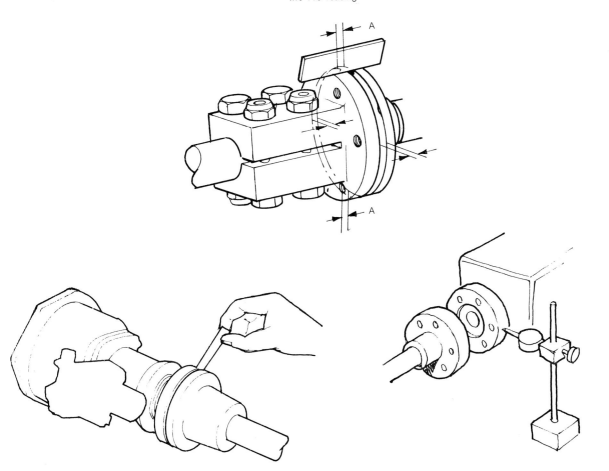

Checking the alignment of the gearbox/reduction box coupling & the propeller shaft coupling

It may be necessary to clock the flanges with an engineer's gauge on first one & then the other coupling face & diameter.

Despite being, in my opinion, a retrograde step, if all else fails there is available, at a price, a shaft coupling that can cope with incorrectable misalignment.

The final line up must be checked after the craft has been launched by running the engine in gear, checking that the temperature of the inboard gland remains cool and 'sighting'. The human eye can detect the smallest wobble.

Bearings or Glands

The inboard bearing is usually bronze whilst the outboard bearing is either bronze or a cutlass rubber insert. This latter is a grooved, hard rubber bearing bonded to a brass sleeve which is clamped in the outboard gland and requires water for lubrication, not grease (Illus. 76). The advantage of a cutlass bearing is that, due to its composition and grooved nature, it is less prone to sand or gritty water damage than a conventional bearing, (nothing like a good mix of grease and sand to provide a nice grinding paste-like mix). A drawback is that a cutlass must be longer than the conventional bronze fitting to give the same bearing effect and there is often not enough room to fit one.

Illustration 76   A Cutlass Bearing

The necessary cooling water is forced through cast lugs or the 'intakes' as the propeller rotates & the craft moves through the water.

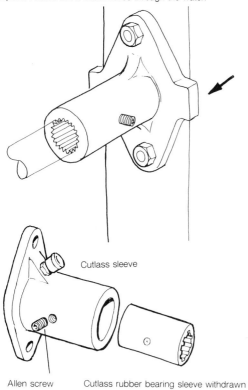

Cutlass sleeve

Allen screw   Cutlass rubber bearing sleeve withdrawn

'A' & 'P' Brackets

Some competition yachts and power craft, fitted with spade rudders (See Illus. 93b), do not have a skeg conveniently positioned for mounting the outboard gland

Illustration 77   A and P Brackets

77a   Alternative Outboard Glands

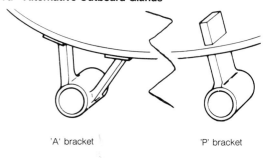

'A' bracket   'P' bracket

of a sterntube. In this case an 'A' or 'P' bracket has to be fitted (Illus. 77a). In installation terms, rather than the skeg 'ruling the angle of installation roost', the engine takes precedence.

The 'A' bracket is fitted to power craft, where the additional staying is required to absorb the greater shaft torque. The 'P' bracket, which causes less underwater turbulence, is usually fitted to yachts, often coupled with a folding propeller, thus reducing to a minimum the interruption to the water flow.

If the thru' hull slot for the bracket shank or flange is cut to give a tight fit, the shank can be easily manoeuvred into the correct position to line up with the propeller shaft. Often the inboard gland used is a composite shaft log casting where the inboard gland and its surrounding simply bolts to the hull. If a proprietary shaft log is not used, then a block must be fashioned on to which the inboard gland may be mounted (See Illus. 69b).

77b   Mounting a 'P' Bracket

Hull mounted fastening block bedded & laminated in position

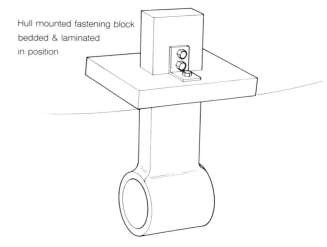

Bolt the bracket to the block & 'glass in'

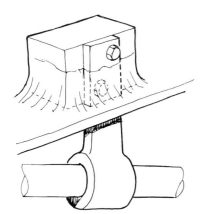

Illustration 78   Fitting the Propeller

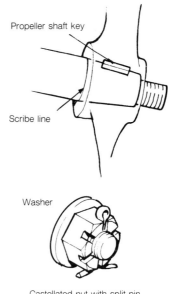

Propeller shaft key

Scribe line

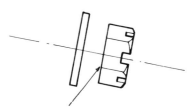

Washer

Castellated nut with split pin

File off the back of the nut

Once the line up is complete, the shank of the bracket(s) can be finally fixed in position. Internally bevel the thru' hull slot to allow the 'laminations' to penetrate as much as possible. Then bed on resin putty a large, hardwood block, slotted out for the shank, and laminate in position with at least 5 layers of 600gms (2oz) mat around the shank or flange of the bracket. Leave as much as 750mm (3″) of the flange projecting internally allowing an 'L' shaped bracket to be bolted to both the shank and the hull mounted block (Illus. 77b).

Propeller Nuts
A couple of hints when fitting sterngear involve the propeller and its holding nut. Check that the propeller is not 'riding' on the key by removing the key, pushing the propeller on the taper and tightening up with the nut. Then scribe a line on the propeller shaft at the rear of the propeller boss, remove the nut and propeller, insert the key and repeat the operation. If, when the propeller is nipped up, the boss does not reach the previously scribed line then the propeller is riding on the key. To remedy, remove the propeller and carefully file a little off the thickness of the key. Repeat the exercise until the scribe line coincides with the propeller boss (Illus. 78).

Often the propeller shaft is pre-drilled through both the propeller nut and the threaded portion of the shaft, or the nut is castellated, in order that a split pin can complete the installation. If, on tightening up, the holes don't coincide, do not drill another hole as it will only weaken this portion of the shaft. The 'knowledge' is to file some off the back of the nut washer or the nut (Illus. 78). Easy when you know how!

Engine Bulkheads & Insulation
Prior to fitting the engine installation equipment, the bulkheads that are (or should be) positioned vertically to the underside of the cockpit sole must be considered. These plywood sheets serve the purpose of stiffening the shape of the cockpit moulding, boxing the engine compartment, as well as acting as a quarter berth and or cockpit locker sub bulkheads (Illus. 79a).

To insulate the engine compartment there are available acoustic sheets of composite rubber, zinc sheet and plastic laminate but they can be difficult to fit when a maze of pipes and wires are all in position, attached to and hung off the side bulkheads. So think now! (Illus 79b).

In planning the route of the various wires and pipes along the engine sub-bulkheads leave as much space as possible for thru' bulkhead engine access traps, especially adjacent to the fuel filters and the stern gland.

Fuel, Electrics & Control Cable Routing
The routing of the exhaust, fuel, cooling water and control cable runs should be kept within the bounds of the engine sub bulkheads. If, as advised, the engine is flexibly mounted, the fuel, water and exhaust runs must have a 'flexible' link let in.

Illustration 79   Engine Bulkheads

79a   Division & cockpit support bulkheads

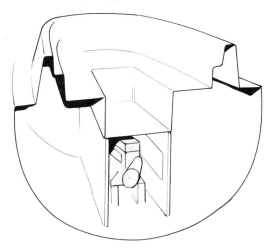

Illustration 80a & b details a couple of suggested fuel installation layouts, as does Illustration 87. Fit a water separator in the fuel line, as water in the fuel is the 'death' of a diesel injection system, causing expensive damage to the pumps and injectors. I am aware that there is usually a filter mounted on the engine but it is very rarely capacious enough to cope with heavily watered diesel fuel, which often occurs due to fuel tank condensation over the years. With the CAV type of filter the water can

79b   Engine compartment insulation

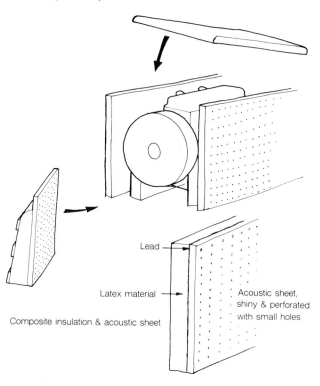

Lead

Latex material

Composite insulation & acoustic sheet

Acoustic sheet, shiny & perforated with small holes

be drained off whilst the engine is running (Illus. 81a).

Mount and clip fuel and water pipe runs on tracks which can be timber battens or, as on larger vessels, galvanised, perforated trays (Illus. 81b). Apart from providing a neat and workmanlike finish to an installation, tracks save accidental damage to the services by their being trodden on or kinked during repairs or routine maintenance. Incidentally, do not group fuel and electrics on the same track.

Nowadays most marine engine units come complete with a pre-wired plug-in wiring loom for the engine electrics to control panel connections, thus taking the guesswork out of what was previously rather a minefield. If a loom is not included in an engine's ancillaries *see* Illustration 82 for an idea of the necessary circuits.

Actuation of the gear lever and throttle controls has advanced considerably from the days of gear lever handles poking through the cockpit sole boards and throttle levers resembling a cross between tram levers and vintage car appendages. The advent of well engineered, push-pull cables and their attachment kits, such as those marketed under the Morse and Teleflex trade names, has revolutionised the installation and operation of the required functions. Cables of this type for actuating manual gearboxes have to be rather hefty but most marine engines are now fitted with hydraulically operated gearboxes, which has reduced the size of the requisite cable to that of the throttle cable.

Steering systems are referred to in Chapter Eleven but here again the advent of the push-pull steering cable has made for much neater installations, even allowing dual steering positions.

Fuel Tanks

Fuel tank installations require special attention. For a start the tank must be very securely fixed, remembering the mass of its contents and the possible consequences if the tank were to break loose in rough seas. Where practicable the tank should be mounted so that an element of gravity feed is present, giving a measure of 'fail safe' if the fuel pump plays up. Obviously the tank should not be positioned too high, otherwise it will have a detrimental effect on the craft's stability. I am in favour of the tank taking up some locker space, if needs be, thus facilitating its boxing. Moreover, if the tank is mounted to one side the filler can be easily fitted on the side-deck so that any spillage does not enter the craft or its confines.

Incidentally, tanks for diesel fuel must not be copper, galvanised or zinc plated but can be constructed of steel plate or fibreglass. This latter option can be built into the hull shape of a GRP craft but I am reluctant to wholeheartedly support this notion, admittedly for somewhat nebulous reasons. If the idea appeals, refer to Chapter Fourteen, in which their construction is detailed.

Illustration 80   Fuel Installations

80a   A typical fuel tank & pipework installation

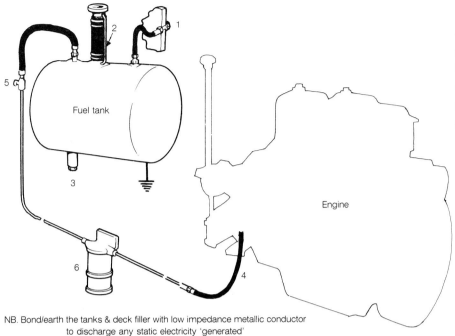

1 Fuel tank vent — fitted with a flame gauze

2 Bonding cable

3 Tank drain

4 Flexible fuel feed pipe

5 Fuel tap

6 Water separation fuel filter

NB. Bond/earth the tanks & deck filler with low impedance metallic conductor
to discharge any static electricity 'generated'

80b   Another fuel tank & pipework installation

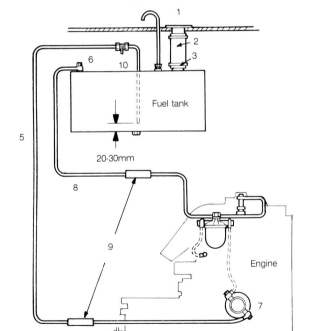

1 Deck filler

2 Semi-rigid, synthetic, fuel resistant pipe

3 Double clipped stainless steel pipe clips

4 Fuel tank vent — fitted with a flame gauze at the outlet

5 Fuel feed pipe

6 Return fuel overspill tank banjo connection

7 Fuel lift pump

8 Return fuel overspill pipe

9 Flexible 'links'

10 Fuel tap

In calculating required tank sizes *see* Chapter Eighteen for useful information.

'Dipping' the tank (establishing the fuel level) can be of the utmost importance. Where installing a single tank, try to fix the filler pipe and deck fitting so that a straight line is achieved. If so a simple dipstick will suffice. Where the filler pipe has to have a bend, or where saddle tanks

Illustration 81   Filters and Tracks

81a   Fuel filter or agglomerator*

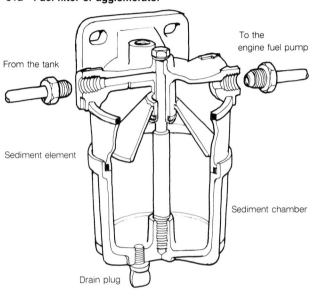

From the tank

To the engine fuel pump

Sediment element

Sediment chamber

Drain plug

* With acknowledgements to CAV, Lucas CAV Ltd.

81b   Supplies track

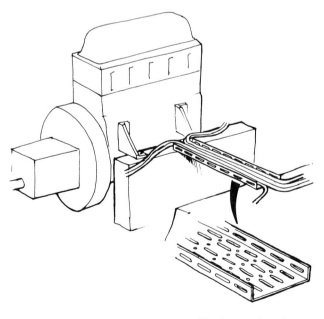

Wooden or perforated tray

Illustration 82   Engine Wiring and Battery Switching

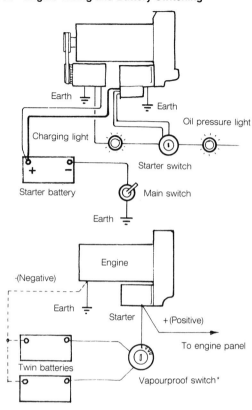

Earth

Earth

Oil pressure light

Charging light

Starter switch

Starter battery

Main switch

Earth

Engine

-(Negative)

Earth

Starter

+(Positive)

To engine panel

Twin batteries

*Vapourproof switch**

* Battering switching — Do not forget to switch off the engine ignition prior to turning the batter switch to 'Off' so as not to open circuit an alternator with possibly irretrievable damage.

are fitted, it is preferable to provide a sight gauge in the manufacture of the tank. Metal tanks can have two elbow pipes welded in position, one top and one bottom, connected by a 6mm (¼") inside diameter, clear fuel pipe. Ensure that the connecting sight pipe is suitable for fuel, is double pipe clipped and has a supporting batten painted with alternate black and white diagonal stripes which aids reading the level (Illus. 83). If fitting the craft out with bungs (*See* Chapter Fifteen & Illus. 162), tie two on here. Fit a fuel tap as close to the tank as is possible, a stipulation that certain Water and Harbour authorities insist upon.

Cooling & Exhausts
Apart from air cooled units, smaller marine engines are usually directly cooled. The raw sea-water is pumped through the intake seacock, passed via the exhaust manifold round the engine block and expelled directly overboard or into the exhaust run (Illus. 84a). In the case of larger horsepower engines, of about 30hp and upwards, the engine coolant is often contained in a closed circuit system. This is cooled in a header tank heat exchanger by sea-water being pumped (sometimes via coolers for the gearbox and engine lubricating oils)

Illustration 83   A Tank Gauge

Angled black and white marked sight card helps to read the level

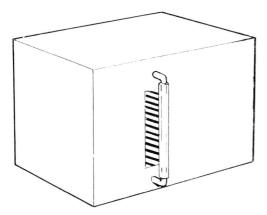

Double clipped clear fuel pipe. And don't forget the bungs if there is not room to fit fuel taps, top and bottom

Illustration 84   Engine Water Cooling

84a   Raw water cooled

Smaller horsepower exhaust layout

Gate valve

Swan neck

Engine

Water pump

Thru' hull skin fitting

NB All exhaust hose pipe clips connections doubled & stainless steel

Water inlet

Bent elbow connector

Strainer

Gate valve

Hull skin fitting

Ensure the seacock is 'grounded' on a well sized internal backing pad

---

through tubes in the header tank and expelled directly overboard or into the exhaust system (Illus. 84b). Other arrangements, more popular on Inland Waterway craft, include keel cooling and swim tanks (*See* Illus. 50).

Modern practice is to run a 'wet' exhaust, piped in suitable flexible rubber hose. The coolant, which has passed round the engine or the header tank, is injected into the exhaust pipe using a water cooled elbow bolted to the exhaust manifold and is expelled with the exhaust gases through the transom exhaust fitting (Illus. 85a). The exhaust run should have at least one 'waterlock' in the line preventing sea-water being sucked back into the engine due to a backfire (Illus. 85b). The waterlock is often combined as a composite unit with an exhaust expansion chamber. Where the engine, or more correctly the exhaust manifold water cooled elbow, is closer than 205mm (8") to the craft's water-line, then an antisiphon vacuum valve must be installed in the engine cooling system between the engine exhaust manifold and the exhaust pipe run. The extra pipework normally takes the form of an upwards loop of about 510mm (20") situated in the connection from the engine and the water intake of the water cooled elbow. The antisiphon vacuum valve is inserted at the top of the loop. (Illus. 85c).

84b   Closed circuit cooling system for a 6 cylinder marine engine

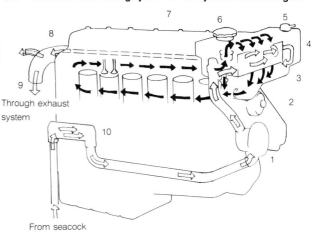

Through exhaust system

From seacock

1 Sea-water pump

2 Circulation pump, fresh water

3 Sea-water inlet to exhaust manifold cooling jacket

4 Heat exchanger

5 Pressure release cap

6 Filler cap for the closed circuit freshwater coolant

7 Thermostat

8 Water-cooled exhaust bend

9 Outlet, cooling water   (Light grey arrows) = Sea-water

10 Oil cooler   (Black arrows) = Fresh water

Illustration 85   Water Cooled Exhausts

85a   Water cooled elbow

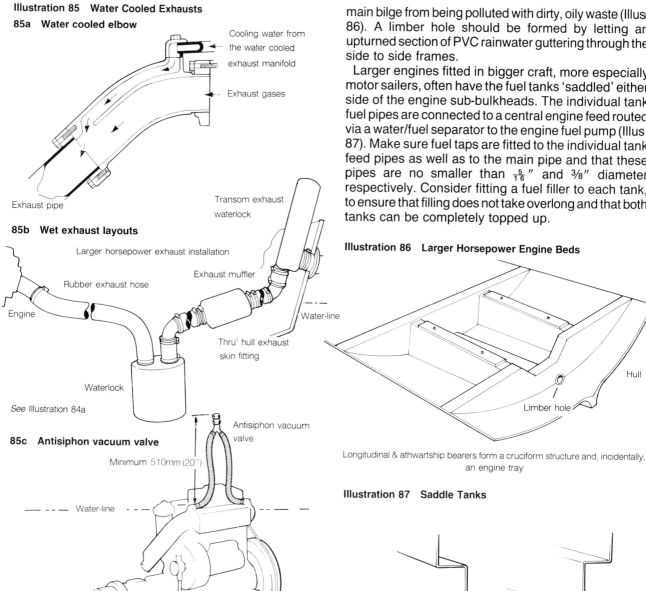

Cooling water from the water cooled exhaust manifold

Exhaust gases

Exhaust pipe

Transom exhaust waterlock

85b   Wet exhaust layouts

Larger horsepower exhaust installation

Rubber exhaust hose

Exhaust muffler

Engine

Water-line

Thru' hull exhaust skin fitting

Waterlock

See Illustration 84a

Antisiphon vacuum valve

85c   Antisiphon vacuum valve

Minimum 510mm (20'')

Water-line

Where fitting flexible exhaust hose, double clip the pipes ensuring the clips are stainless steel

Composite Engine Beds & Saddle Tanks

Larger engine installations require a number of departures from the installation details described above. Firstly, it is usual to make a composite engine bed where the longitudinal bearers are formed into a framework with the addition of athwartship frames. This framework is then laminated into the hull not only forming a very strong and rigid structure but incidentally, an engine tray which can be separately pumped out, thus saving the

main bilge from being polluted with dirty, oily waste (Illus 86). A limber hole should be formed by letting an upturned section of PVC rainwater guttering through the side to side frames.

Larger engines fitted in bigger craft, more especially motor sailers, often have the fuel tanks 'saddled' either side of the engine sub-bulkheads. The individual tank fuel pipes are connected to a central engine feed routed via a water/fuel separator to the engine fuel pump (Illus 87). Make sure fuel taps are fitted to the individual tank feed pipes as well as to the main pipe and that these pipes are no smaller than $\frac{5}{16}$" and ⅜" diameter respectively. Consider fitting a fuel filler to each tank, to ensure that filling does not take overlong and that both tanks can be completely topped up.

Illustration 86   Larger Horsepower Engine Beds

Hull

Limber hole

Longitudinal & athwartship bearers form a cruciform structure and, incidentally, an engine tray

Illustration 87   Saddle Tanks

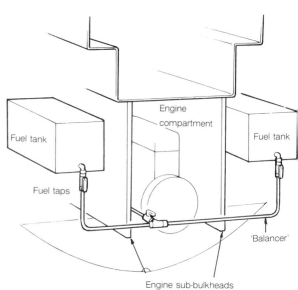

Engine compartment

Fuel tank

Fuel tank

Fuel taps

'Balancer'

Engine sub-bulkheads

Illustration 88   Propeller Shaft Couplings for Larger Engines

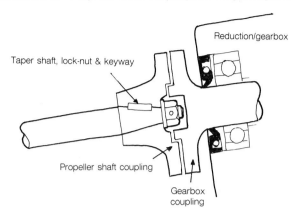

I suggest, nay insist, that the inboard end of the propeller shaft of larger horsepower engines is tapered, keywayed and threaded for a nut so that the drive coupling is fitted on to a keywayed taper held on by a coupling nut (Illus. 88). This should guarantee that the connection will not come adrift.

Batteries

Batteries must at least be mounted in a tray and strapped down to save any possible damage by electrolytic spillage. Preferably they should be fitted in a ventilated, acid proof box (Illus. 89).

Smaller horsepower engines may be fitted with a single battery whilst larger units require twin batteries and a switching system, one battery being used for starting

Illustration 89   Battery Boxes

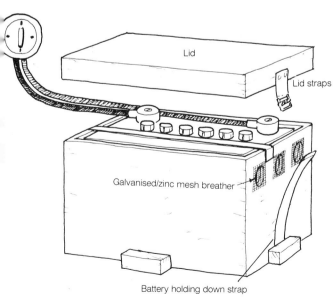

and the engine requirements, the other servicing the 'domestic' electrics. It is a 'must' to fit any battery installation with an isolating switch to prevent drain, feed back and any possible electrolytic couples (See Illus. 82). For further information refer to Chapter Twelve.

Remote Greaser

To take the agony out of 'greasing' the inboard stern gland, why not fit a remote greaser complete with bulkhead mounting bracket (Illus. 90)? The more conventional grease cap often has to be approached through a cockpit sole locker lid or some other tortuous route via the engine sub bulkheads — not always an easy task in bad weather with pitching seas and a badly leaking stern gland. Apart from which the wretched little cap is bound to slip through the fingers and finish up in an inaccessible part of the bilge, beneath the engine!

Illustration 90   A Remote Greaser

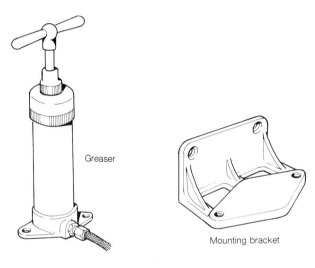

Engine venting

One other point to consider carefully is the aspiration and venting of the engine compartment which requires hot, noxious fumes to be expelled and replaced by fresh air, whilst not letting water in. The heat developed in an unventilated engine compartment can be detrimental, especially to a diesel units operation. I have even observed battery casings that have melted in a poorly ventilated installation. On smaller yachts a trunking can be brought up to the main cockpit bulkhead. On larger craft, with more freeboard, it is often possible to fit an exhaust fan connected to the ignition switch and exhausted through a deck ventilator, mounted to the rear of the craft (Illus. 91).

Illustration 91   Engine venting

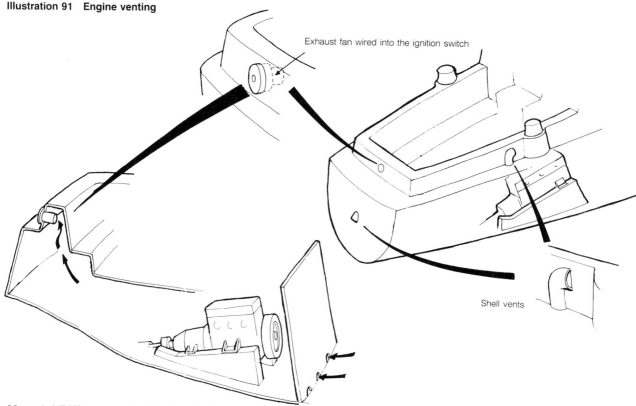

Exhaust fan wired into the ignition switch

Shell vents

Material Differences in Engine Beds

The engine beds of hulls manufactured of steel and aluminium will almost without doubt, be fabricated of a similar material and welded in position. They can be constructed from L shaped angle bar with athwartship frames and the longitudinal bearers laid on the hull frames. This saves undue strain to the hull in the way of the fore and aft engine bearer to hull weld. The arrangement is immeasurably strengthened by fabricating tanks to the outboard side of the bearers (Illus. 92).

Naturally, plywood and timber hulls have wooden beds glued and thru' bolted.

Ferrocement boats usually have the engine beds and sterntube built in during the construction of the hull. If the beds are incorrectly spaced then fabricated, angled steel capping can be thru' bolted to the existing ferro beds. If the sterntube was not cored then, as ferrocement vessels are straight thru' keeled, it will be almost impossible to drill through on the centre line and the engine will have to be:-

   (1) Offset, with an inboard shaft log and 'P' gland bracket fitted.
   (2) Mounted on the centre line, and 'V' belts and pulleys used to drive an offset prop shaft (*See* Illus. 64f).

Or:
   (3) Fitted with a hydraulic drive.

The shaft log must be bedded on doublers, sealant, thru' bolted and laminated in position. Lack of engine beds built into the original construction does not bear thinking about but might be overcome by the thru' hull clamping of suitable plates, to which wooden bearers could be bolted, and then totally laminated in position.

Illustration 92   Metal Craft Engine Beds

Saddle tanks to outboard of the engine beds

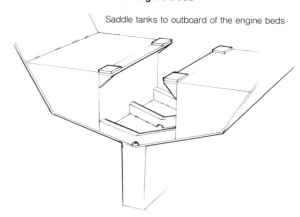

After completing the engine installation polythene wrap and tape up the unit thus preserving its appearance till construction is complete.

11

THE STEERING GEAR

There are various types of rudder gear which fall into four basic types of installation.

a) Transom fitting: generally fitted to smaller sailing craft or older river boats. (Illus. 93a).

b) Cast spade rudder: with inboard rudder gland, generally fitted to high performance powered craft (Illus. 93b)

c) Aerofoil section rudder: with inboard stock, generally fitted to sailing craft (Illus. 93c).

d) Rudder plate: with inboard rudder tube, generally fitted to sailing craft (Illus. 93d).

e) Rudder plate: with inboard gland, generally fitted to powered craft and motor sailers with wheel steering (Illus. 93e).

The type of installation, is determined by the designer but a few comments will not go amiss:-

1. It is sound practice to fit a remote greaser to an inboard rudder gland or tube, similar to that fitted to the propeller stern gland and for the same reasons.

2. The rudder should have up to $\frac{1}{16}$ th of its total area in front of the centre line of the rudder stock, to achieve a balanced feel to the helm.

3. When fabricating rudder gear remember that the rudder may have to be withdrawn at some time in the future! To facilitate this a flange connection to the stock saves, in some cases, either having to dig a very big hole or lifting the craft's stern to a height which might well prove impracticable (*See* Illus. 93d & e).

4. To aid 'drawing' the propeller shaft, place a hole in the rudder plate adjacent and in line with the shaft's angle of withdrawal (*See* Illus. 93d & e).

5. Rudder stops should be fitted, maybe to the rudder deck plate or to the skeg shoe, which allow about 35° movement either side of the craft's centre line (Illus. 94a). This curbs the effect of negative rudder response incurred when the helm is put too far over.

6. The bottom bearing of a rudder housed in a skeg shoe takes a fair amount of hammering. It is worth

Illustration 93   Steering Systems

93a   Transom hung rudder — gudgeoned, pintled & tiller

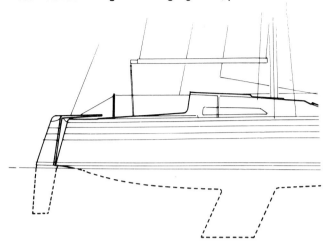

93c   Aerofoil section rudder — stock & bottom bearing

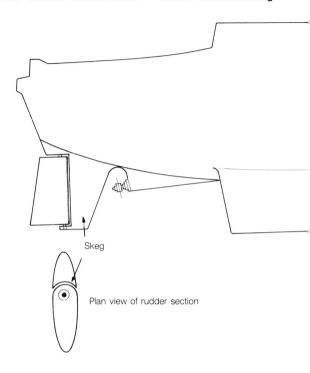

Skeg

Plan view of rudder section

93b   Spade rudder — inboard rudder gland & cable

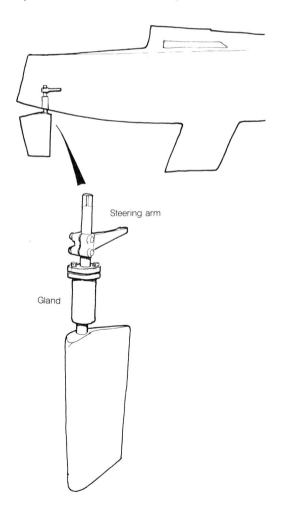

Steering arm

Gland

considering fabricating the bearing portion of the skeg shoe so that the housing unbolts and can be removed without detaching the whole skeg (Illus. 94b).

7.   Where a skeg shoe is fitted and bolted through the skeg moulding, to save 'pinching' the moulding, laminate a wooden block in position to take the pressure when the skeg bolts are tightened up.

8.   Sailing craft fitted with aerofoil rudders may, under power, experience an annoying tendency to incur a juddering helm. This is caused by the aerofoil rudder acting in the same manner as an aircraft's wings — that is causing lift, which in a boat is a tendency to move the rudder to one side or the other. This deviation can be alleviated by fitting a bar on the 'propeller hand' side of the rudder section (Illus. 95). Unfortunately, only trial and error determines the exact size but usually the dimensions are quite surprisingly small and for a craft of 8m (26ft) might well involve a slat measuring 6mm (¼") deep by 20cm (8") long.

9.   Stainless steel is recommended for rudder stocks where a GRP aerofoil foam filler rudder is standard, but mild steel can be used for other types of rudder plate installation, as long as the anodic protection is adequate.

10.   Ensure that rudder stocks are squared off at the top end in a diamond fashion, thus facilitating the provision of a tiller head or steering arm.

93d Rudder plate, stock & tube

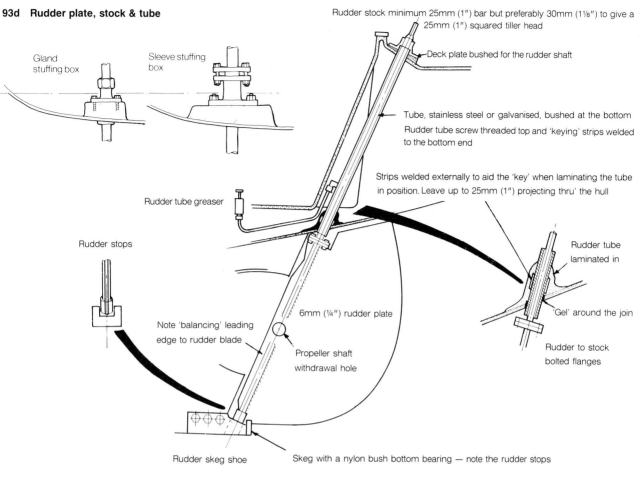

Gland stuffing box

Sleeve stuffing box

Rudder stock minimum 25mm (1″) bar but preferably 30mm (1⅛″) to give a 25mm (1″) squared tiller head

Deck plate bushed for the rudder shaft

Tube, stainless steel or galvanised, bushed at the bottom
Rudder tube screw threaded top and 'keying' strips welded to the bottom end

Strips welded externally to aid the 'key' when laminating the tube in position. Leave up to 25mm (1″) projecting thru' the hull

Rudder tube greaser

Rudder stops

Rudder tube laminated in

6mm (¼″) rudder plate

Note 'balancing' leading edge to rudder blade

Propeller shaft withdrawal hole

'Gel' around the join

Rudder to stock bolted flanges

Rudder skeg shoe

Skeg with a nylon bush bottom bearing — note the rudder stops

93e Rudder plate & inboard gland

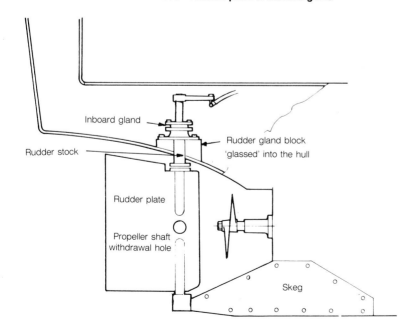

Inboard gland

Rudder gland block 'glassed' into the hull

Rudder stock

Rudder plate

Propeller shaft withdrawal hole

Skeg

Illustration 94 Rudder Stops and Removable Skeg Bearing

94a Various rudder stops

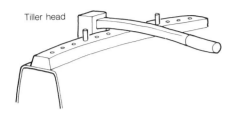

Tiller head

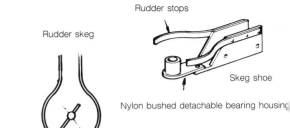

Rudder stops

Rudder skeg

Skeg shoe

Nylon bushed detachable bearing housing

Rudder

35°

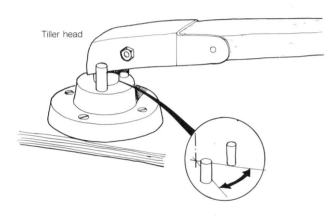

Tiller head

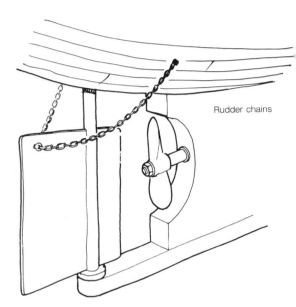

Rudder chains

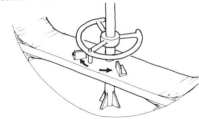

Quadrant Rudder arm

94b Detachable skeg bearing

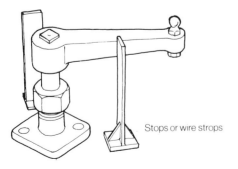

Rudder lever stops

Stops or wire strops

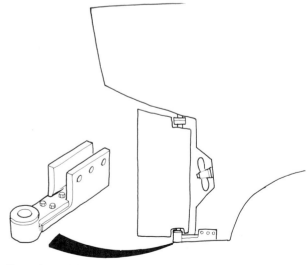

Bearing holder bolted to the skeg

Illustration 95   Aerofoil Rudder Bars

Left hand propeller

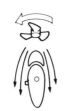

Results in 'lift' & a
steering bias to the
port hand

Fit the bar & the
bias/lift is countered

NB With a right hand propeller the bar is fitted to the right or starboard side
of the rudder moulding. This will counter a starboard steering tendency

STEERING

The method of transmitting the helmsman's
requirements to the rudder depends on the type of craft
and style of rudder. Alternatives include a tiller (*See* Illus.
52a), wheel (*See* Illus. 52b & c), and pedestal (Illus. 96).

Tillers
Ash provides a good looking tiller handle whilst
laminations of ash and mahogany make an extremely
attractive article. A folding tiller head gets the wretched

Illustration 96   Pedestal Steering

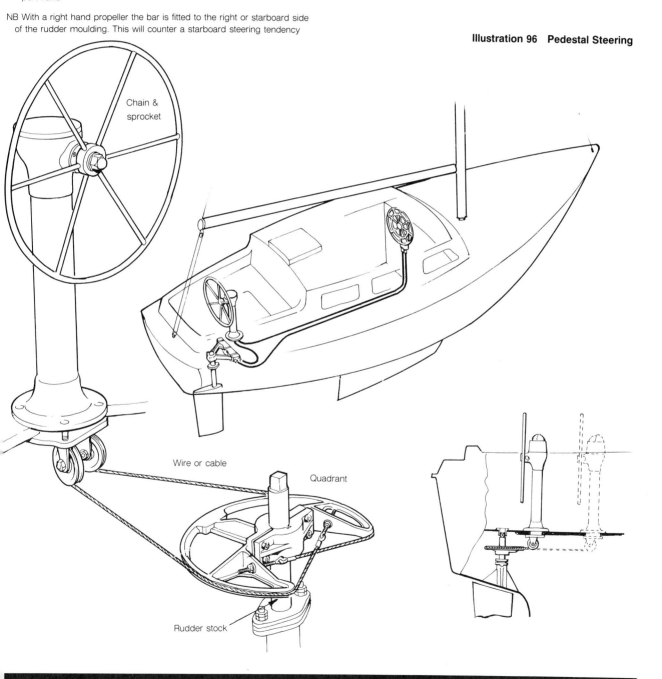

Chain &
sprocket

Wire or cable

Quadrant

Rudder stock

thing out of the way when not in use (Illus. 97). Illustrations 98b & c detail suggested emergency tiller arrangements but the layout depends on the design of the craft. Some motor sailers require an extension rudder stock brought up through the cockpit coaming or seat mouldings on to which a spare tiller and head can be quickly positioned. If the extension rudder stock projection would cause a nuisance or obstruction, by emerging through the cockpit sole, bring the 'offending' stock to just below the surface and fit a large screwed brass fishing boat style deck plate for access (Illus. 98c).

Wheels

Wheel steering may be made up of wire, chain, sprockets and pulleys but any saving in costs over and above a cable system is more than offset by the fiddly

Illustration 97 Folding Tiller Heads

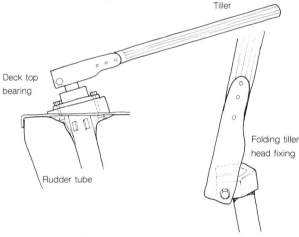

Tiller

Deck top bearing

Folding tiller head fixing

Rudder tube

Illustration 98 Wheel Steering and Emergency Tiller Arrangements

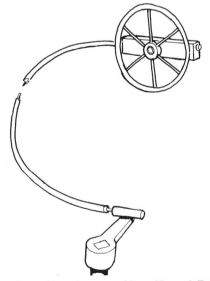

98a Proprietary inner & outer cable — Morse & Teleflex type

nature of the installation. Cable steering utilises a rack and pinion to operate a heavy duty, single spiral wound inner cable sliding in a fixed outer, the rudder arm being connected directly to the inner cable (Illus. 98a). Where possible, motor sailers should be fitted with an alternative steering capacity and the wheel, usually fitted in the wheelhouse, be capable of speedy disconnection for the secondary arrangement to be put into operation (Illus. 98b & c).

Pedestals

A wheel mounted on a pedestal is becoming a popular addition to sailing craft but is a comparatively expensive 'bolt on goody'. The layout requires a pedestal complete with radial wheel drive, stainless steel wheel, recessed sheaves, wire and chain assembly and mounting bolts (See Illus. 52 & 96). The amount of 'advantage' gained depends upon the radius of the quadrant and the number of teeth on the chain sprocket. Generally, a 0.6m (24") diameter wheel system can be said to equate to a 2.4-3m (8-10ft) tiller. The wire system has the advantage of being easily adapted to two station steering.

Apart from other wheel steering benefits, it is jolly difficult to steer a centre cockpit craft without one because the rudder stock usually ends beneath the aft cabin berths. (See Illus. 98c). To continue the stock through the cabin to the coach roof would result in an incumbrance to the accommodation. Furthermore, most of the major controls, sheet winches and engine controls will be in or around the cockpit so it is desirable that the steering be placed within the same area.

Hydraulic systems are available but, being comparatively expensive, are probably outside the scope of this book.

Anodic or Galvanic Protection

All craft must have serious attention paid to anodic protection due to the electrolytic action set up in water between dissimilar metals.

Many marine engines have sacrificial anodes fitted into the cooling waterways. Sacrificial anodes must be fitted to the hull of a vessel, the rudder and skeg shoe, propeller shaft, the sterngear and the engine. The rudder and skeg should be fitted with thru' bolted bar anodes whilst the sterngear and engine can be protected by bolt on and thru' hull anodes fitted with bonding cables (Illus. 99a).

Metals have various voltage conductivity and if different metals are used for fastenings, especially below the water-line, it is best to ensure that their voltage difference is as small as is possible. The table for corrosion is expressed in terms of a metal's 'Nobility' (See Chapter Eighteen). The more likely a metal is to corrode, the less Noble it is, i.e. zinc; the less the metal corrodes the more Noble it is, i.e. some of the stainless steels. But beware as many stainless steels are subject to crevice corrosion

98b Aft cockpit motor sailer — suggested auxiliary steering assembly

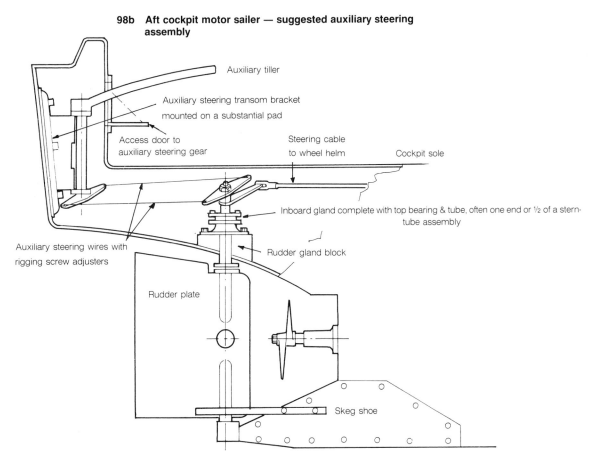

Auxiliary tiller

Auxiliary steering transom bracket mounted on a substantial pad

Access door to auxiliary steering gear

Steering cable to wheel helm

Cockpit sole

Inboard gland complete with top bearing & tube, often one end or ½ of a stern-tube assembly

Auxiliary steering wires with rigging screw adjusters

Rudder gland block

Rudder plate

Skeg shoe

98c Aft cockpit motor sailer — suggested auxiliary steering assembly

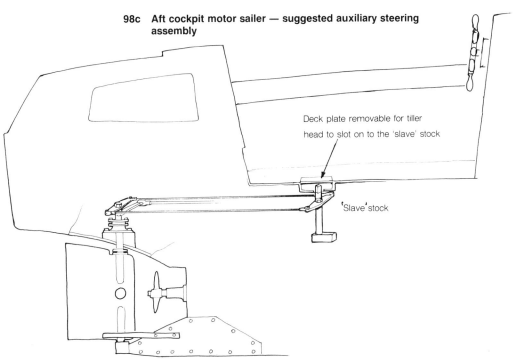

Deck plate removable for tiller head to slot on to the 'slave' stock

'Slave' stock

in sea-water and so generally speaking should not be used underwater in any circumstances.

The safest course of action is to use Admiralty Brass or Manganese Bronze fastenings below the water-line, more especially as the majority of the thru' hull skin fittings are manufactured in a similar material. Where totally dissimilar metals must be used it is advisable to have the less Noble metal of a much larger size than the more Noble metal which is exactly the case where a steel rudder plate and stock are fitted adjacent to a bronze outboard stern gland bearing. Sea-water anodes are cast in zinc.

Inland Waterway craft should be fitted with magnesium alloy anodes suitable for freshwater cruising (Illus. 99b).

Illustration 99 Anodic Protection

99a

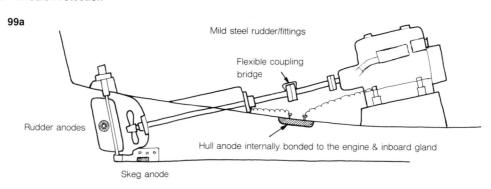

Mild steel rudder/fittings

Flexible coupling bridge

Rudder anodes

Hull anode internally bonded to the engine & inboard gland

Skeg anode

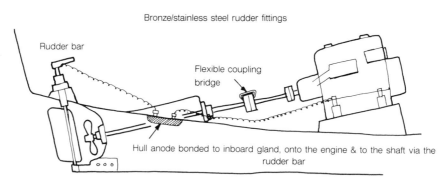

Bronze/stainless steel rudder fittings

Rudder bar

Flexible coupling bridge

Hull anode bonded to inboard gland, onto the engine & to the shaft via the rudder bar

99b Inland Waterway craft

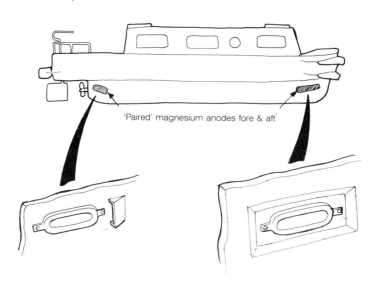

'Paired' magnesium anodes fore & aft

12

DOMESTIC ELECTRICS

None of us seems to 'like' electrics and boat domestic electrics are usually approached with a great deal of caution.

But, failing a friendly auto-electrician or a friend with knowledge which more often than not can be a very dangerous solution, an owner must set to and do the job himself.

BATTERIES

For serious cruising twin batteries are recommended, wired into a fourway isolator/change-over switch. These are vapourproof and allow for off, one or the other of the batteries or both to be connected into the circuit (*See* Illus. 82 & Chapter Ten, Batteries,). 'Handraulic' I know, but I am not entirely convinced as to the eternal infallibility of switching and blocking diodes (Illus. 100). These devices allow the charge to each battery to be metered proportionately to that particular battery's state of discharge, without allowing either battery to discharge into the other. If not properly ventilated, switching and

blocking diodes fail due to the heat generated. They also have a voltage drop of some 0.75 volts.

Incidentally, if an alternator is fitted, the hand operated type of master switch must NOT be used when the engine is running, otherwise the alternator will be open circuited and damaged.

I maintain that the minimum battery amperage size is 65 ampere hour for engines up to 20hp and 125 ampere hour for power units of 30hp and over. The quoted amperages may seem to be in excess of the 'recommended' but take into account a craft's requirements for a typical ten hour period without the engine being run. Do purchase batteries with built in carrying handles, an 'extra' that is a great help when an owner has to leg the 'hellish' thing ashore for winterization.

Wiring should be run in PVC or rubber insulated and sheathed, twin core, stranded copper cable. To achieve a neat and professional looking job, purchase a proprietary fused switch panel with the switches purpose labelled or engraved. Mount the panel as close as

possible to the power supply, i.e. the appropriate battery.
Certain supplies may well be required to be fitted 'upstream' of the batteries and the isolating switch, including automatic bilge pumps, burglar alarms and fire fighting equipment, all of which must be separately and adequately fused.

WIRING CABLES

To ensure that the cables for each run have sufficient current capacity, bear in mind that it is better to choose a thicker rather than a thinner cable, for the thicker the wires the less resistance. The maximum recommended voltage drop on a 12 volt system is 0.75 volt.
Metrification of wire sizes has taken much of the 'black magic' from cable sizes and the required functions. The table below gives some outline details.

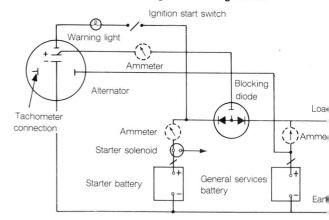

Illustration 100   Switching and Blocking Diodes*

* With acknowledgements to Lucas Marine

Cable Type	Conductor*	Size mm²	Current Rating	Voltage Drop Factor	Voltage Drop per metre
Single core PVC flex	14/0.25	0.7	6	0.059	0.0272
	14/0.30	1.0	8.75	0.043	0.0188
	28/0.30	2.0	17.5	0.023	0.0094
	44/0.30	3.0	27.5	0.015	0.0060
	65/0.30	4.5	35.0	0.009	0.0041
Twin core PVC flex, insulated & sheathed	2x16/0.20	2x0.5	3	0.083	0.0544
	2x24/0.20	2x0.75	6	0.059	0.0272
	2x14/0.25	2x0.7	6	0.059	0.0272
	2x14/0.30	2x1.0	8.75	0.043	0.0188
	2x28/0.30	2x2.0	17.5	0.023	0.0094
	2x44/0.30	2x3.0	27.5	0.015	0.0060
Triple core starter cable	3x14/0.30	3x1.0	8.75	0.043	0.0188
	37/0.90	25	170	0.0026	0.000762
	61/0.90	40	300	0.0016	0.000462
	61/1.13	60	415	0.0011	0.000293

* by courtesy of Ripaults Ltd.

Consumption calculations
The formula to calculate voltage drop is E = I x R where E is the voltage drop, I is the units amperage consumed and R is the resistance in ohms along the wire length (the resistance per foot x the length of wire). Incidentally watts = amps x volts and is the electrical unit in which, for instance, light bulbs are expressed.
A 12 volt 8 watt neon tube consumes (W = A x V) ie. 8 = X x 12 or X x 8/12th = ²/₃ amp. Now with 5 neon lights in series, four of 8 watt and one of 13 watt the total amperage is 4½ or say 4 amps. To calculate the required cable size for this lighting run, use the table or the

formula E = I x R. Checking on the table, the twin core cable 14/0.25, with an amperage rating of 6 amps, would seem to be suitable. The controlling factor is the length of cable required and the resultant voltage drop. If the run totals say 12 metres, allowing for the return distance, then E = 4 x (0.0272 x 12) where E is the voltage drop, 4 is the lighting amperage consumed, 0.0272 is the voltage drop per metre and 12 is the cable length. The calculation gives an E or voltage drop figure of 1.2976 volts which is well in excess of the allowable figure of 0.75 volts. Taking a cable one size up (i.e. 14/0.30) gives the equation E = 4 x(0.0188 x 12) or 0.9024 volts. This is still not quite large enough but the twin core cable 2 x 28/0.30, with an amperage rating of 17.5 amps, more than adequately carries the required current.

Two important points to remember are:
1. That voltage drop must be calculated from the battery and not the distribution panel, and
2. The 'Diversity Factor' which takes into account, when considering the total loads on the battery, that not all the services will be switched on at the same time and is usually allowed for at 20% of the possible, maximum voltage demand.

One other example will suffice and involves the supply from the battery to the main switch panel. If the panel has 6 switches rated at 4 amps each, then a cable with a rating of 24 amps is required (ie. 6 switches x 4 amps). If the cable length from the battery is 3 metres, or a 6 metre return run, then a cable of 27½ amp rating would appear to be adequate but the calculated voltage drop

is $E = 24 \times (0.0060 \times 6)$ or 0.9840, which is over the limit. In this case it is possible to fit a cable of greater amperage or it might well be advisable to split the supply to the panel, thus halving the rating required. A 12 amp and 17½ amp rated cable gives a voltage drop of 0.6788 volts $(E = 12 \times (0.0094 \times 6))$ well within the maximum allowable voltage drop of 0.75 volts. But the voltage drop must be calculated over the total supply, that is from the source to the service point or from the battery to say a masthead navigation light. To allow for the total loadings it would be necessary to fit far heavier cable from the battery to the switch panel.

Domestic Wiring
From the schematic wiring diagram in Illustration 101 it will be noted that similar services are wired on the fused circuit in parallel.

The cabin or domestic wiring is easiest installed prior

Illustration 101   Schematic Domestics Wiring Diagram

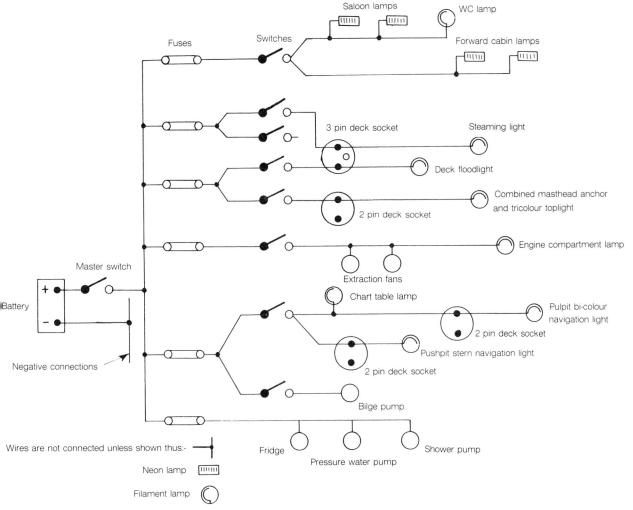

NB The negative return wires are not shown for sake of clarity

Illustration 102   Cable Routes and Runs

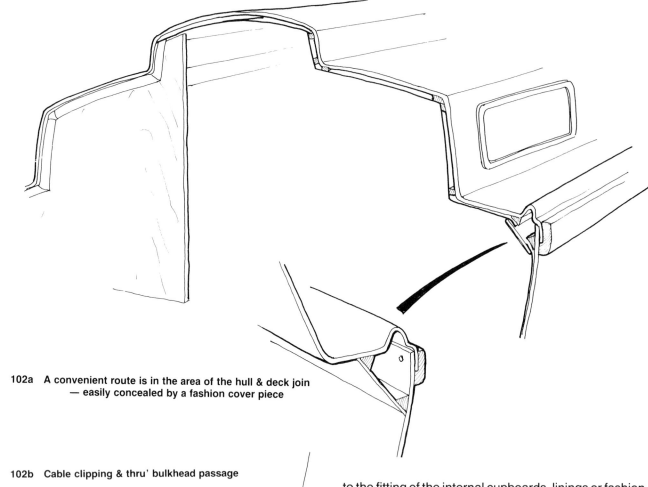

102a   A convenient route is in the area of the hull & deck join
— easily concealed by a fashion cover piece

102b   Cable clipping & thru' bulkhead passage

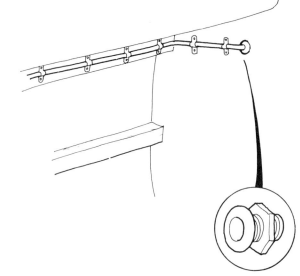

to the fitting of the internal cupboards, linings or fashion pieces. One of the avenues through which to lead the cables is up under the inwale, that is the internal area in the way of the hull to deck join (Illus. 102a).

Wiring must be clipped on to a timber track or ducted in a plastic conduit. Where a wire or wires pass through a bulkhead ensure that the edges of the bulkhead are rounded off and that the cables are well fastened, either side of the bulkhead (Illus. 102b).

Connection of cables should be via a connector box (Illus. 103a) but if needs be a 'chocolate' block or crimped connectors will suffice (Illus. 103b). Incidentally crimped fittings benefit from running some solder into the connection. Please do not simply wrap bare cable ends around each and then wrap in insulation tape. Where cables are led into a fitting form a drip loop (Illus. 103c).

When cable runs cannot be fixed on a track route them through spiral wound wrapping or polythene tubing. Do not run domestic and navigation instrument services adjacent to each other.

Illustration 103   Connections

103a   A connection box

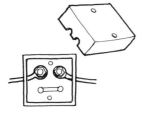

103b   A 'chocolate' block & or crimped connectors

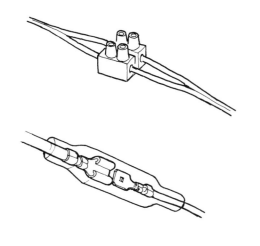

Ensure the connectors are soldered

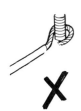

Oh & don't wrap wires around a fitting or round each other

103c   Drip loops

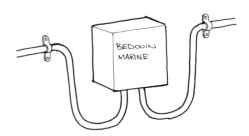

Fittings

There are some extremely attractive 8 & 13 watt neon lamps available for cabin illumination. In the toilet compartment a 15cm (6") rim switch is probably favourite and don't forget to fit two, strategically placed 15cm (6") rim switch lamps in the engine compartment. The mast lights should be led via deck sockets and plugs, one 2 pin for the combined masthead anchor light and tricolour top light and one 3 pin for the deck flood light and steaming light. The use of 2 and 3 pin plugs is to ensure the pins and plugs are not muddled (Illus. 104a). Ensure the sockets are fitted to the fore side of the mast to save being kicked when working at the inner end of the boom, are well bedded on sealant and have a 'blind' in the form of a timber upstand. This should be as tight as possible to the fore end of the sockets, but leaving enough room to unscrew the plug and screw on the sealing cap when they are disconnected. The

Illustration 104   Deck Mounted Pins and Plugs

104a   Waterproof deck sockets & plugs

104b

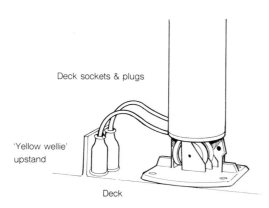

Deck sockets & plugs

'Yellow wellie' upstand

Deck

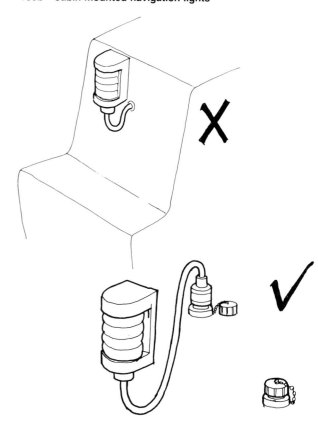

upstand helps save the deck stepped sockets and plugs from involuntary kicks from 'yellow wellies' (Illus. 104b).

Also connect pushpit and pulpit mounted navigation lights via deck sockets and plugs (Illus. 105a) as well as cabin-side mounted navigation lights. It is not good enough to simply poke the wire thru' the mouldings (Illus. 105b). Illustration 105c gives an idea of the navigation light cable runs required.

Motor sailers fitted with a wheelhouse often have additional electrical circuits wired from the console engine instrument switch panel, itself connected to the batteries. These may well include the navigation, wheelhouse and engine compartment lights, as well as the ventilator fan and windscreen wipers.

Illustration 105   Navigation Lights

105a   Pulpit & pushpit mounted lights

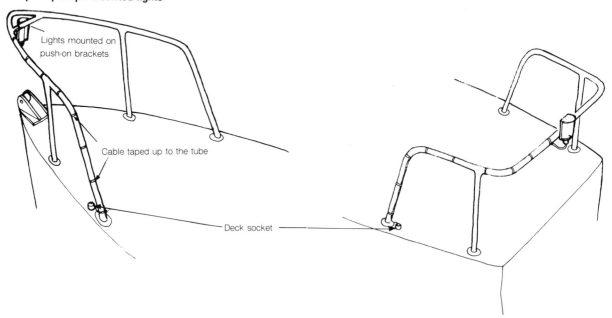

Lights mounted on push-on brackets

Cable taped up to the tube

Deck socket

105c Cable Runs

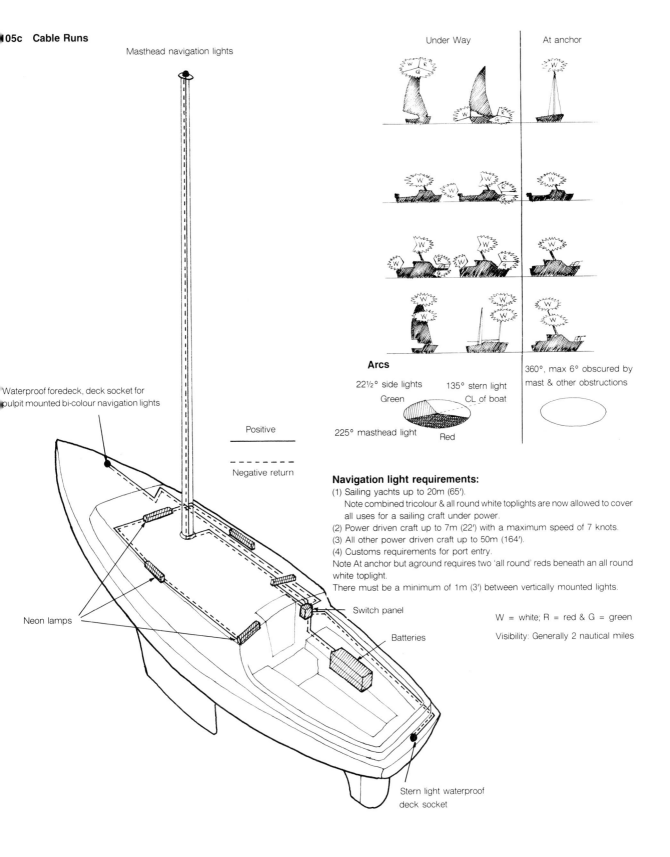

Masthead navigation lights

Waterproof foredeck, deck socket for
pulpit mounted bi-colour navigation lights

Neon lamps

Positive

— — — — — — —
Negative return

Under Way

At anchor

Arcs

22½° side lights

Green

135° stern light

CL of boat

225° masthead light

Red

360°, max 6° obscured by
mast & other obstructions

Navigation light requirements:
(1) Sailing yachts up to 20m (65′).
   Note combined tricolour & all round white toplights are now allowed to cover
   all uses for a sailing craft under power.
(2) Power driven craft up to 7m (22′) with a maximum speed of 7 knots.
(3) All other power driven craft up to 50m (164′).
(4) Customs requirements for port entry.
Note At anchor but aground requires two 'all round' reds beneath an all round
white toplight.
There must be a minimum of 1m (3′) between vertically mounted lights.

W = white; R = red & G = green

Visibility: Generally 2 nautical miles

Switch panel

Batteries

Stern light waterproof
deck socket

A pair of small horse power engine beds bedded on resin putty & ready for laminating. Just perceptible are the surrounding berth units protected with brown paper & sticky tape.

Motor Sailer engine beds dry fitted to the hull with the timber tube in position.

Right A large inboard marine engine installed in a Motor Sailer viewed thru' the cockpit sole hatch. Note the stainless steel waterlock in the exhaust run & the well insulated engine side bulkheads.

Below.A neatly installed, flexibly mounted 12hp inboard marine engine.
Don't miss the inboard stern gland remote greaser.

13

FINISHES, TIMBER LININGS & FITTING OUT — THE COMMENCEMENT

I recognise that an owner completing a craft is involved in the task as a labour of love as well as, quite possibly, a dream to create the perfect boat. Consequently, whilst involved in the Herculean task, it is unlikely that the possibility of ever selling the repository of all this toil and money will be a factor in the innumerable and various considerations to be weighed in the balance. But one day and for whatever reason, she just might have to be sold.

Now it is said that beauty is in the eye of the beholder, thus an owner can quite easily ignore the most eye catching faults in the construction of the craft. But will guests, fellow yachtsmen and, more importantly, potential purchasers? Accordingly it is not only aesthetically but economically prudent to concentrate on achieving a professional look to the construction and finishing work. This can quite often be achieved with little extra material cost but does require thought and effort which, although demanding and time consuming, are comparatively inexpensive. Incidentally, the above strictures must be nowhere more uppermost than when

considering the selection of the motive power but those considerations have been discussed in Chapter Ten.

The reason for introducing the subject of finishes here is that the installation of the major bulkheads has already been dealt with but, prior to fitting the minor and sub-bulkheads, the question of framing, cover strips, rails, edging and cappings must be given attention. Rather like the Victorian adage that 'Table legs should not be left uncovered' — nor should the edges of any timber! More importantly perhaps, a carefully rebated hardwood section not only achieves the required objective of covering a main bulkhead end grain but accommodates a return bulkhead (Illus. 106a). Illustration 106b sketches other possible methods of capping bulkhead edges. Obviously the general layout will have been sorted out by now but decisions as to the detail may not have been decided (Illus. 107a & b).

BUNKS, SUB & SUPPORT BULKHEADS

With the major bulkheads in position, the method of

Illustration 106   Plywood Edgings

106a   Rebated bulkhead capping

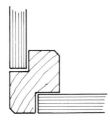

Hardwood section for not only edging the main bulkhead but to accommodate
the return bulkhead

106b   Other plywood cappings

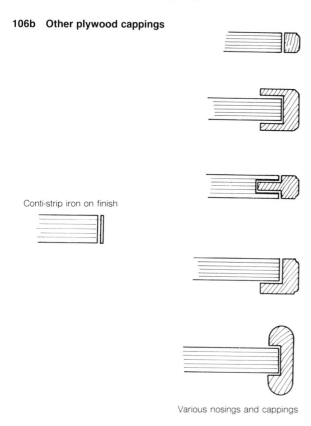

Conti-strip iron on finish

Various nosings and cappings

construction of the bunks, positioning of the galley, chart table, form of dining table and seating arrangements must be finalised.

If available, were internal headlinings, sole, berth and side lining mouldings purchased? To have made this decision, both the extra cost as well as the inflexibility of slavishly following a builders' layout will have been weighed against the extra work and time involved in fitting out a completely bare shell. If some or all of the standard mouldings are being used, the scope to alter the interior is very limited.

Presuming an owner has gone his own way, sub bulkheads, which should be constructed of a minimum of 9mm (⅜″) and preferably 12mm (½″) plywood, are usually fitted at berth divisions, galley unit and navigation table ends. The height and shape will be determined by the position, purpose and aesthetic appearance. For instance, where a main cabin berth runs into a quarter berth, the height above the bunk top may vary from nothing to the thickness of the berth cushion. On the other hand a galley or chart table bulkhead may be quite substantial in size, in the case of the galley to keep any spillage within the compartment.

Beneath berth, plywood sub-bulkheads should stiffen the construction and double up as dividers for storage. If a false sole or floor is fitted, and the various joints laminated in, a 'dry locker' is created. Loose GRP mouldings and custom built berth units require to be supported by battens screwed and glued athwartship to the main and sub-bulkheads, as well as by under berth bulkheads scribed into the hull. Fasten the outboard bottom face to the hull stringers and the trailing vertical edge to hull and sole bearers (Illus. 108). The framework for berth units may appear a comparatively basic task as the joints are simple. On the other hand, the number of overlapping joints requires the project to be thought through carefully, otherwise the same piece of timber will be half lapped twice or more (Illus. 109a)!

Most of the concealed framing throughout the craft can be of 50mm x 25mm (2″ x 1″) whitewood but do treat the timber with a preservative prior to installation. Keep joints simple (See Chapter Five); glued, brass screwed or gripfast nailed and blocked. A whitewood framework tied into the hull stringers and covered with 9mm or 12mm (⅜″ or ½″) ply fastened all the way round the edges will, with mattress fiddles in place, form a sound, good looking unit. Berth tops may be plain faced ply, whilst the visible fronts should be of an appropriately veneered or faced ply.

I prefer top to front access to the bunk storage as it is less fiddly and more capacious than drawers. If carefully jigsawed the top aperture cut-outs can be re-used as the access lids. The underside of the berth top will require to be battened, preferably with a hardwood section screwed and glued in position. Dummy hardwood surrounds fixed to the berth fronts break up bare expanses of GRP or plywood (Illus. 109b).

It may be useful to be reminded of some approximate minimum dimensions suitable for a berth unit for which See Chapter Seven.

CHAIN LOCKER COMPLETION

The chain locker compartment and bulkhead, but for a few details, should now be almost finished. If the chain locker can be accessed via a foredeck hatch, then fair enough. All that is required is to laminate the anchor

Illustration 107   'Typical' Craft Layouts   107a   General arrangement interior layout plan & elevation for an 8.5m (26ft) Sailing Yacht

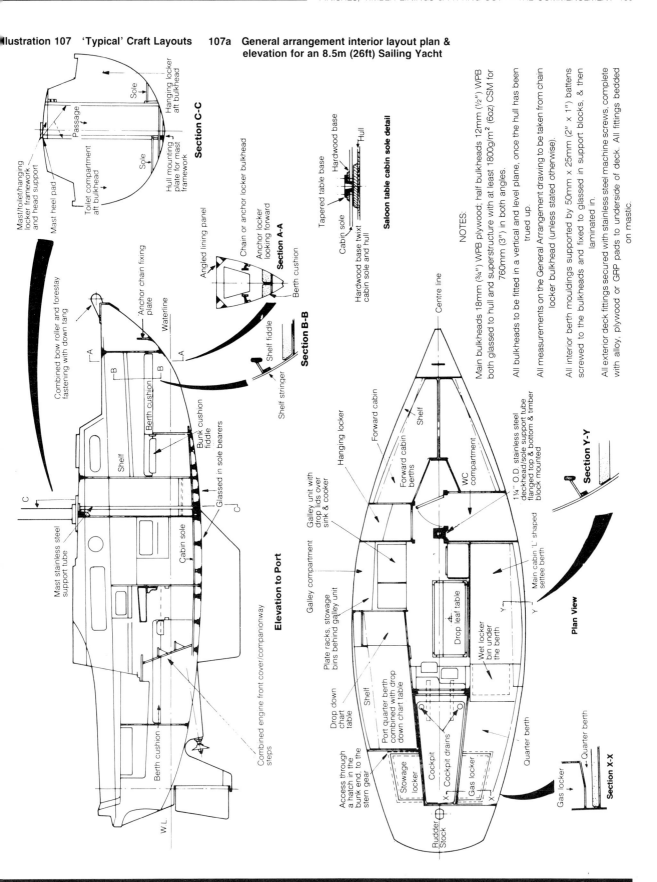

Section C-C

Mast/toilet/hanging locker framework and head support

Mast heel pad

Sole

Passage

Hanging locker aft bulkhead

Toilet compartment aft bulkhead

Hull mounting plate for mast framework

Sole

Section A-A

Chain or anchor locker bulkhead

Angled lining panel

Anchor locker looking forward

Berth cushion

Section B-B

Shelf fiddle

Shelf stringer

Combined bow roller and forestay fastening with down tang

Anchor chain fixing plate

Waterline

Berth cushion

Bunk cushion fiddle

Shelf

Glassed in sole bearers

Cabin sole

Mast stainless steel support tube

Berth cushion

Combined engine front cover/companionway steps

W L

Elevation to Port

Saloon table cabin sole detail

Tapered table base

Hardwood base

Hull

Cabin sole

Hardwood base twixt cabin sole and hull

Centre line

NOTES:

Main bulkheads 18mm (¾") WPB plywood; half bulkheads 12mm (½") WPB both glassed to hull and superstructure with at least 1800g/m² (6oz) CSM for 760mm (3") in both angles.

All bulkheads to be fitted in a vertical and level plane, once the hull has been trued up.

All measurements on the General Arrangement drawing to be taken from chain locker bulkhead (unless stated otherwise).

All interior berth mouldings supported by 50mm x 25mm (2" x 1") battens screwed to the bulkheads and fixed to glassed in support blocks, & then laminated in.

All exterior deck fittings secured with stainless steel machine screws, complete with alloy, plywood or GRP pads to underside of deck. All fittings bedded on mastic.

Forward cabin

Shelf

Hanging locker

Forward cabin berths

WC compartment

1¼" O.D. stainless steel deckhead/sole support tube flanged top & bottom and timber block mounted

Section Y-Y

Galley unit with drop lids over sink & cooker

Galley compartment

Plate racks, stowage bins behind galley unit

Shelf

Drop down chart table

Port quarter berth combined with drop down chart table

Access through a hatch in the bunk end, to the stern gear

Stowage locker

Cockpit

Cockpit drains

Gas locker

Rudder Stock

Drop leaf table

Wet locker bin under the berth

Main cabin 'L' shaped settee berth

Quarter berth

Plan View

Gas locker

Quarter berth

Section X-X

107b   General arrangement of a 13m (42′) canal cruiser *

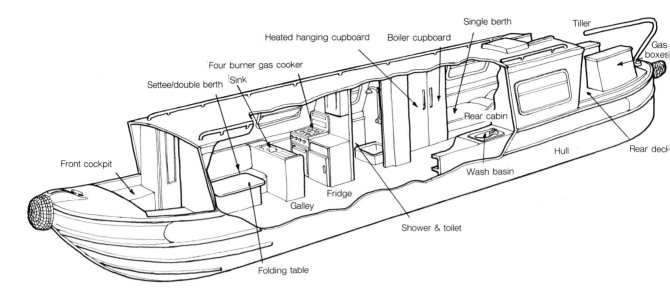

Single berth

Tiller

Heated hanging cupboard   Boiler cupboard

Gas boxes

Four burner gas cooker

Settee/double berth   Sink

Rear cabin

Front cockpit

Wash basin

Hull   Rear deck

Fridge

Galley

Shower & toilet

Folding table

* With acknowledgements to Wyvern Shipping Co, Leighton Buzzard

Illustration 108   A Dry Locker and Berth Construction

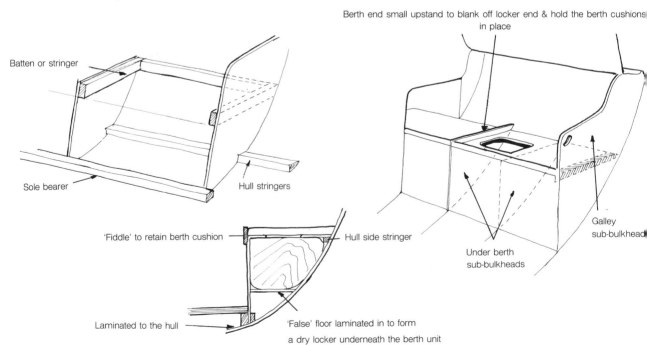

Berth end small upstand to blank off locker end & hold the berth cushions in place

Batten or stringer

Sole bearer

Hull stringers

Galley sub-bulkhead

'Fiddle' to retain berth cushion   Hull side stringer

Under berth sub-bulkheads

Laminated to the hull

'False' floor laminated in to form a dry locker underneath the berth unit

Illustration 109 More Berth Construction

109a Berth framing

Best

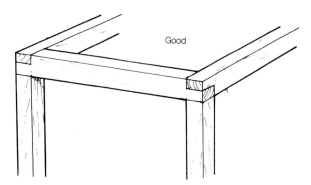

Good

No! Far too complicated — and what's left to fasten to which?

chain fixing plate on the hull centre line. The plate can be a plywood upstand with a hole to accommodate the chain end D shackle. After which cut the locker drain holes through the hull, making sure they are close to the bottom of the locker and of an adequate size (we don't want seaweed or rubbish blocking off the drains and leaving the chain locker filled with water). Gel over the exposed hull laminate edges and fit shell mouldings to cover the rawness of the drilling. Lastly, headlining material, stuck down in the compartment protects the inner forepeak skin from chain damage.

Where deck entry is not available, then a tight fitting hatch will have to be let into the chain locker bulkhead, thus allowing access via the forecabin (*See* Illus. 107a).

DOOR FURNITURE FASTENINGS, LIPPINGS, SHELVES & FIDDLES

Wherever hanging, say, a toilet compartment door on a plywood sheet, the fastenings should be thru' bolted

109b Top access & dummy surrounds

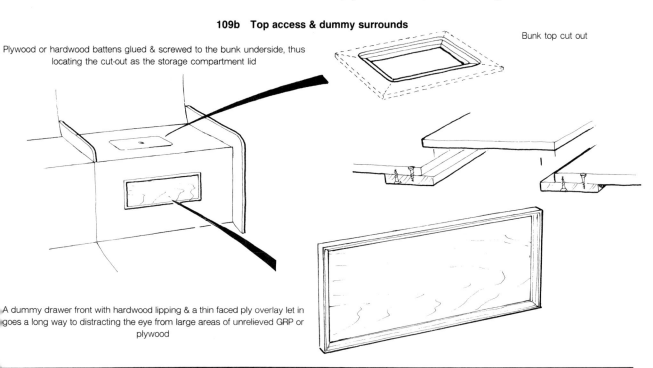

Plywood or hardwood battens glued & screwed to the bunk underside, thus locating the cut-out as the storage compartment lid

Bunk top cut out

A dummy drawer front with hardwood lipping & a thin faced ply overlay let in goes a long way to distracting the eye from large areas of unrelieved GRP or plywood

rather than screwed (Illus. 110a). Which reminds me that another advantage of hardwood lipping or capping is that, where screws are to be used for fixing, there will be something solid into which to securely fasten (Illus. 110b). Please never, never screw into plywood end grain (or for that matter any end grain) unless, say, a dowel of hardwood has been let into the ply to accommodate the fastening (Illus. 110c).

Illustration 110   Door Furniture Fastenings

110a   Bolting thru' ply

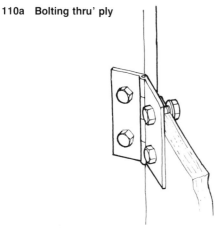

If a bolthead will appear unsightly, use round head fastenings

110b   Solid fixing for screws

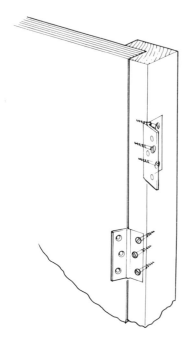

Where fastening into a hardwood section, screws are acceptable for fixing door furniture

110c   A hardwood plug or dowel

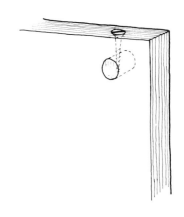

Where no other alternative is possible let in a hardwood plug or a dowel. Mind you, despite the illustration detail, a screw cup might be a desirable, aesthetic addition!

Where it is inconvenient to persuade a timber capping or edging to fit a sharp curve, it is permissible to use a synthetic stick-on strip. They are available in various widths and matching finishes and can be utilised, for instance, on heavily rounded bulkheads or sharply radiused plywood fascia cut-outs (Illus. 111a). To employ a timber lipping requires square edges to the cut-out to facilitate angled joints or, alternatively, that a timber finish is laid on the surface of the fascia (Illus. 111b).

Cut-outs can be either left open or converted into cupboards and, where situated at the correct height, the doors may be covered with material, doubling up as a padded backrest (Illus. 112a). Conventional cupboard doors look best if the edge lipping protrudes slightly, as should the capping of the surrounds into which it fits. Very convenient fastenings for this type of door are the finger hole and lever catch for which timber rings can be purchased in matching teak or mahogany finishes

If at all possible, ensure internal doors are the more substantial panel construction rather than unbraced plywood, which may well warp with time and damp. Shelves, should be deep and angled so that, even when the craft is heeled over, the contents cannot spill out. If not behind a fascia, the shelf fiddle must be deep and not some piddling apology for an upstand (Illus. 113a). Do not forget to leave a 'crumb' gap so that dirt and dust can easily be cleaned away (Illus 113b).

Illustration 111   Alternative Cut-out Treatment

111a   A stick-on strip ironed in place

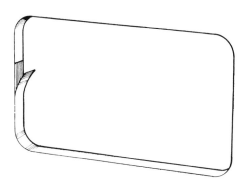

111b   Angled joint lipping & face timber overlays

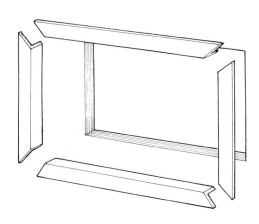

Illustration 112   Cupboard Doors and Fastenings

112a   Possible cut-out cupboard doors

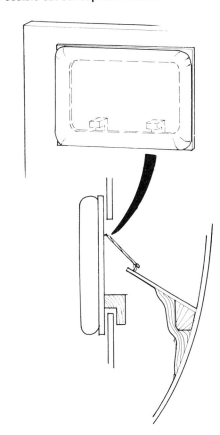

112b   Cupboard door fastenings

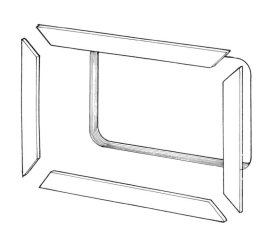

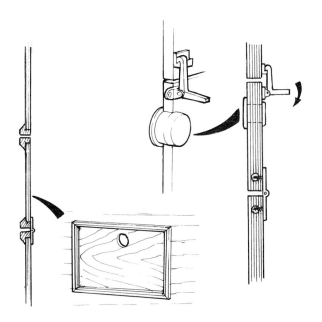

Illustration 113   Shelf Fiddles and Crumb Gaps

113a   A sensible, substantial shelf fiddle

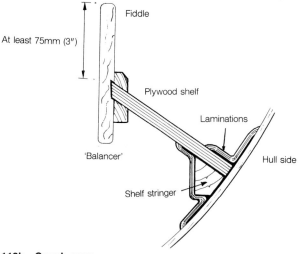

Fiddle

At least 75mm (3″)

Plywood shelf

Laminations

'Balancer'

Hull side

Shelf stringer

113b   Crumb gaps

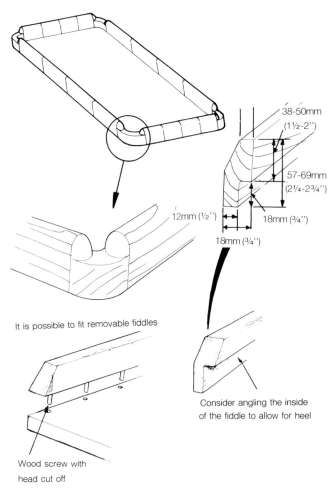

38-50mm
(1½-2″)

57-69mm
(2¼-2¾″)

12mm (½″)

18mm (¾″)

18mm (¾″)

It is possible to fit removable fiddles

Consider angling the inside
of the fiddle to allow for heel

Wood screw with
head cut off

COVERINGS

In considering the internal aspects of a boat an owner must plan and visualise how each section of the internal shell is to be treated. For instance, will the exposed 'bits' be left bare or be covered with foam backed headlining glued directly to the sides of the hull and deck; will material covered, shaped plywood sheets be fixed in position; will marine grade hessian or carpet finish be stuck to the interior; will fascia panels and cupboard units be used to both conceal portions of the hull, or will a mixture of all or some of these possibilities be utilised (Illus. 114)?

Illustration 114   Facias and Coverings

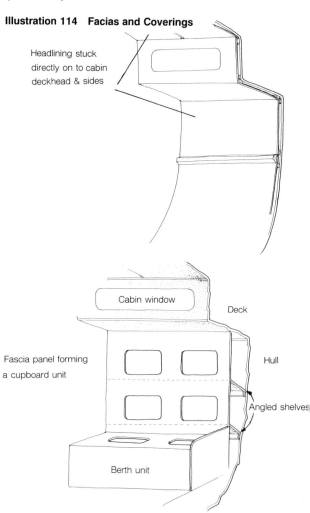

Headlining stuck
directly on to cabin
deckhead & sides

Cabin window

Deck

Fascia panel forming
a cupboard unit

Hull

Angled shelves

Berth unit

Note the cupboard front forms a fiddle or upstand for the well angled shelves

Where an area is large enough, make use of material covered 4mm plywood sheet and cut the panel slightly oversize so it can be sprung into position. On craft up to about 8.5m (28ft) the necessity to keep the maximum headroom available usually precludes the extensive use

Illustration 115   'Springing' Headlining Panels and Coverings for Metal Frames

115a   Cover strips to hold deckhead panels in position

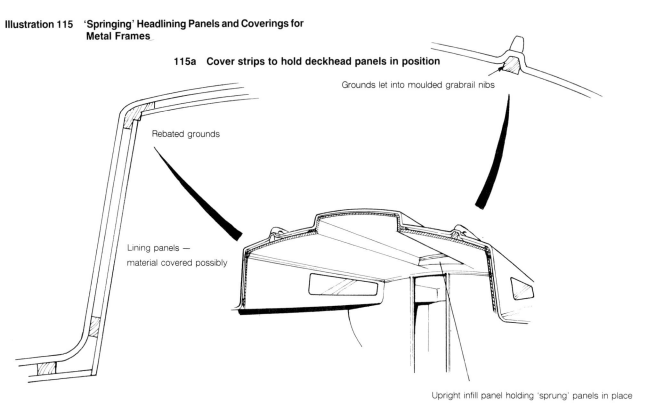

Grounds let into moulded grabrail nibs

Rebated grounds

Lining panels — material covered possibly

Upright infill panel holding 'sprung' panels in place

of 'grounds' to which panels can be fastened but does not limit their use on the hull sides. It may be possible to strategically position thin plywood slats and to laminate blocks into external grabrail 'nibs' moulded in the superstructure. The use of judicious 'springing' and adequate bulkhead cover strips will more than adequately hold a deckhead lining panel in position (Illus. 115a) and this subject is more fully set out in Chapter Fifteen (See Illustrations 172a, b, c, d, e, f, & g.)

Coverings for Steel & Aluminium Shells
The internal deckhead beams and stiffeners should be hardwood capped. Not only does this help trap headlinings but a knock on the head with a rounded piece of wood is, although unpleasant, not nearly so serious as the impact of a cold metal edge (Illus. 115b).

Fastenings
If fastenings have to be face fitted, and look unsightly, there are a number of proprietary means to neaten them, one such being Snap Caps which have a plastic base rather like a cup washer with a snap on cap (Illus. 116). Very ingenious.

115b   Metal edges hardwood capped

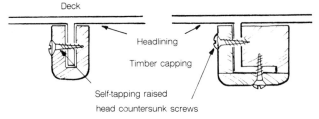

Deck

Headlining

Timber capping

Self-tapping raised head countersunk screws

Internal deck stiffners & frames timber capped for the eye of the beholder & safety as well as trapping headlinings

Illustration 116   'Snap Caps'

Plastic cup washer & snap on cap for concealing screw heads

Settee berth with an offset table & large drop down leaf. Well it's easier on larger yachts! The table support doubles up as a deckhead to hull support. Also visible are the internal grabrails & a massive athwartship main bulkhead beam, blocked at either end.

Main cabin berth/chart table hooked onto the galley bulkhead & dropping down to complete the berth end when required. One of the chart table support knees is just visible.

The 'business' or deckhead end of a pipe cot berth where the back rest inner lining, to the right, hinges up to form the berth. The forward strap (in view) is snap-shackled back onto itself when not in use.

14

FITTING OUT — THE COMPLETION, DETAILED DRAWINGS, SKETCHES, IDEAS & FINISHING OFF

Fitting out is very much a matter of personal choice and cannot be subject to hard and fast pronouncements. Having said that, some suggested guide lines will not go amiss.

FORECABIN

Remember when planning the forecabin that it may well have a dual purpose on a sailing craft. Whilst under sail, (I nearly wrote canvas but terylene would be more appropriate) this area often becomes a sail store — discarded spinnakers, genoa's or general purpose foresails being bundled below from the foredeck. Apart from 'aiding this activity', through ventilation and safety occasions the fitting of a forehatch. Why not a good quality, aluminium framed unit, fully glazed with bars to protect the toughened glass and an opening of about 51 x 51cm (20″ x 20″)? This type of hatch allows light (in a cabin which can often be rather murky), ventilation (where very much required, especially when trying to introduce a draught) and an excellent point of exit in case

the main cabin is blocked by bodies or, more frighteningly, by some disaster. Where the hatch cannot be conveniently bolted directly to the deck surround, it is usually possible to construct a hardwood frame to marry the two together (Illus. 117a).

Although the designer's mind occasionally goes blank and little detailed assistance is given, a GRP hull and deck quite often comes complete with a moulded forehatch. This is especially so when the hatch is fitted in an area of compound curves and a proprietary article would not easily fit. The hatch moulding may well require stiffening with additional layers of GRP applied to the inside. It is not at all rare to hear tales of forehatch's being blown away — most regrettable in any weather, let alone a gale when all openings should be battened down. A little thought usually enables the hatch moulding to be top hinged which, combined with a sensible, internally mounted catch, should provide a workmanlike job (Illus. 117b). Sealing also requires attention, especially if the moulded upstand is not of sufficient depth or width to enable the hatch to make a good grounding. It may be

Illustration 117 Fore-hatches

117a Anodised aluminium hatch framework

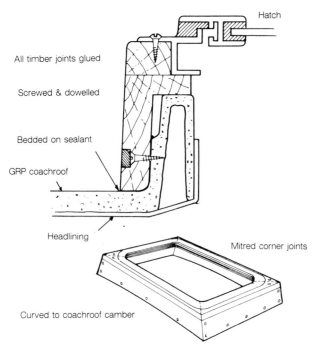

All timber joints glued

Screwed & dowelled

Bedded on sealant

GRP coachroof

Headlining

Hatch

Mitred corner joints

Curved to coachroof camber

Hardwood frame counterbored, screwed, dowelled & glued up

117b   Fixing a moulded fore-hatch

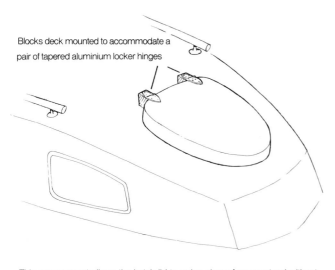

Blocks deck mounted to accommodate a
pair of tapered aluminium locker hinges

This arrangement allows the hatch lid to swing clear of any upstand without
binding

necessary to fit a timber or metal upstand on to which a rubber or neoprene strip seal can be affixed (Illus. 117c).

An opening porthole or two in the forecabin might be a thought, and a static ventilator a necessity (*See* Illus. 136).

Where the forecabin contains two angled berths, a worthwhile wrinkle is to make a wooden infill complete

117c   Fastening & sealing moulded fore-hatches

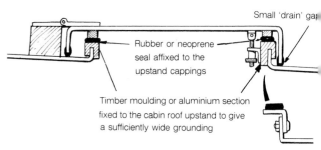

Small 'drain' gap

Rubber or neoprene
seal affixed to the
upstand cappings

Timber moulding or aluminium section
fixed to the cabin roof upstand to give
a sufficiently wide grounding

Fore-hatch catches should be bolted in position towards the corners to save
unnecessary snagging

with a shaped drop-in section of mattress so that the whole area can be made into one enormous berth (Illus. 118). Fit a fiddle upstand on the open side to retain the mattress infill in position. This arrangement is very suitable for children, more especially if, in the evenings, a door can shut the cabin off from carousing adults.

Where space precludes fitting a door, a zipped vinyl panel let into the forecabin entrance will more than suffice (Illus. 119a) as it will for any open fronted, hanging locker (Illus. 119b).

Illustration 118   Forebunk Infill

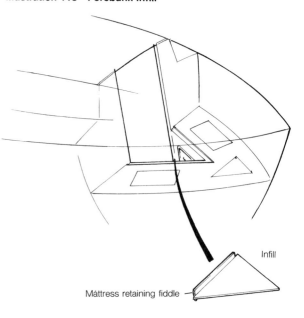

Infill

Mattress retaining fiddle

Illustration 119   Zipped Vinyl Panels

119a   As a cabin door

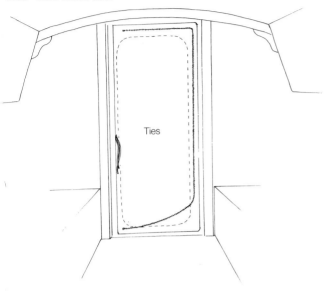

Illustration 120   A Toilet Plinth

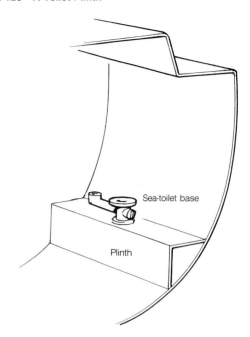

119b   As a hanging locker door

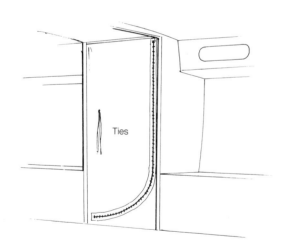

THE TOILET COMPARTMENT

Position and choice of the toilet is of paramount importance when considering the space available. To get the right 'sitting' height it may well help to place the toilet on a plinth. This may be a necessity, due to the rise of the hull sides (Illus. 120).

The siting of sea-toilet seacocks needs care. They must be easily accessible but the reinforced pipes, necessary to connect the inlet and outlet to the toilet unit, are not easily pushed out of the way. It may be an idea to have fabricated a bend where the pipe has to execute more than a slow curve (Illus. 121). The water inlet must be in front of the outlet otherwise flushing simply recycles the stuff . . . ! If the craft's layout is fairly standard, it is conceivable to install the seacocks beneath one of the fore or main cabin berths. Clearly mark the 'on' and 'off' positions — it is surprising how often crew get it wrong and wonder why 'the . . . . thing won't work'.

Whilst mulling over the toilet valves (and why not?) resist the temptation to buy cheap items. It is no good congratulating oneself on how smart one has been to save so much money and there really is no difference . . . . There is a difference between inexpensive and costly valves and it's in the engineering (Illus. 122a). When the tapered sleeve on a cheaper valve is tightened up to stop leaking it usually distorts the angled and ground tapered seat. This tends to bind, so the securing nut has to be slackened off, which results in the valve leaking more furiously, so the securing nut has to be tightened, which binds more, so . . . !

Tighten the seacocks down on internal pads in order to spread the load on the hull (Illus. 122b). After 'bedding' down, check that excess sealant is cleaned from the bores, otherwise the loo won't work!

Fitting reinforced hoses to the seacocks can be a struggle unless you 'have the knowledge'! In this case it involves immersing the end of the pipe in a bowl of very hot water and applying a little, light oil to the spigots.

Illustration 121   A Sea-toilet Pipe Fabrication

122b   Seacock grounds

See Illustration 26c for backing pad composition to suit various shell material

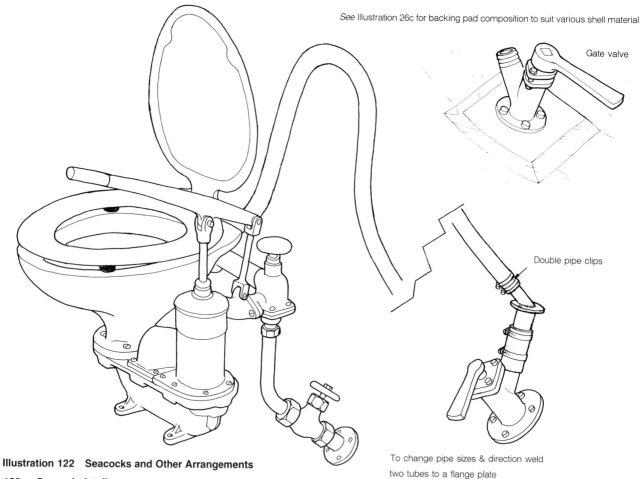

Gate valve

Double pipe clips

To change pipe sizes & direction weld
two tubes to a flange plate

Illustration 122   Seacocks and Other Arrangements

122a   Seacock detail

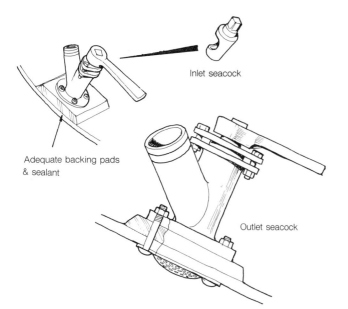

Inlet seacock

Adequate backing pads
& sealant

Outlet seacock

122c   A Porta-Potti

Modern design has done away with the old 'bucket & chuck-it'!

Hey presto! Double stainless steel clip the pipes.
   Other installations include the Porta-Potti type of
portable unit with an integral holding tank (Illus. 122c)
and a sewage holding tank system (Illus. 122d).

122d Waste water & sewage holding tanks

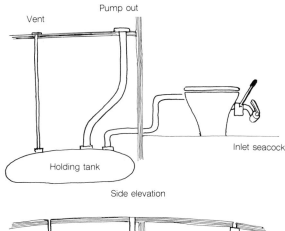

Vent

Pump out

Holding tank

Inlet seacock

Side elevation

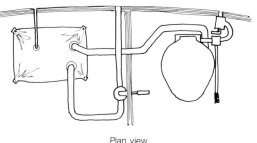

Plan view

Illustration 123 Showers

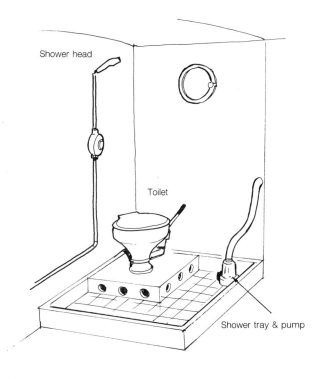

Shower head

Toilet

Shower tray & pump

If a shower can be fitted the extra cost will be amply repaid in both onboard comfort and onshore costs. Most marinas charge for showers! The systems now available enable an inexpensive and a really worthwhile installation to be fitted, especially when coupled to a suitable galley sited water heater (Illus. 123). The shower head is best placed in the corner closest to the door of the compartment or over the toilet unit, so giving the maximum amount of room for a 'hose down'. The shower tray, constructed of marine ply and laminated in position if necessary, should be sloped and watertight with a recess to facilitate a drain pump (we don't want soapy suds straying into the bilges, do we?) One of the small, hull mounted electric bilge pumps piped via a non-return valve and a thru' hull gate valve does the job excellently.

Should a vanitory unit be incorporated, it is a space saving thought to mount it on slides so that it pushes away under the side-deck when not in use. Brass 'shoots' lock the unit in the relevant position and the waste can be emptied into the toilet bowl when the basin is in the 'out' position — which does save on another thru' hull skin fitting (Illus. 124).

Illustration 124 Vanitory Units

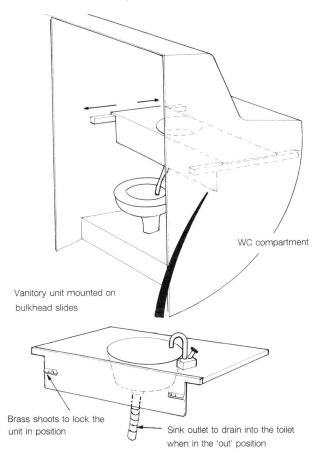

WC compartment

Vanitory unit mounted on bulkhead slides

Brass shoots to lock the unit in position

Sink outlet to drain into the toilet when in the 'out' position

Illustration 125 Schematic Fresh Water and Low Pressure Bottled Gas Installations

125a Domestic water system

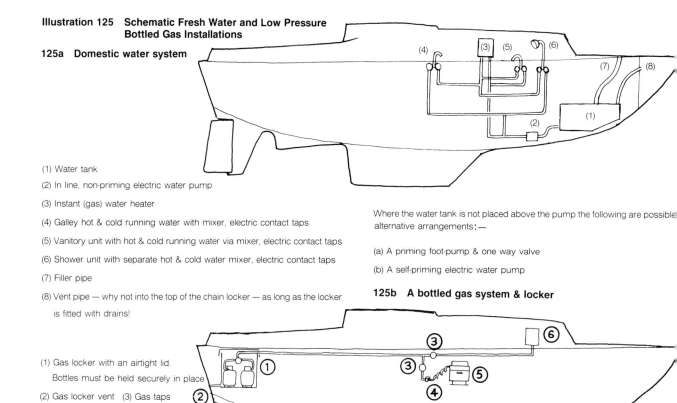

(1) Water tank

(2) In line, non-priming electric water pump

(3) Instant (gas) water heater

(4) Galley hot & cold running water with mixer, electric contact taps

(5) Vanitory unit with hot & cold running water via mixer, electric contact taps

(6) Shower unit with separate hot & cold water mixer, electric contact taps

(7) Filler pipe

(8) Vent pipe — why not into the top of the chain locker — as long as the locker is fitted with drains!

Where the water tank is not placed above the pump the following are possible alternative arrangements:—

(a) A priming foot-pump & one way valve

(b) A self-priming electric water pump

125b A bottled gas system & locker

(1) Gas locker with an airtight lid. Bottles must be held securely in place

(2) Gas locker vent   (3) Gas taps

(4) Flexible pipe from a bibcock fitting

(5) Cooker

(6) Instant gas water heater

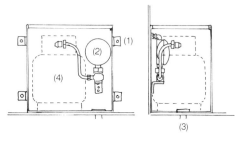

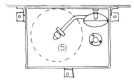

*by courtesy of Calor Gas Ltd

(1) The gas bottle box

(2) Regulator

(3) Box gas tight drain

(4) Gas bottle

(5) Gas bottle to regulator connection

A 3.9kg propane bottle locker* 381mm high, 267mm deep & 381mm wide

An opening porthole is essential, as is at least a static ventilator. On larger craft, with an adequate battery capacity, wherever static ventilators are recommended why not replace them with electric 'driven' units (See Illus. 137).

THE GALLEY

Illustrations 125a & b sketches a schematic fresh water system and a low pressure, bottled gas installation. In order to make the galley slave's job as pleasant as possible it is necessary to pay close attention to the required dimensions. For instance to fit a gas cooker with 2 rings, grill and half oven, as well as a reasonable sized stainless steel sink, the galley unit requires a width of about 101-102cm (3' 4") (Illus. 126).

Other worthwhile dimensions include:-

Worktop height	86 ½cms (2' 10")
Main worktop width	56cms (1' 10")
Shelf above worktop distance	40½cms (1' 4")
Shelf above worktop width	30½cms (12")
Maximum 'lean forward' distance (for the back of a locker etc . . .)	76cms (2' 6")

Minimum depth for a working aisle 56cms (1' 10")

125b (contd)

Gas bottle box & piping detail

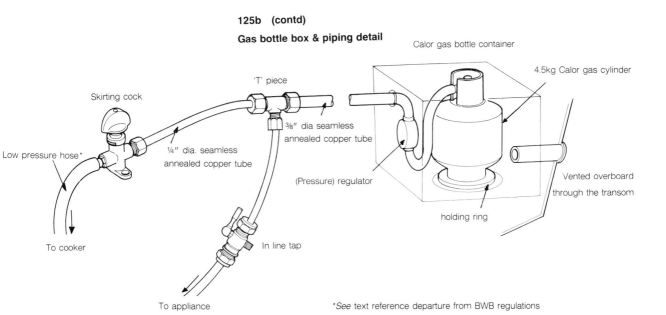

Calor gas bottle container

Skirting cock

'T' piece

4.5kg Calor gas cylinder

⅜" dia seamless
annealed copper tube

Low pressure hose*

¼" dia. seamless
annealed copper tube

(Pressure) regulator

Vented overboard

through the transom

holding ring

To cooker

In line tap

To appliance

*See text reference departure from BWB regulations

Illustration 126   The Galley Compartment

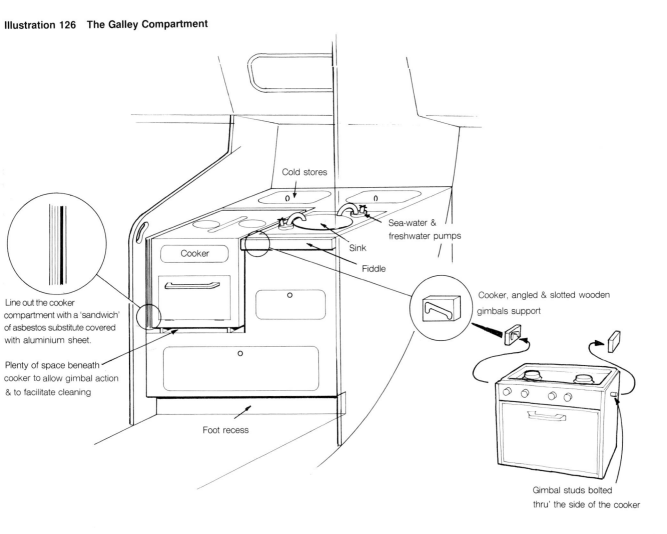

Cold stores

Line out the cooker
compartment with a 'sandwich'
of asbestos substitute covered
with aluminium sheet.

Cooker

Sea-water &
freshwater pumps

Sink

Fiddle

Cooker, angled & slotted wooden
gimbals support

Plenty of space beneath
cooker to allow gimbal action
& to facilitate cleaning

Foot recess

Gimbal studs bolted
thru' the side of the cooker

Line out the cooker compartment with a 'sandwich' of aluminium and asbestos substitute. Seagoing vessels should have the cooker gimballed. One of the proprietary cooker fiddle rails, with pan clamps, can be thru' bolted on to both sides of the cooker. If the bolts are heavy quality, say 19mm (¾") and sleeved, they can be used to gimbal the cooker in conjunction with a pair of wooden, angled slots fitted to either side of the cooker compartment. The slotted bearers should be positioned so that when the cooker is back on its lower position, it is at rest in the compartment, whilst when pulled up and forward, it is free swinging and gimballed (Illus 126).

In planning the galley, it is desirable to have a lipped flap swung off the galley bulkhead and/or the front of the galley, both ideas furnishing additional working surfaces, of which there can never be enough on a small boat (Illus. 127). Incidentally, where possible galley, table and shelf fiddles should be as much as 7½cm (3") in height, not forgetting to leave 'crumb gaps' (See Illus. 113).

The cold water pump or tap is plumbed into the fresh water tank but it is an idea to fit a sea-water pump for rinsing and washing up, so saving on precious fresh water.

Where a water heater is fitted, the system requires to be fitted with an electric pump. Two of the pumps connected in line gives sufficient head to a shower as well as a safety factor in the unlikely event of one of the pumps breaking down.

Useful additional items to fit in the galley include providing the sink with a purpose made, loose top which gives additional working surface whilst cooking (See Illus. 158); provision for a jumbo paper roll (marvellous for wiping up greasy frying pans) and a galley webbing strap. This latter aids cooking in rough weather, when snap shackled into position, being laid in or on, depending which beat the cook is 'fighting' against (Illus. 128).

Behind the cooker and sink units there might be room, well at least 20cms (8"), to fit a couple of store bins which will, if insulated, keep provisions cool. Do not omit to slope the bottom and fit a 13mm (½") sink drain size, skin fitting, coupled to a tap and drain pipe led into the bilges. This enables the locker to be washed out. Food storage lockers can get surprisingly 'interesting' and sticky due to interfusions of burst tea-bags, spilt milk, sugar and cooking fat.

Bottled Gas (Low pressure)

The bottled gas plumbing requires much care and attention. The gas bottle must be firmly mounted in a vented, gas tight box* which should be large enough to hold two bottles if possible (one spare). Often this

* Although this is not a mandatory stipulation of the BWB regulations.

Illustration 127   Galley Flaps

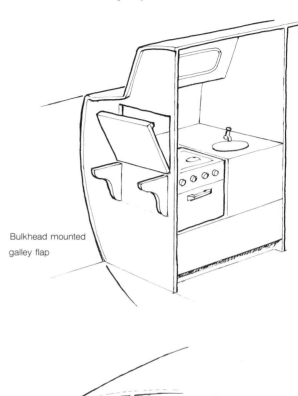

Bulkhead mounted galley flap

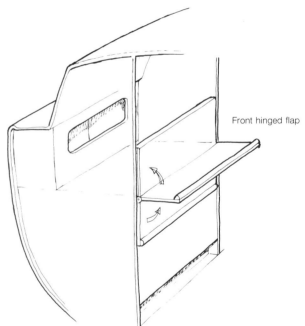

Front hinged flap

arrangement cannot be accommodated and the spare bottle must be stowed elsewhere, in another gas tight box. It is not entirely safe to rely upon shock cord to hold the bottle(s) upright and is preferable to fix a 'doughnut' or timber ring so as to locate the small upstand of the 4.5kg (10lb) bottle, or the circular bottom of the 15kg (32lb) bottle. Make the box a snug fit to the bottle(s). Vent overboard with a copper pipe diameter of at least ½″, via the transom, keeping the drain as low down as is possible, if this can be achieved (*See* Illus 125b).

Follow, say, the British Waterways Board recommendations for bottled gas installation (*See* Chapter Eight), but guide lines include the following, noting that gas pipes are only available in Imperial sizes:-

a) Pipe the main run in seamless, annealed copper tube of a minimum of ⅜″ diameter if the craft is fitted with more than one device, ie. a cooker and water heater. Otherwise ¼″ tube will suffice.

b) In the gas bottle locker form some horizontal coils in the copper pipe to absorb any movement of the bottle. Better still fit a pigtail which is a length of pre-made rubber pipe with the appropriate fittings crimped on each end.

c) Ensure the pipe run is kept as high as possible and is well clipped, more especially in the way of any bulkheads which should be rounded off where pipes pass through them.

d) Keep joints to an absolute minimum using a tee-piece to branch off to the cooker and water heater.

e) Fit a bibcock tap/skirting cock in the pipe run to a gimballed cooker with a length of low pressure hose completing the connection.

f) SWITCH OFF at the bottle every time after use**

Calor Gas bottle details include:

Butane (blue bottles)

4.5kg   (10lb); weight empty, approx. 6kg (13lb), full 10.5kg (23lb); overall height 35cms (13¾″) x width 25.5cms (10″).

15kg   (32lb); weight empty, approx 16kg (35lb), full 31kg   (68lb); overall height 63cms (24¾″) x width 33cms (13″).

19kg (42lbs); weight empty approx 20kg (44lbs), full 39kg   (86lbs); overall height 82cms (32¼″) x width 33cm (13″).

Propane (red bottles)

3.9kg   — as for 4.5kg butane but ½kg weight less for a full bottle

13kg   — as for 15kg butane but 2kg weight less for a full bottle

19kg   (42lbs); weight empty approx 20kg (44lbs), full 39kg (86lbs); overall height 82cms (32¼″) x width 33cm (13″).

I have not discussed alternatives to low pressure bottled gas for cooking and heating. If an owner plans to undertake extensive continental cruising it might be as well to consider fitting Camping Gaz appliances as the chances of picking up replacement U.K. Calor Gas

**This recommendation is contrary to BWB regulations but is necessary in the case of seagoing gimballed cookers.*

Illustration 128   Galley Slave Strap

cylinders is slight to non existent. An adaptor is available to convert Camping Gaz appliances to run off Calor Gas, but not the other way around as generally they do so without the need for one.

I am not over enthusiastic about the various pressure stoves fired by paraffin and other highly combustible liquids. On the other hand, recent developments of calibrated and computerised paraffin cookers and cabin heaters, where the fuel is sucked up to a metering device and is not therefore under pressure, look interesting and would appear to be foolproof and safe. Excess fuel is piped back to the fuel tank, in much the same way as a diesel engine fuel metering system works and exhaust gases are vented overboard. The cooker hot plates are solid with the sealed combustion chambers located underneath.

TABLES — CHART & CABIN

If the craft is not large enough to accommodate a specific chart table/navigation compartment, part of the main cabin berth can, with a little thought, be converted into a navigation area. One of the possibilities is to utilise the galley bulkhead off which to hang a chart table. There are attachments suitable for fitting to the leading edge of a detachable table and a bulkhead but they require additional support in the shape of swing out knees (Illus. 129). This type of table can only take folded, large size charts. The chart drawer needs to be about 68½cms (2′3″) wide by 46cms (1′6″). Two dozen, closely folded charts require a draw depth of about 12½ cm (5″). Other minimum measurements include an overall height of 76cm (2′6″), a seat height of 46cm (1′6″), a seat depth of 43cms (1′5″) and clear height between seat top and table top of 30 ½cms (1′), not forgetting to allow for any berth cushion thickness. Chapter Fifteen sketches some possible chart stowage options.

The main cabin table, its size and fitting is always a difficult choice and boils down to the great British compromise, much depending on the main cabin layout. A dinette berth arrangement is now rather unfashionable but does give a reasonable double berth/dining table (Illus. 130). The problem is that it is difficult to increase the number of seats and fitting a quarter berth behind the dinette is troublesome.

Minimum dimensions to seating four are:-

Table length 101½cms (3′4″) and width 71cms (2′4″)

The more fashionable 'L' shaped settee/double berth layout allows flexible seating arrangements and numerous variations of table columns, drop down flaps and folding leaves. On smaller craft a suggestion is to fit a table support tube which comes complete with tapered base, table fitting and fixed length tubes with tapered ends (Illus. 131a). One of the advantages of this particular system is that by splashing out for a spare base it is possible to fix it in the cockpit sole, thereby enjoying the luxury of a cockpit mounted dining table for those sunny days, whilst at berth. One can dream, can't one.

Another type of table post doubles up as a deckhead/cabin roof support. The column is cut to the required length for mounting to the hull (or cabin sole if well supported) and the deckhead. These fittings

Illustration 129   A Chart Table

An alternative hingeless table top leaves an uncluttered finish

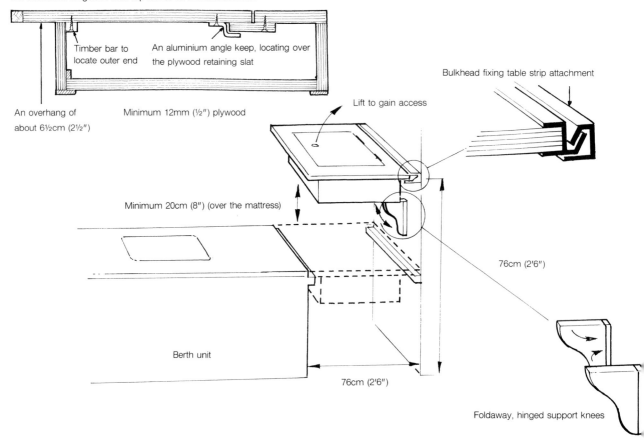

Timber bar to locate outer end

An aluminium angle keep, locating over the plywood retaining slat

An overhang of about 6½cm (2½″)

Minimum 12mm (½″) plywood

Lift to gain access

Bulkhead fixing table strip attachment

Minimum 20cm (8″) (over the mattress)

76cm (2′6″)

Berth unit

76cm (2′6″)

Foldaway, hinged support knees

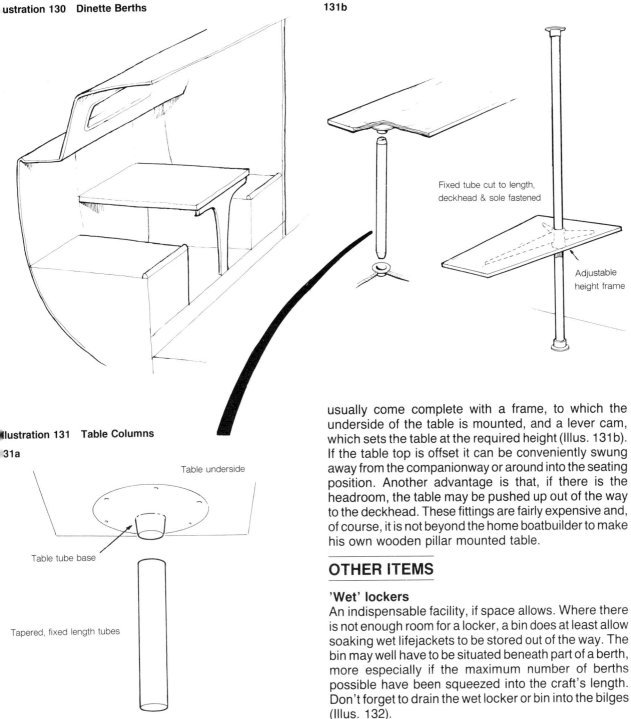

ustration 130 **Dinette Berths**

131b

Fixed tube cut to length,
deckhead & sole fastened

Adjustable
height frame

Illustration 131 **Table Columns**

31a

Table underside

Table tube base

Tapered, fixed length tubes

Sole fitting for table tube

usually come complete with a frame, to which the underside of the table is mounted, and a lever cam, which sets the table at the required height (Illus. 131b). If the table top is offset it can be conveniently swung away from the companionway or around into the seating position. Another advantage is that, if there is the headroom, the table may be pushed up out of the way to the deckhead. These fittings are fairly expensive and, of course, it is not beyond the home boatbuilder to make his own wooden pillar mounted table.

OTHER ITEMS

'Wet' lockers
An indispensable facility, if space allows. Where there is not enough room for a locker, a bin does at least allow soaking wet lifejackets to be stored out of the way. The bin may well have to be situated beneath part of a berth, more especially if the maximum number of berths possible have been squeezed into the craft's length. Don't forget to drain the wet locker or bin into the bilges (Illus. 132).

Access Hatches
When building saloon cabin berths against the cockpit main cabin bulkhead and or quarter berths, allow for hatches through the berth ends to give access to the various lockers as well as the stern and rudder gear (Illus. 133).

Illustration 132   Wet Lockers

Hanging . . .

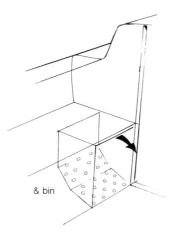

& bin

Illustration 133   Access Hatches

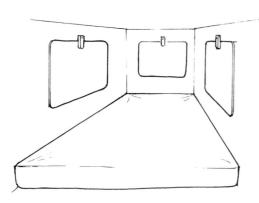

Main saloon cabin berth end

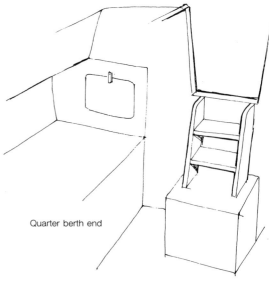

Quarter berth end

Pipe Cots

Pipe cot (or root) berths have 'fallen' out of fashion but for little cost and effort an extra berth can easily be accommodated (oh dear!). Reminiscent of those old fashioned, wartime stretchers, bulkhead mounted blocks locate the berth poles (Illus. 134a). A more sophisticated arrangement may be incorporated by top hinging and stiffening up a hull side lining which, when raised and 'hung' from the deckhead, forms a very acceptable berth (Illus. 134b).

Do not forget to provide a lee cloth (it's a long way down), not only to this berth but to all other single, main cabin berths (Illus. 135).

WINDOWS

The ultimate in cabin windows are those constructed of toughened glass fitted into anodised aluminium, alloy flanges. A mix of fixed and half sliders as well as opening 127mm (5″) and 152 ½mm (6″) portholes and a hatch or two set in the cabin deckhead supply more than adequate light and ventilation. If buying proprietary windows, ensure the finished articles are inspected prior to purchase. There are windows and windows!

That is the ultimate! Now, to save costs consider fitting perspex bolted thru' the cabin sides. Perspex is expensive and some effort may have to be made to locate a supplier with the particular requirements in stock. As the perspex will have to be individually cut, the windows can be made to the exact outline that pleases the eye. To pattern them, tape brown paper to the desired shapes on to the cabin sides and stand back to view the result.

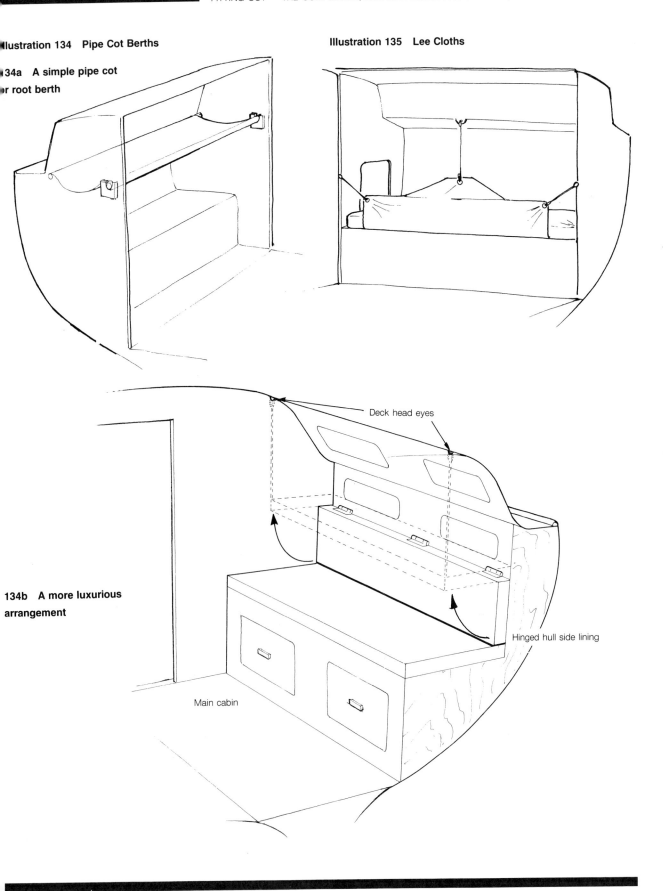

Illustration 134   Pipe Cot Berths

134a   A simple pipe cot or root berth

Illustration 135   Lee Cloths

134b   A more luxurious arrangement

Deck head eyes

Hinged hull side lining

Main cabin

The perspex should be no less than 9mm (³⁄₈″) thick; consider tinted acrylic and remember to have the edges chamfered to give them a professional appearance. If a 'friendly supplier' will not machine the perspex then it's down to the builder. When cutting perspex with a jigsaw, keep the blade cool using a liquid detergent bottle full of water and don't strip the covering paper off the perspex until all machining is entirely finished, thus saving scratches and scuffs. Grind off the edges to smooth out irregularities and use an electric drill, 'handy bolt on' bevelling attachment to make the chamfer. Allow at least 25mm (1″) overlap all the way round the cabin side cut-outs. Prior to drilling the fastening holes, test the bit on a scrap of perspex to check if the 'rake' of the drill is correct and doesn't chip and snatch. If it does, this can be overcome by grinding a slight negative rake on the drill flutes. It will also be necessary to decide what, if any, cover strips are to be fitted to the interior of the windows. If none, then select the pitch centre and distance apart of the fastening holes and drill them slightly oversize. Back off the inside with a counter bore and bed the windows on sealant prior to fastening down (Illus. 136).

Despite fabricating and fitting fixed cabin windows, if it can be helped do not attempt to save on the purchase of manufactured portholes or the forecabin hatch. Apart from their ventilation qualities, which must not be disregarded, they are very difficult items for an amateur owner to make without their declaring the matter!

Some window manufacturers conveniently supply paired, stainless steel screws and fasteners, called 'inter-screws', which make a neat job of fitting the windows. Purchase them overlong and crop to the correct length prior to fixing into the female fastener. The window fasteners or interior cover strips can be used to 'trap' cabin linings, for further details of which refer to Headlining, towards the end of Chapter Fifteen and Illustration 172.

If there is no intention to use window trims, delay finally fitting the windows until the headlining is in position. It is preferable to have a neat ring of fastening heads showing through the headlining, thus trapping it, than a row of uneven bumps beneath the surface.

VENTILATION

Why not substitute solar powered ventilators for static units? Other commendable ventilators include the PVC vents with screwed bezels and blanking caps as well as the 'Dorade' type ventilator (Illus. 137a, b, c, & d).

Observed, but to be decried on seagoing craft, is the fitting of louvred doors in the main hatch entrance. A craft must be able to take a 'knock down' and to do so the number of open 'holes' in the shell have to be kept to the minimum. If ventilation must be provided in the main hatch dropboards or doors, suitable alternatives include

Illustration 136   Window Fastenings

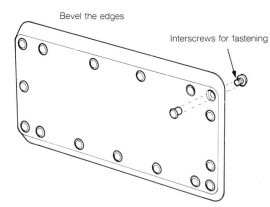

Bevel the edges

Interscrews for fastening

Evenly space the fastening holes from each other & the edge of the perspex

Methods of fastening windows & types of internal window trims

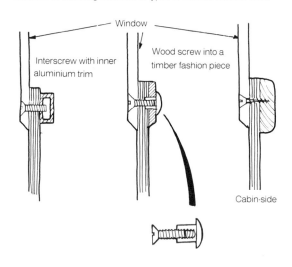

Window

Interscrew with inner aluminium trim

Wood screw into a timber fashion piece

Cabin-side

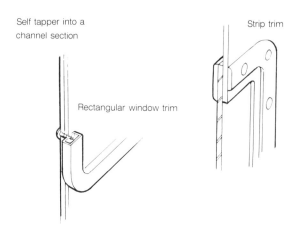

Self tapper into a channel section

Strip trim

Rectangular window trim

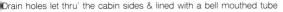

Drain holes let thru' the cabin sides & lined with a bell mouthed tube

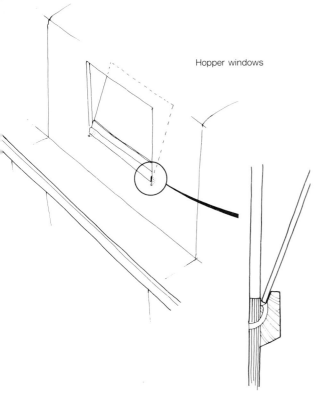

Hopper windows

a small hooded 'cut out', a butterfly ventilator or a louvred, stainless steel pressing complete with insect gauze all fitted with closures and let into the top washboard (Illus. 138).

Whilst on the subject of ventilation, I am unhappy about fitting plastic mushroom ventilators, having seen them break around the screw spindle on a number of occasions.

BILGE PUMPS

A fairly ideal bilge pumping system (Illus. 139a) can be achieved by fitting:-

1. A thru' bulkhead, cockpit mounted, self-priming diaphragm bilge pump. The main suction pipe should be led to a two-way valve with one pipe routed down into the skeg and the other through or around the engine compartment to the main cabin bilge. The pipe end must be fitted to a strum box (which gives a rather neater ending than a beaten out and drilled copper pipe).

and

2. A hull mounted electric bilge pump which, if the craft is left for long periods unattended, can be coupled to an automatic switch. The bilge water rises and the pump switches on, the bilge water level falls and

Illustration 137 Ventilators

137a Flexible PVC vents

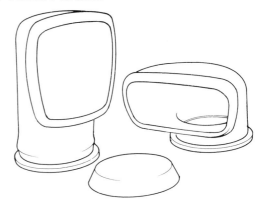

137b Electrical ventilators

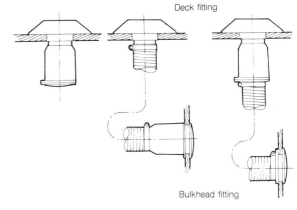

Deck fitting

Bulkhead fitting

Fan & motor switch

137c Static ventilator

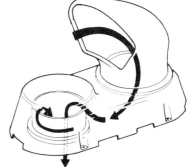

137d 'Dorade' ventilator

Illustration 138   Dropboard Ventilators and Thru' Craft Circulation

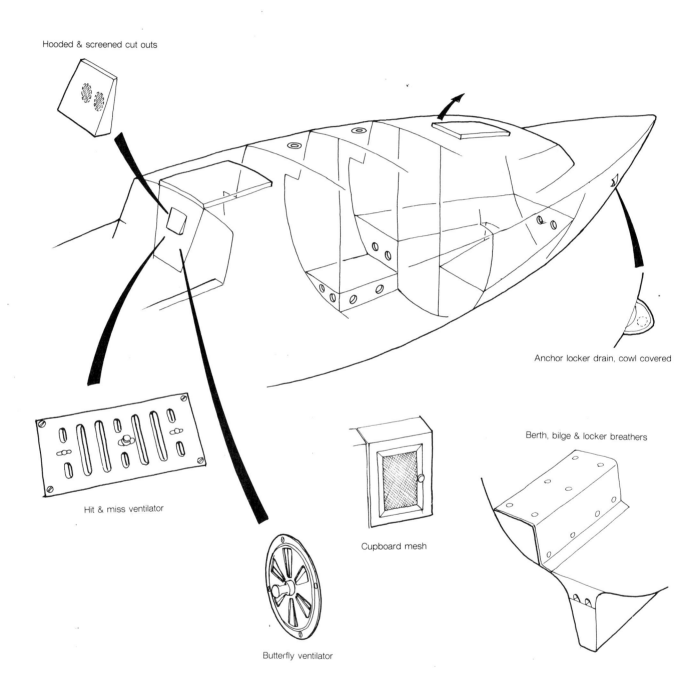

Hooded & screened cut outs

Anchor locker drain, cowl covered

Hit & miss ventilator

Cupboard mesh

Berth, bilge & locker breathers

Butterfly ventilator

Illustration 139   Bilge Pumps

139a   Bilge pumping systems & schematic layout

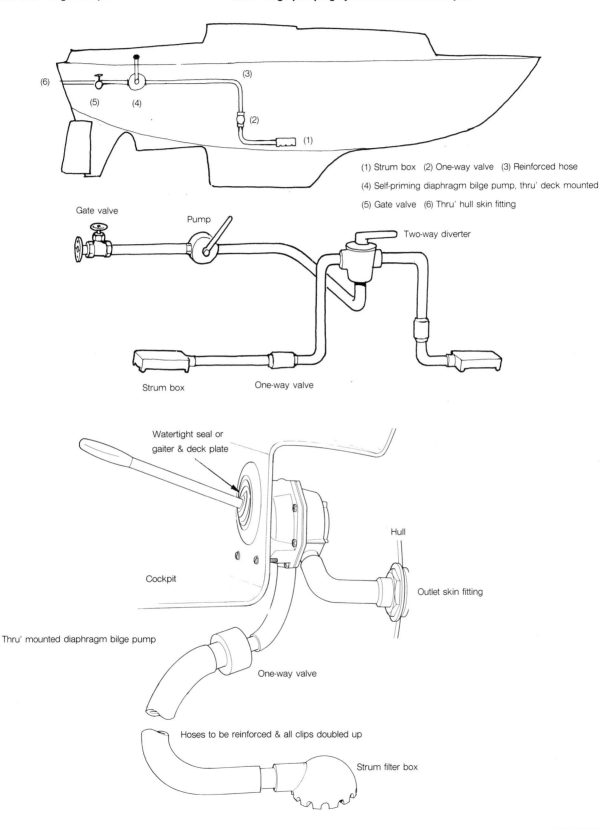

(1) Strum box   (2) One-way valve   (3) Reinforced hose

(4) Self-priming diaphragm bilge pump, thru' deck mounted

(5) Gate valve   (6) Thru' hull skin fitting

Gate valve

Pump

Two-way diverter

Strum box

One-way valve

Watertight seal or
gaiter & deck plate

Hull

Cockpit

Outlet skin fitting

Thru' mounted diaphragm bilge pump

One-way valve

Hoses to be reinforced & all clips doubled up

Strum filter box

the pump switches off; magic! (Illus. 139b). Super as long as you have a dual battery system, both are well charged and the pump is wired 'upstream' of the battery master switch. (*See* Chapter Twelve).

Manual bilge pumps should have non return valves in the pipe run as must the hull mounted electric bilge pumps, as they can 'back syphon' with disastrous results!

In case I haven't detailed the fact more than a dozen times, ALL skin fittings must be fitted with gate valves and ALL flexible pipes fastened with double, stainless steel pipe clips.

TANKS

In considering tank sizes remember that the daily consumption of fresh water per person on a boat is about 4.5 litres (1 gallon) which weighs some 4.53 kilos (10lbs).

The advent of flexible water tanks has greatly aided the professional and amateur boatbuilder for they can be fitted in awkward shaped recesses, saving having to fabricate complicated shapes in metal. Two flexible tanks may be connected in series, some distance apart and, as long as the pipe runs are practical, they can be positioned so as to balance up the weight of the craft's internal fittings. A possible layout includes a bow tank under the forecabin berth connected to another tank under one of the main cabin berths and from there to the various supply points (*See* Illus. 124). The filler pipe is usually 38mm (1½″) and the connection and outlet pipes 13mm (½″) diameter (Illus. 140). But one word of warning, do line out compartments in which flexible tanks are to be installed so that any internal hull protrusions cannot cut through the synthetic skin of the water bag. Pipe runs should be of non toxic hose fastened with (doubled) stainless steel pipe clips.

It may well be that a GRP tank or tanks are chosen for water storage, or for that matter for fuel. I am, as previously expressed, loathe to recommend GRP tanks but nonetheless they are extensively used so here goes . . . . It is quite often the case that the tanks will be situated up against the hull, the inside of which, on a GRP craft, can form one side of the tank. Two basic methods of construction may be used, the one using flat sheets of GRP and the other by laminating in shaped plywood. To make panels of GRP, 'mould wax' or tightly stretch polythene over a suitably sized, flat former which allows the resultant sheets to 'release' easily. Then roll on resin, lay down an already 'wetted out' layer of mat, stippling through the resin. Continue with layers of resin and mat until the requisite thickness for the required sheet is achieved (*See* Chapter Two for GRP 'basics'). Whichever material is used, it must be cut to the required shape, fitted to the hull, bedded on resin putty and laminated in position with 450 gms (1½oz) CSM (Illus. 141a). If using plywood, fit battening to the inside

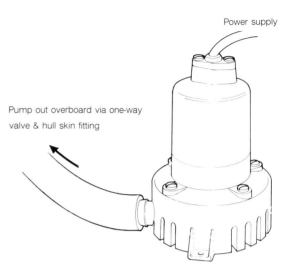

Power supply

Pump out overboard via one-way valve & hull skin fitting

Submersible free standing bilge pump

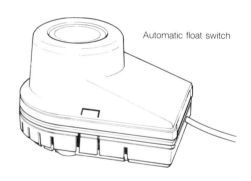

Automatic float switch

top edge and laminate with at least three layers of CSM, applied 'all over', thus completely encapsulating the plywood. The battening gives a satisfactory base on to which the top cover can be affixed. Any tank in excess of 30½cm (12″) in length should be fitted with surge baffles at spacings of about 30½cms (12″). The baffles, which can be used to support the top of the tank, are also laminated in and encapsulated. Prior to fitting the top, gelcoat the whole of the interior. Cut manholes in the tank lid, to allow access to the inside, fastening and sealing them down on a rubber gasket. The manhole fastenings must be drilled, positioned and the bolt heads glassed in. This ensures they do not turn when the nuts are tightened down and stops any liquid creeping up the threads. After the lid has been encapsulated with laminations and gelcoat, access through the manhole covers and gelcoat the internal joints.

Illustration 140   Flexible Water Tanks

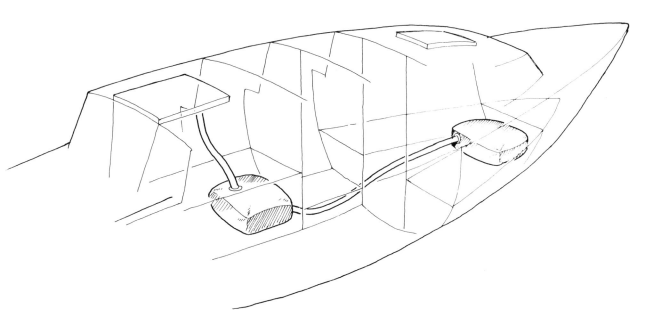

Illustration 141   GRP Tanks

Framed plywood structure, laminated *in situ*

141a   Manufacture of a GRP tank

6mm (¼″) bolt holes — drilled at 75% tapping thread size in the tank top, clearance drilled in the lid — 18mm (¾″) in from the access edge at 50mm (2″) centres

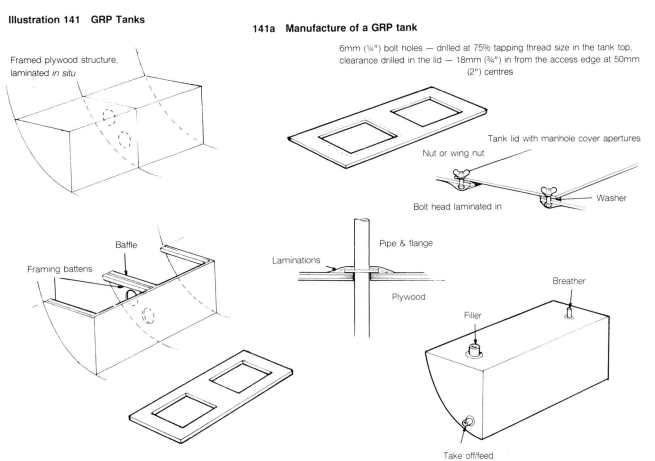

Tank lid with manhole cover apertures

Nut or wing nut

Washer

Bolt head laminated in

Baffle

Framing battens

Pipe & flange

Laminations

Plywood

Breather

Filler

Take off/feed

Depending upon the position of the tank, and where is the most convenient, the pipe take-off points must be flattened with a disc sander prior to drilling out with a tank cutter. Gunmetal or nylon thru' hull skin fittings can be used, as can a copper pipe with brazed collars. Laminate them in position.

Ensure saddle tanks are coupled with a balance pipe and shut off valves at each tank. It may be important to be able to stop the flow of liquids from one tank to another, especially whilst heeled over (Illus. 141b).

141b   Saddle tank connections

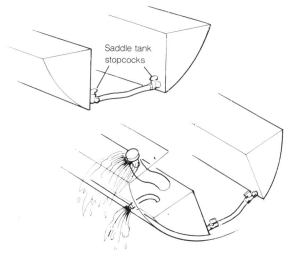

Ensure coupling feed pipe stopcocks are turned off so that tank contents do not spill out when craft heeled over

COMPANIONWAY DOORS, DROPBOARDS, HATCHES & STEPS

The main cabin companionway steps must be solidly made and mounted as a lot of 'traffic' thumps up and down them. Certainly they should be well trapped at the bottom and securely fastened at the top. Conversely, as they are probably in the way of the engine compartment, they must be able to be removed from their position reasonably easily. It is quite remarkable how, on a long haul, one or other crew member appears to spend the entire sea passage perched on the top step, so why not angle the sides to allow for heeled passages (Illus. 142).

The main companionway can be shut off with doors but the traditional and well tried method for yachts is the dropboard (washboards) frame and assembly. By slightly tapering the side frames and angling the individual dropboard top and bottom edges, the whole forms a very durable, strong and rigid construction when all in place (Illus. 143). Since the notorious and ill-fated Fastnet Race of a few years ago, it has been considered ˙ advisable for dropboards to be secured in position. Lanyarded brass pins can be used, or better still, brass

Illustration 142   Companionway Steps

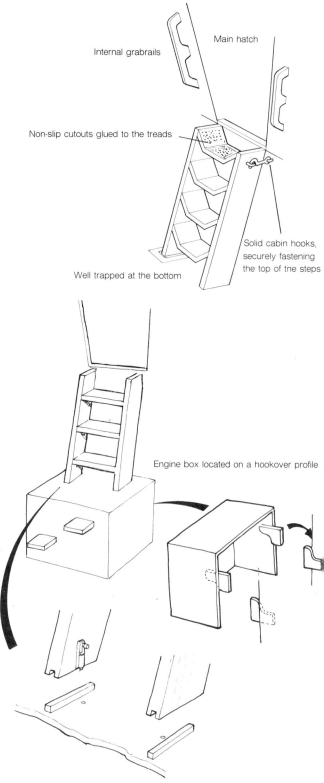

Main hatch

Internal grabrails

Non-slip cutouts glued to the treads

Solid cabin hooks, securely fastening the top of tne steps

Well trapped at the bottom

Engine box located on a hookover profile

Step foot grooved to slot on a matching slat & fixed in position with shoot bolt

Illustration 143   Dropboard Frame Assembly

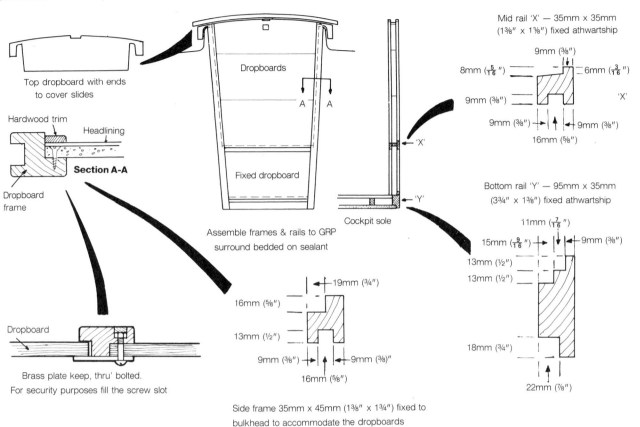

Top dropboard with ends to cover slides

Hardwood trim

Headlining

Section A-A

Dropboard frame

Dropboards

Fixed dropboard

A   A

Assemble frames & rails to GRP surround bedded on sealant

Cockpit sole

'X'

'Y'

Mid rail 'X' — 35mm x 35mm (1⅜″ x 1⅜″) fixed athwartship

9mm (⅜″)

8mm ($\frac{5}{16}$″)

6mm ($\frac{3}{16}$″)

9mm (⅜″)

'X'

9mm (⅜″)

9mm (⅜″)

16mm (⅝″)

Bottom rail 'Y' — 95mm x 35mm (3¾″ x 1⅜″) fixed athwartship

11mm ($\frac{7}{16}$″)

15mm ($\frac{9}{16}$″)

9mm (⅜″)

13mm (½″)

13mm (½″)

18mm (¾″)

22mm (⅞″)

Dropboard

Brass plate keep, thru' bolted. For security purposes fill the screw slot

19mm (¾″)

16mm (⅝″)

13mm (½″)

9mm (⅜″)

9mm (⅜)″

16mm (⅝″)

Side frame 35mm x 45mm (1⅜″ x 1¾″) fixed to bulkhead to accommodate the dropboards

GRP sliding main hatch

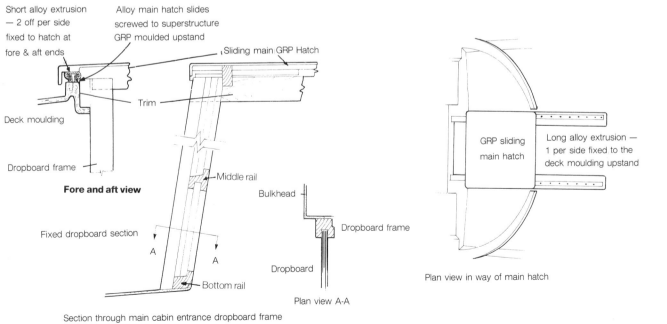

Short alloy extrusion — 2 off per side fixed to hatch at fore & aft ends

Alloy main hatch slides screwed to superstructure GRP moulded upstand

Sliding main GRP Hatch

Trim

Deck moulding

Dropboard frame

Fore and aft view

Fixed dropboard section

A   A

Middle rail

Bulkhead

Dropboard frame

Dropboard

Bottom rail

Plan view A-A

Section through main cabin entrance dropboard frame

GRP sliding main hatch

Long alloy extrusion — 1 per side fixed to the deck moulding upstand

Plan view in way of main hatch

shoots and clips (Illus. 144). Smaller companionways may have a single sheet of ply instead of a number of dropboards.

If doors are required, it is best to fit double doors with lift off hinges so they can be stored away below when not in use (Illus. 145). This type of arrangement must be capable of being securely fastened in the event of bad weather, as detailed above for the dropboards (*See* Illus. 144).

Illustration 144   Dropboard Fastenings

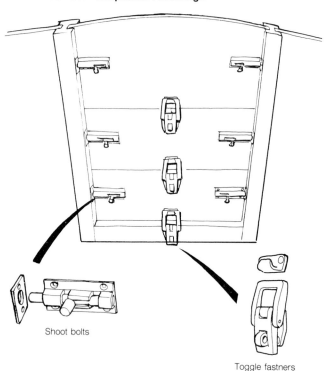

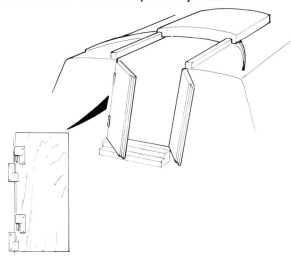

Shoot bolts

Toggle fastners

Illustration 145   Lift Off Companionway Doors

COCKPITS, COCKPIT LOCKERS & DRAINS

To save irritating knocks and bumps to the back of the crews' calves, hold closed the cockpit locker lids with internal drawstrings threaded around bull's-eye lead blocks and fastened with clam cleats (Illus. 146). This arrangement requires any marauder to break into the craft to get to the lockers. But don't leave the main cabin keys at home!

Hinge the cockpit locker lids with simple, anodised aluminium hinges, which are both utilitarian and efficient. Check for binding and seat on thick rubber strip to ensure water tightness. On the other hand, locker lids can be constructed of oiled teak and the cockpit sole fitted with a teak cockpit grating (*See* Chapter Fifteen).

Illustration 146   Fastening Cockpit Locker Lids

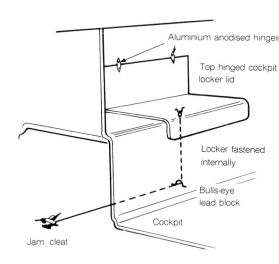

Aluminium anodised hinge

Top hinged cockpit locker lid

Locker fastened internally

Bulls-eye lead block

Cockpit

Jam cleat

This is a practicable alternative only if (a) an owner is a good carpenter, (b) the cost will not be too much, and (c) cut out and rounded off composition deck coverings will not more than adequately do the job of covering those 'acres' of cockpit surfaces (*See* Chapter Fifteen & Illus. 175a).

Although cockpit drains were referred to very early on (*See* Illus 23 & Chapter Six), it is most important that the drains are of adequate size, number, and are installed correctly. An average 8m-8.5m (26/28ft) yacht should have a minimum of two cockpit drains of at least 4cm (1½″), but preferably 5cm (2″) diameter, with crossed over reinforced pipes, double stainless steel clipped, and gunmetal thru' hull fittings fitted with gate valves and tails. The cockpit sole drains can be nylon (Illus. 147).

Where a beam has to be fitted to support split cockpit sole boards it may be necessary to make arrangements to drain away any water. The framework should be

Illustration 147   Cockpit Drains

147a   Cockpit seat & crossed over cockpit drains

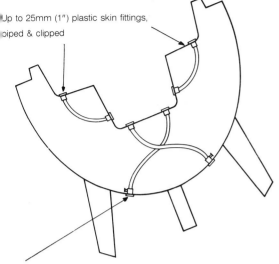

Up to 25mm (1″) plastic skin fittings, piped & clipped

Minimum of 38mm (1½″) gunmetal thru' hull skin fitting complete with gate valve & tail connection piped to the cockpit sole skin fitting (Don't forget to fit double pipe clips & gate valves)

'guttered' with grooves led to drain tubes fed into the cockpit drain pipework (Illus. 147b). Cockpit seat drains are well worth fitting if the locker lid arrangement is not moulded in such a way as to take away storm water (Illus. 147a).

HANDRAILS

Deckhead grabrails, where possible, should be matched internally and externally. Old fashioned, but good looking, wooden handrails still do not look out of place and lend themselves to be thru' fastened to each other and it will not go amiss to fit a grabrail, or section of one, to either side of the main companionway, inside and out (Illus. 148a). Certainly any bulkhead that can take a 'hand hold' cut out should be so treated (Illus. 148b).

147b   Cockpit sole beams

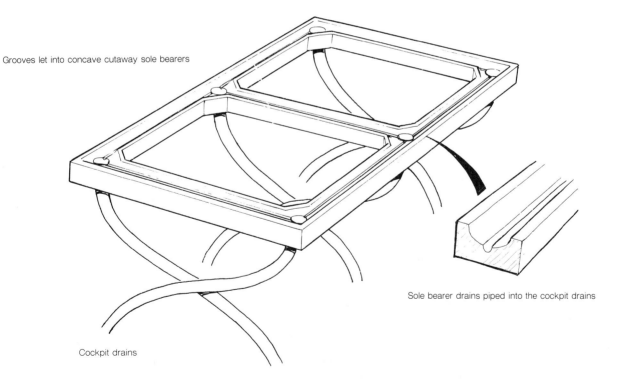

Grooves let into concave cutaway sole bearers

Sole bearer drains piped into the cockpit drains

Cockpit drains

Illustration 148   Grab and Handrails

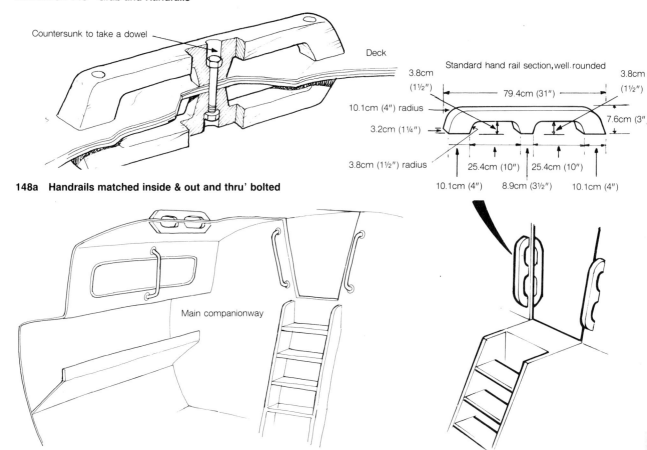

Countersunk to take a dowel

Deck

Standard hand rail section, well rounded

3.8cm
(1½")

79.4cm (31")

3.8cm
(1½")

10.1cm (4") radius

7.6cm (3"

3.2cm (1¼")

3.8cm (1½") radius

25.4cm (10")   25.4cm (10")

10.1cm (4")   8.9cm (3½")   10.1cm (4")

148a   Handrails matched inside & out and thru' bolted

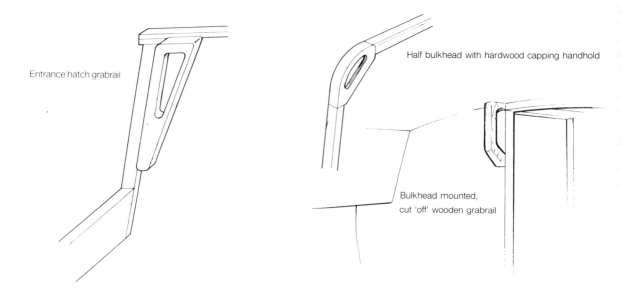

Main companionway

Stainless steel grabrails bridging a window cabin side cut-out

148b   Grabrails

Entrance hatch grabrail

Half bulkhead with hardwood capping handhold

Bulkhead mounted,
cut 'off' wooden grabrail

15

NOW TO THE FINAL FINISHING OFF

It would make the book long and tortuous if all the ideas sketched and annotated in this Chapter were to be fully detailed in the text. I believe that well executed drawings with a full description can be easier to follow than pages of descriptive matter.

Thru' bulkhead boxes are extremely useful for storing big and deep items where 'headcracking' would result from fitting an over-large, bulkhead mounted cabinet. An ideal position through which to mount them is the toilet/main cabin bulkhead (Illus. 149).

Drawers should have a lift and pull arrangement to save the contents involuntarily spilling out whilst the craft is heeled over (Illus. 150). Instead of making fiddly and time-consuming drawer dividers, purchase a suitable plastic household cutlery container and make the drawer to fit!

The pull-out double berth has almost disappeared from use but is worth consideration as a replacement for the more conventional saloon or dinette berth arrangement (Illus. 151).

An over foot berth locker and shelf achieves extra storage neatly, without interfering with the effective berth dimensions (Illus. 152).

Hopper drawers are very useful if there is not enough room for a drawer to be slid in and out, more especially where the hull draws in, close by the bilges. They can be used for garbage, particularly when the weather is too inclement for the more usual (?) cockpit located cardboard box, as well as for the storage of vegetables. Why not fit two? (Illus. 153).

The detachable hanging clothes locker is a development of the airline suit bag and is especially suitable for fitting in the forecabin where space is often at a premium. They can be removed by fitting press studs to the bulkhead and deckhead. The depth of the bag should be not more than 23cms (9″) (Illus. 154).

Additional chart stowage can be arranged in convenient places other than the navigation table (Illus. 155 & *See* Chapter Fourteen & Illus. 129).

Netting is very useful for magazine storage and can be bulkhead, cabin side or shelf mounted. If fitted with fold down arms, they will conveniently stow away and

Illustration 149   Thru' Bulkhead Boxes

The bulkhead is cut out either side of the vertical divider

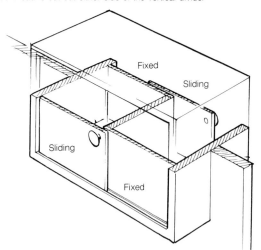

See Illustration 150 (Drawer Unit) & 159 (Book Rack) for construction detail & dimensions

Illustration 150   Drawers

The whole is glued & screwed

Groove & rebate joint

Back stop bar

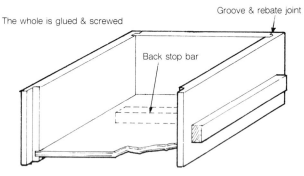

Back, front & sides — 18mm (¾" ply)   Bottom - 9mm (⅜") ply

150a

Inset the front stop bar to allow slight pull forward prior to lifting the drawer as in C.

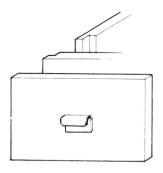

150b

Hardwood 'fashion' drawer front overlapping all the way round to cover the drawer aperture

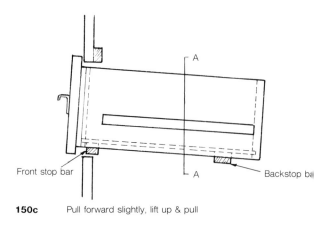

150c   Pull forward slightly, lift up & pull

Front stop bar

Backstop ba

A

A

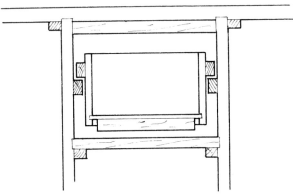

150d   Section through A-A   Front view with the fascia removed

Illustration 151   Pull-out Double Berth

The outboard end can be supported by a drop down leg. Hopefully one er will be adjacent to a bulkhead which makes for ease of fixing

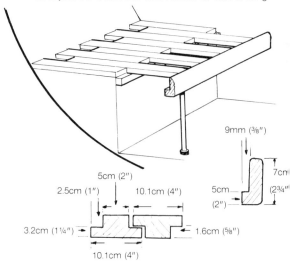

9mm (⅜")

7cm

2.5cm (1")   5cm (2")   10.1cm (4")   5cm (2")   (2¾")

3.2cm (1¼")   1.6cm (⅝")

10.1cm (4")

Illustration 152   Over Foot Berth and Locker

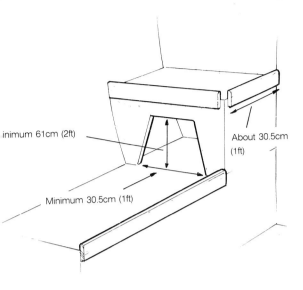

inimum 61cm (2ft)

About 30.5cm (1ft)

Minimum 30.5cm (1ft)

Illustration 153   Hopper Drawers

Slot for 'plaky' bag to be able to sit over the edge all the way round

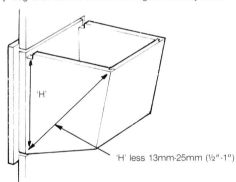

'H'

'H' less 13mm-25mm (½"-1")

o save the unit falling out on a beat, fit a finger catch

or joints and construction details *See* Drawer detail Illustration 150

ut the unit can be butt jointed and internally stiffened

esin coat the internal joints to save unsavoury leakage

Illustration 154   Detachable Hanging Clothes Locker

Press studded to the deckhead & bulkhead

Sail bag material with piped edges & zip fronted

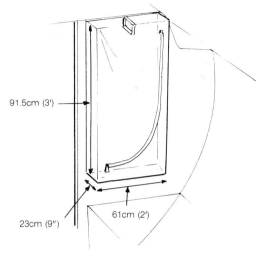

91.5cm (3')

23cm (9")

61cm (2')

Thin plywood let into the top & bottom material & the rail suspended from the ply top

Illustration 155   Chart Stowage

Main companionway

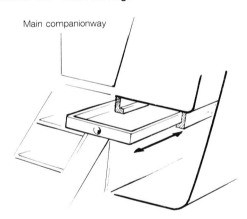

9mm (⅜") ply bottom let into 12mm (½") ply sides, back, front & internally framed up in 9mm (⅜") square whitewood. The draw supported on simple 'L' shaped drawer slides

Minimum width 56cm (22"), length 73.5cm (29") & drawer depth up to 7.5cm (3")

Pull out chart drawer mounted underneath the cockpit sole or cockpit locker seating

Cabin deckhead

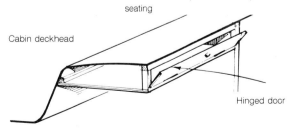

Hinged door

9mm (⅜") ply bottom let into 12mm (½") ply sides & internally framed in 9mm (⅜") square whitewood

may be fitted in the place of shelving (Illus. 156).

Portable radios really must have a permanent home. They have a nasty habit of crashing to the cabin sole, falling from this or that table or shelf when a new tack is made (Illus. 157).

As a galley aid it is disproportionately useful to make a sink cover/chopping board, more especially if the reverse side has an open topped box fitted. This locates the chopping board securely in the sink recess and, when reversed, contains vegetables or an extra saucepan (Illus. 158).

Illustration 156 Netting

Netting can also be deckhead 'hung'.

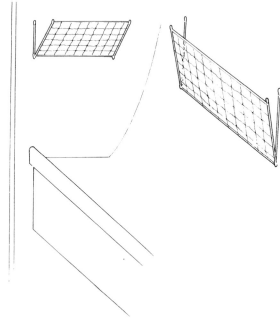

The cotton netting can be held in place with elastic shock cord. If used in place of shelves, hem & grommet the edges

Illustration 157 Portable Radio Boxing

The box sides can be made of 19/25mm (¾"/1") hardwood, the bar 19/25m (¾"/1") thick & 25/38mm (1"/1½") deep

Recessed to hold square end of retaining bar

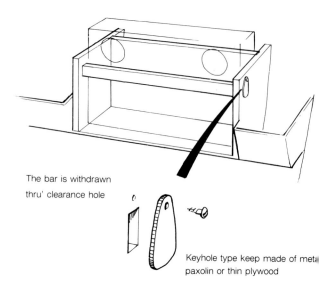

The bar is withdrawn thru' clearance hole

Keyhole type keep made of met paxolin or thin plywood

If there is not enough room to be able to easily withdraw the retaining bar, hing one of the retaining sides so it can lay down & keep in an upright position w a barrel bolt

Illustration 158 Sink Cover/Chopping Board

Minimum 18mm (¾") ply complete with Formica top face

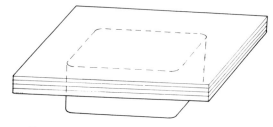

The open top box must fit into the sink compartment

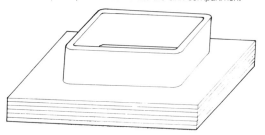

When reversed the sink locater becomes a pan/container holder

A book rack is well worth the time and effort and is usually located in the main cabin, hull side mounted shelving. It's worth considering letting a book locker into an athwartship bulkhead for, if the fiddle rail is of ample dimensions, a retaining bar may well not be required (Illus. 159).

Lockers fitted with sliding doors give secure storage and if the panels are made of perspex, the contents may be easily seen (Illus. 160).

Alternative anchor chain stowage can be organised by leading the chain aft to store under the forebunks (Illus. 161)

Softwood bungs are a safety factor worth incorporating, and almost compulsory for long distance cruising. Round off the tapered bungs at both ends and drill out the larger end to take the lanyard, for which oiled leather

Illustration 159   Book Rack

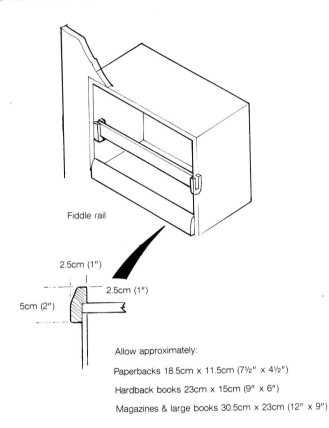

Fiddle rail

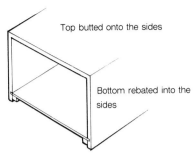

Top butted onto the sides

Bottom rebated into the sides

9mm (⅜") sq. battening

2.5cm (1")

2.5cm (1")

5cm (2")

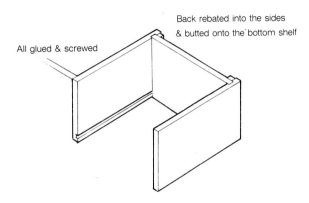

Back rebated into the sides & butted onto the bottom shelf

All glued & screwed

18mm (¾") ply box sides, 12mm (½") ply box back, top & bottom

Allow approximately:

Paperbacks 18.5cm x 11.5cm (7½" x 4½")

Hardback books 23cm x 15cm (9" x 6")

Magazines & large books 30.5cm x 23cm (12" x 9")

Illustration 160   Sliding Door Lockers

Mullion 4.5cm x 4.5cm (1¾" x 1¾")

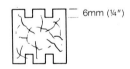

6mm (¼")

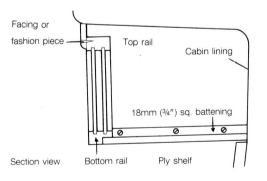

Facing or fashion piece

Top rail

Cabin lining

18mm (¾") sq. battening

Section view   Bottom rail   Ply shelf

Top rail 4.5cm x 2.9cm (1¾" x 1⅛")

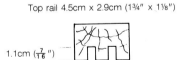

1.1cm ($\frac{7}{16}$ ")

All slides for perspex doors to be 3mm (1/8") wide plus sliding clearance

Bottom rail 4.5cm x 2.9cm (1¾" x 1⅛")

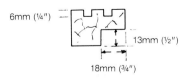

6mm (¼")

13mm (½")

18mm (¾")

Locker front view

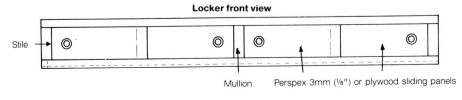

Stile

Mullion   Perspex 3mm (⅛") or plywood sliding panels

Illustration 161   Alternative Chain Stowage

Illustration 162   Softwood Bungs

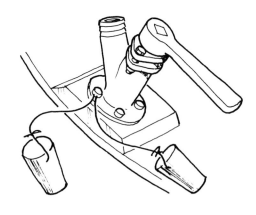

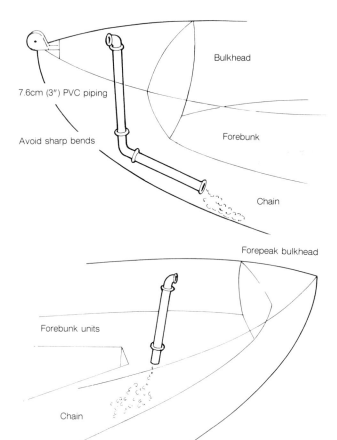

Bulkhead

7.6cm (3″) PVC piping

Avoid sharp bends

Forebunk

Chain

Forepeak bulkhead

Forebunk units

Chain

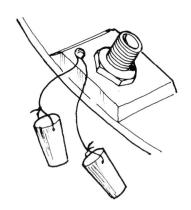

A metal pipe here as the chain pipe is exposed in the forecabin & may be subject to accidental knocks

boot laces are ideal (Illus. 162). Wire or lanyard them to each thru' hull skin fitting in order to seal it off should disaster strike. This not only warrants they are to hand when required but adjusting the length of the lanyard ensures the bungs cannot be vibrated out of position. Thru' hull skin fittings possibly include the rudder stock, exhaust outlet, sterntube gland, engine cooling inlet, cockpit drains, sink and bilge pump outlets and the WC seacocks.

A table-top locker can be fabricated with a suitable cut-out panel that will take spirit and wine bottles and the glasses. Don't make all the bottle holes circular, for as an Irish, Surgeon-Captain friend of mine pointed out, "quite a lot of whisky bottles are square in shape"! If the lip edging is omitted for at least 7·8cm (3″) at both sides and ends, the locker lid can be lifted with finger tip pressure at one end (Illus. 163).

Cabin soles tend to swell and bind with the surrounding woodwork, however dry the bilges. To help stop this annoying cause and effect, and to present a workmanlike appearance to the cabin, lip the boards and match with a rebated hardwood surround (Illus. 164a). Similarly timber access hatches should have surrounding hardwood margin boards (Illus. 164b). Most of the devices sold as sole board lifting rings are no more than finger breakers and usually have a derisory method of fastening. A number of practical solutions are sketched in Illustration 164c.

The engine compartment profits from sympathetic thought and treatment. Smaller sailing craft are restricted for space and access but motor sailers, where more room is available, benefit from the provision of stowage shelves and a thwart plank on which to crouch, clamp a vice or just rest a few tools. Well appreciated . . . especially if one has spent a fair amount of time sweating over a hot engine, balancing spanners on the

Illustration 163   Table-top Locker

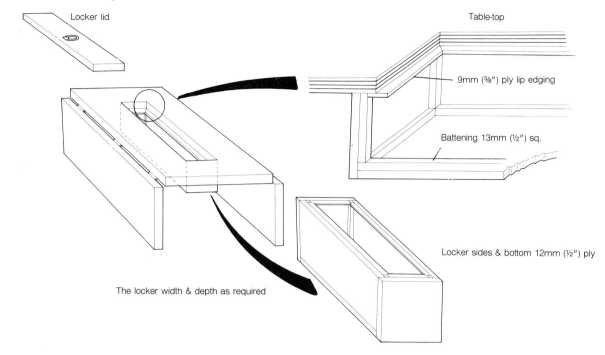

Locker lid

Table-top

9mm (⅜″) ply lip edging

Battening 13mm (½″) sq.

Locker sides & bottom 12mm (½″) ply

The locker width & depth as required

Illustration 164   Cabin Soles, Access Hatches and Sole Board Lifting Rings

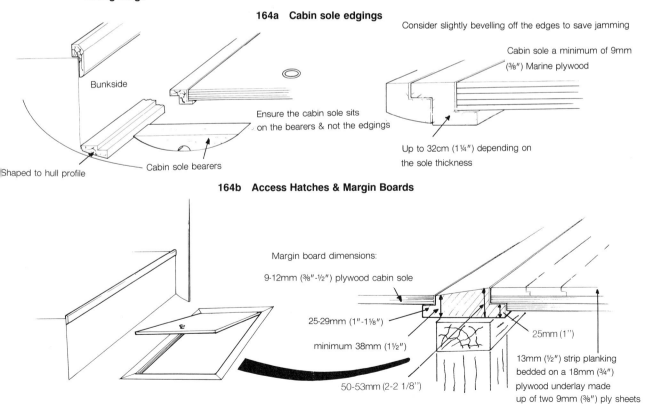

164a   Cabin sole edgings

Consider slightly bevelling off the edges to save jamming

Cabin sole a minimum of 9mm (⅜″) Marine plywood

Bunkside

Ensure the cabin sole sits on the bearers & not the edgings

Up to 32cm (1¼″) depending on the sole thickness

Cabin sole bearers

Shaped to hull profile

164b   Access Hatches & Margin Boards

Margin board dimensions:

9-12mm (⅜″-½″) plywood cabin sole

25-29mm (1″-1⅛″)

minimum 38mm (1½″)

50-53mm (2-2 1/8″)

25mm (1″)

13mm (½″) strip planking bedded on a 18mm (¾″) plywood underlay made up of two 9mm (⅜″) ply sheets

164c   Sole board lifting rings

Why not fit a drawer handle which have a large enough base plate to allow machine screws to be used for the fastenings?

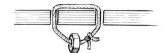

Cord weighted with a nut or three

Illustration 165   Engine Compartment Stowage

gearbox and seeing them slide gracefully an irretrievably beneath the engine in an unfathomable poo of oily water — know the feeling! (Illus. 165).

I'm surprised that more yachts do not have dec mounted mast pulpits fitted. It does save having to han on for dear life whilst stationed at the base of the mas with the yacht well heeled over (Illus. 166a). Another iter

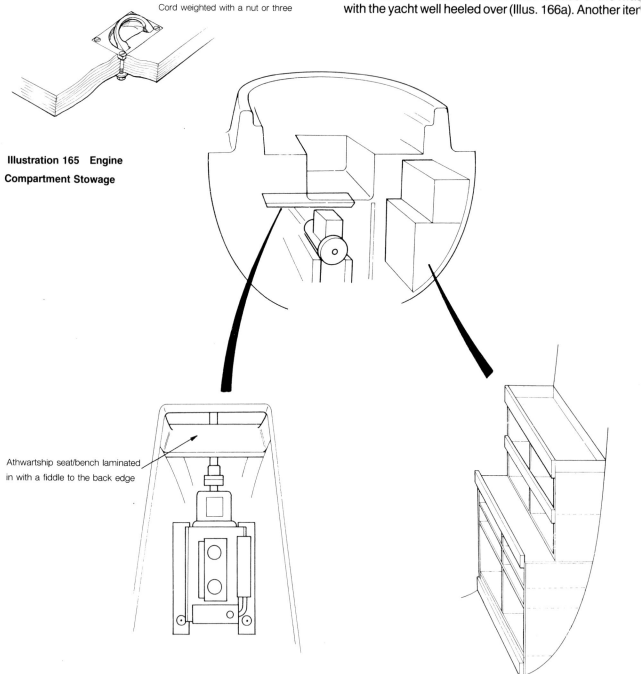

Athwartship seat/bench laminated in with a fiddle to the back edge

Hull mounted shelf storage in the engine compartment

Illustration 166   Mast Pulpits and Safety Line 'Hitching Rails'

166a   Mast pulpit

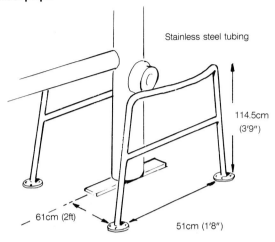

Stainless steel tubing

114.5cm
(3'9")

61cm (2ft)

51cm (1'8")

166b   Foredeck Hanking points for safety lines

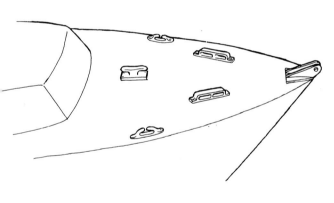

Cockpit coaming lockers save possible storage space going to waste. Cut through the coamings and create lockers for winch handles, the odd sheet, halyards, mainsail ties, cans of beer and other odds and sods (Illus. 168).

Illustration 167   Pulpit Nets

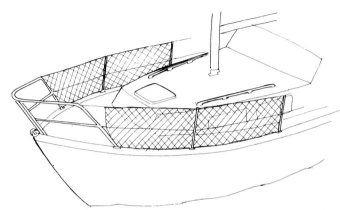

Illustration 168   Cockpit Coaming Lockers

Ensure the box is larger than the cut-out thus giving a fiddle all the way round

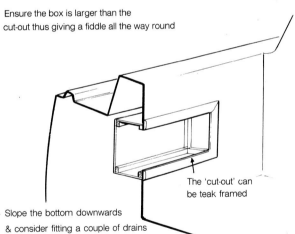

The 'cut-out' can be teak framed

Slope the bottom downwards & consider fitting a couple of drains

worthy of consideration are safety line hanking points mounted on the foredeck (Illus. 166b). The usual safety lines tend to peter out at the outset of the foredeck but these 'hitching rails' are a possible solution, allowing an unaccustomed amount of foredeck freedom of movement.

Pulpit nets make a welcome safety addition to the cruising inventory. 'Beneficiaries' include beleaguered foredeck crew and 'dropped' foresails that will not be able to slip through the guard rails and get a thorough soaking. The nets should be fixed to the pulpit and guardrail stanchions and fastened at deck level with small fender eyes (Illus. 167).

The box can be made up of 9mm (⅜") plywood boxed with 9mm (⅜") square whitewood framing

Expanses of cockpit locker tops can be fitted with teak seating slats instead of applying deck paint or composition deck covering. Why not teak cap the coamings, but don't overdo it (Illus. 169)?

To match teak clad cockpit seating and coamings, an owner might consider constructing a teak cockpit grating. Prior to embarking on the project think first, then if you've come to any decision other than to abandon the idea, think again! 'No seriously folks' . . .

Illustration 169   Teak Seating Slats and Coaming Capping

Fastenings counterbored 6mm (¼″) stainless steel machine screws & dowelled at 15.2cm (6″) centres

Bed the coaming capping on sealant. The thickness of the capping should be between 13mm (½″) and 18mm (¾″) depending upon the 'look of the thing'

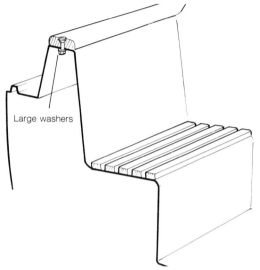

Large washers

The hardwood slats should be about 13mm (½″) thick by 4.5cm (1¾″) wide with well rounded top corners & bedded on sealant with an 18mm (¾″) gap between the edges & fastened at 7.5cm (3″) centres

Single skin — screw up from underneath

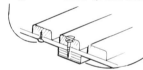

If the cockpit has a balsa core top fasten (counterboring and pelleting) into a plywood slat on the underside

TEAK GRATINGS

Illustration 170 is broken up into sections (to hopefully) guide the prospective 'grating' maker through the various stages of manufacture. Illustration 170a is a plan view of a completed cockpit grating and the rest of the drawings take the operation from the teak plank through to the finished article. Prior to fixing the machined sections together (170f), sparingly apply glue to the channels and ensure the excess is quickly wiped off. When the grating sections are fitted together, turn over and fasten the sections to each other using 13mm (½″) x 6 brass, countersunk head woodscrews. Plug or stop up. Clean prior to fixing into the frame which can now be 'dry' fitted. Make the side pieces full length so as to be able to fix to the athwartship top and bottom pieces with a half lap joint. Round off the edges, clean again and place the frame around the grating before marking where the grating butts up to the frame (170h). The marking must be accurate as dowels are used to joint the grating to the frame, let into the full square grating ends and the frame (170i, j & k). It is probably best to

Illustration 170   Teak Gratings

170a

Surround frame

Plan view

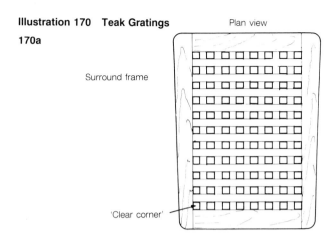

'Clear corner'

The teak grating must be square therefore the outside of the teak surround will have to take up any tapering or irregularities in the cockpit shape. The frame width should not go below 5cm (2″) plus. The size of the grating must be such that the four corners are 'clear space'

170b

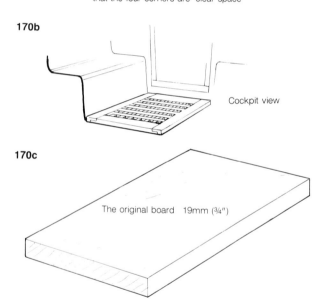

Cockpit view

170c

The original board   19mm (¾″)

The usual finished timber thickness is 19mm (¾″) & the width as near as possible divisible by 19mm (¾″) making allowance for the width of the saw blade cuts

To save unnecessary waste, the teak plank length should be such that it will give multiples of a grating length & a width section of 2 lengths & widths (all will be made plain I hope!)

170d

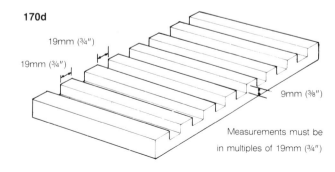

19mm (¾″)

19mm (¾″)

9mm (⅜″)

Measurements must be in multiples of 19mm (¾″)

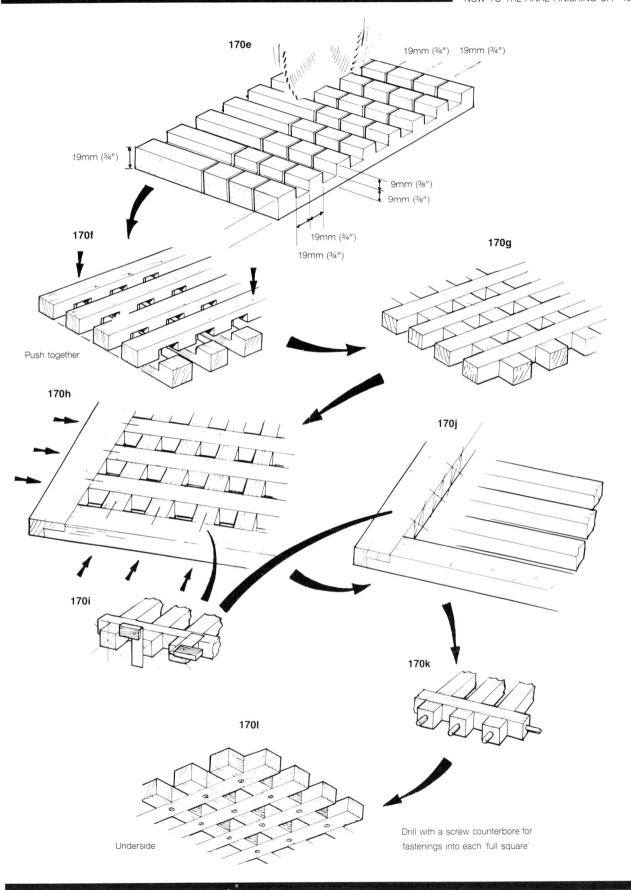

170e

19mm (¾")   19mm (¾")

19mm (¾")

9mm (⅜")

9mm (⅜")

19mm (¾")

19mm (¾")

170f

Push together

170g

170h

170j

170i

170k

170l

Underside

Drill with a screw counterbore for
fastenings into each 'full square'

use a dowelling jig to ensure the dowel holes are not only drilled to a constant depth of no more than 13mm (½″) but are square, which is very important. Fix the dowels to the grating and offer up the frame which is similarly drilled. If there is difficulty in lining up, the 'trick' is to carefully ease out the frame dowel holes till the frame fits to the grating and the other frame pieces. The whole can then be glued, screwed and clamped together.

TEAK DECKING

Teak decking is probably the most prestigious appendage that can be fitted to a craft but if my words in respect of cockpit gratings rang warning bells, then the sounds now echoing in a readers ears should resemble sirens!

The 'knack' is to underlay the teak planking with a plywood deck overlay (if you see what I mean) rebated into teak margin/edging boards (171a). The advantage of a ply deck covering is that the seal between the planks and shell will be watertight, the planks may be fastened by either screwing into the overlay or by thru' fastening and the thickness of the planks can be reduced to 13mm (½″). This not only makes it easier to shape the planking to the necessary curves but means that they can be fastened to the ply deck with, say, No. 10 stainless steel, countersunk head wood screws (171g).The plywood and margin boards should be dry fitted first, removed to clean away swarf and drill waste and then well bedded on deck caulking sealant. If it is intended to screw the decking into the plywood overlay, then the overlay must be securely fastened to the deck and a number of thru' fastenings should be fitted. If, on the other hand, it is intended to thru' fasten all over, then the plywood need only be temporarily fastened down with self-tapping screws which are removed as the deck is laid.

The decision must be made as to the style of decking. Is it to be 'straight laid' (171c), 'half' (171d) or 'full sprung' (171e)? The final choice is then drawn on the overlay enabling consideration to be given to the position of decking joints and fastenings. Where possible, joints should be arranged on the straight with butt or stepped scarfs rebated for the caulking sealant (171f).

A 'straight' teak deck is laid from the inner side outwards, a sprung deck from the outer edge inwards. The outer edges of straight and half-sprung decking have to be let into the outer edge margin boards. To save an awful lot of chisel work set a router just short of the requisite depth, routing out most of the waste and finishing with a chisel for the final fit. For the sake of neatness, arrange the fastenings in line and plug or dowel. The boards must be as long as possible, knot free and be approximately 5-7½cm (2″/3″) wide for a straight laid deck and 4-5cm (1½″/2″) wide for half and full sprung decks, with a minimum thickness of 13mm

(½″). The inboard edge of each plank is rebated for the sealant groove (171b). This saves laying the deck with removable, equal sized fillets of timber set in between each plank in order to enable the caulking to penetrate. To lay the decking it is necessary, even on the straight, to force the planks together with wedges and then fasten down (171h).

The centre line of the foredeck of sprung decks can be treated in two ways. One is to utilise a herringbone pattern (171i) and the other is by letting the decking into a kingplank (171j), which requires the same 'nibbing' as the outer margin boards.

Illustration 171   Teak Decking

171a

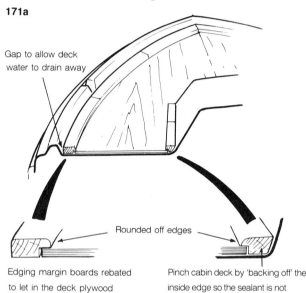

Gap to allow deck water to drain away

Rounded off edges

Edging margin boards rebated to let in the deck plywood

Pinch cabin deck by 'backing off' the inside edge so the sealant is not completely squeezed out

171b

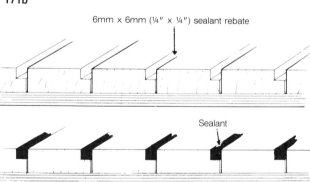

6mm x 6mm (¼″ x ¼″) sealant rebate

Sealant

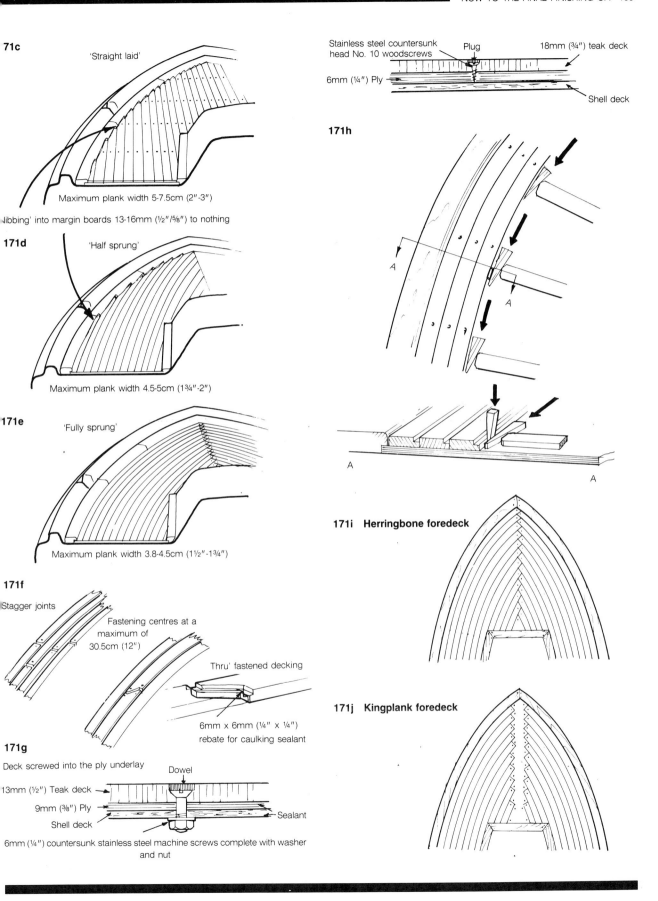

71c

'Straight laid'

Maximum plank width 5-7.5cm (2"-3")

'Nibbing' into margin boards 13-16mm (½"/⅝") to nothing

171d

'Half sprung'

Maximum plank width 4.5-5cm (1¾"-2")

171e

'Fully sprung'

Maximum plank width 3.8-4.5cm (1½"-1¾")

171f

Stagger joints

Fastening centres at a maximum of 30.5cm (12")

Thru' fastened decking

6mm x 6mm (¼" x ¼") rebate for caulking sealant

171g

Deck screwed into the ply underlay

Dowel

13mm (½") Teak deck

9mm (⅜") Ply

Shell deck

Sealant

6mm (¼") countersunk stainless steel machine screws complete with washer and nut

Stainless steel countersunk head No. 10 woodscrews

Plug

18mm (¾") teak deck

6mm (¼") Ply

Shell deck

171h

A

A

A

A

171i   Herringbone foredeck

171j   Kingplank foredeck

HEADLINING

As touched upon in earlier chapters (*See* Chapters Thirteen & Fourteen), the choice and method of internal lining is determined at a very early stage of the project, but now is the time to elaborate.

The size of the task depends on how much of the interior is left unclad by fitted furniture and the type of craft.

Three basic methods are available to the amateur boatbuilder (I say this because the professional might have electrostatic flocking available):

1. Painting out with a gelcoat wash or an anti-condensation paint. Often found on racing craft where unnecessary weight and frills are not required.

2. Direct application of one of the wide variety of cabin and headlining materials and hessians. Opting for a foam backed vinyl or leather cloth not only gives a finish but very adequately copes with condensation due to the foam backing forming a thermal barrier. The minimum thickness of foam, for satisfactory insulation, is 4mm and the manner of fixing is with an impact adhesive. Prior to 'gluing up', grind down unacceptable bumps and lumps and 'clean up' the surfaces using resin putty to smooth out dips, holes and uneven surfaces.

3. Where space, headroom and money allows, some builders opt for panelled linings fastened to grounds or battens, as well as the other numerous blocks and pads 'littered about' for some other purpose. The hull & deck material controls the method of fixing softwood grounds in position. Naturally in GRP craft they can be secured with occasional straps or 'bandages' of GRP, not requiring a continuous application of laminate (*See* Illustration 115). For other materials refer to Chapter Three.

Decorative faced, or material covered ply can be sprung into position using the natural curvature of the shell, edging trims and by fastening to the aforementioned battens (Illus. 172a & *See* Illus. 115). Prime the back of the panel prior to stretching the headlining over the sheet and stapling down the return edges.

Trimming, edging and finishing off is achieved in a number of different ways. Where possible trap the edges of the headlinings with interior furniture, main structural timbers and beadings. In the berth areas bunk cushions mask the edges. The most eye catching quarter, which thus requires detailed attention, is where the cabin deckhead headlining butts up to the bulkheads. Some builders bring the headlining down over the bulkhead and cut off with a straight edge (Illus. 172b), others employ fashion pieces and trims scribed to the necessary contours. If the trim is not covered, then

Illustration 172   Headlinings

172a   Panelled internal linings

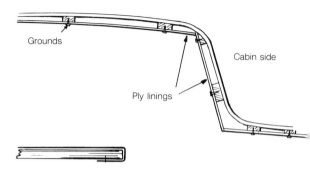

Covering material glued in position, folded over the edge & stapled down

172b   Cabin headlinings, straight edge cut

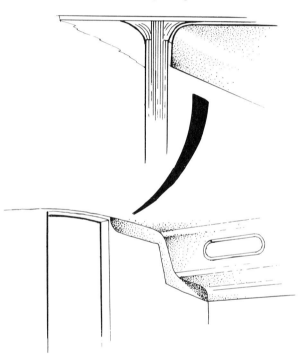

hardwood is the more pleasing finish (Illus. 172c). Plywood can be used when it is covered in matching material to the headlining (Illus. 172d) for which obtain unfoamed material or strip the foam backing off some headlining. Be bold and make the trims of adequate width, not footling scraps of matchstick. Don't forget that all interior headlining and panels must be removable where thru' deck fastened fittings are 'in the way' and might require replacement, re-sealing or re-fastening at some time in the future.

Portholes and cabin windows should, if at all possible, be purchased complete with matching, internal fastening trims as, apart from tidying up the installation, they can be utilised to trap headlinings. (*See* Illustration 136). If these are not available, approach another window manufacturer! Alternatively, hardwood or plywood trims may be machined using a router but they very rarely look anything but amateurish. It is possible to turn the cabin lining around the window cut-out and pinch it in position with the inner face of the external window flange. But this holds the window frame off the cabin-sides with the consequential need to use a heavy application of sealant — not a satisfactory method (Illus. 172e).

The gunwale/side deck area may require treatment where not covered by cupboards and other internal joinery. A solution is to 'smooth out' the area with angled, material covered panels (Illus. 172f).

Quarter berths must not be forgotten and should be lined out whilst lockers, beneath berth mouldings and bilges benefit from at least a coat or three of paint.

When using headlining glue, do be careful. I've seen grown men having to be pulled out of a boat, almost unconscious. You've heard of 'sniffing', well when shut in a confined space, maybe with a fan heater switched on and . . . .!

172e If you must . . .!

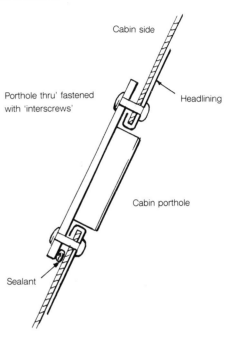

Cabin side

Porthole thru' fastened with 'interscrews'

Headlining

Cabin porthole

Sealant

172c Hardwood trim

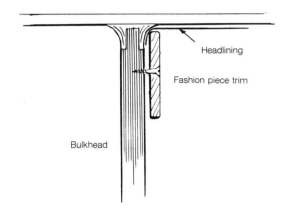

Headlining

Fashion piece trim

Bulkhead

172d Material covered plywood trims

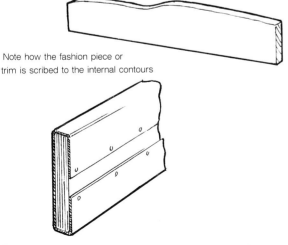

Note how the fashion piece or trim is scribed to the internal contours

The material covering glued, pinned or stapled at the back of the trim

172f Smoothed out inwale

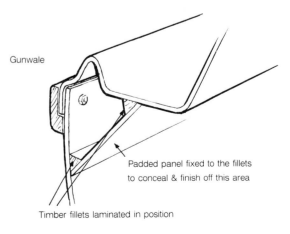

Gunwale

Padded panel fixed to the fillets to conceal & finish off this area

Timber fillets laminated in position

This type of inner lining gives a very neat & accessible trunking for services

BERTH CUSHIONS

Berth cushions and their coverings have a very definite effect on the interior look of a craft. Whether purchasing a tailor-made set or making them, do not settle for less than 10cms (4″) thick foam and 5-7½cms (2″-3″) thick backrests. The choice of covering material is usually influenced by the depth of an owner's pockets, but what isn't? The cheapest, but perhaps the most undesirable method, owing to its 'stickiness' quality, is to use vinyl plastic. Dralon is a suitably inexpensive alternative, but, if possible, fit an upholstery woollen fabric, which are available in a wide variety of finishes.

In making paper patterns for the upholstery foam, remember that at berth height, over the thickness of the foam, the hull probably widens out. This requires the hull side of the mattress to be angled, sometimes quite considerably, so watch out when pattern cutting!

To save costs the underside covering of the mattress can be a scrim cloth; 'pipe' the 'topside' edges to achieve that professional look and do fit a zip in the side of the cushions to allow the covers to be cleaned every so often.

FLOOR COVERING

Marine grade, rubber backed, man-made fibre carpet is ideal and may be run up the bunk sides to cover any unsightly bunk front to hull joins. Whatever is used, only lightly fasten down.

Don't forget that all bare plywood edges should be capped, headlining fitted with trims, fastening heads dowelled, surplus sealant trimmed off, bilges vacuumed and unclipped wires or pipes tidied up.

Sea toilet positioned on a plinth to overcome the steep rise of the hull.

A 'finished' interior. Of note are the very solid companionway steps built into the engine box front, headlinings sprung into place & 'snapcapped', companionway handrails, the window trims used to trap the headlining & the swingout bracket for the echo sounder & log.

16

PAINTING

The various paint manufacturers produce a veritable welter of sometimes (dare one say) conflicting and certainly confusing information. To overcome this I have based my advice and instructions on the products of one company pre-eminent in the yachting field — International Yacht Paints. The decision was based not only on their all encompassing product range but their comprehensive and informative back up literature. *

One thing is certain, the basic fundamentals for any good finish must be a dry, clean and dust free surfaces, as well as correct preparation.

The following are in the nature of jottings to supplement the plethora of data available.

In addition to the purchase of a range of items including brushes, rollers, masking tape, mutton cloth, various

*I would reiterate that I have no connection with any company listed in this book, other than a normal commercial one as a partner of a small marine business, nor have I received any 'freebies' — yet! Furthermore that a particular manufacturer is not listed or mentioned does not infer any criticism of that company.

grades of sandpaper, wet and dry paper, a sanding block, a scraper or three, an orbital sander, goggles and a face mask, make a Tak-Rag. This is a cheese or mutton cloth damped out with warm water and lightly soaked in a thinned down varnish mix. It wipes surfaces very clean of dust.

Of the three power sanders usually available, do not use the disc type as it tends to dig in and only use a belt sander on continuous, fairly flat surfaces. The orbital sander is the least likely to cause damage and can achieve a fine surface finish. (Illus. 173). Mahogany keeps its indigenous colour much longer when treated initially with raw, linseed oil.

To heat a tin of paint in order to make application easier, place it in a bowl of hot water. It's much safer than applying a blow torch.

Although it may seem astonishingly obvious, clean down, prepare and paint from the top downwards. This saves double work by having to clean hull paintwork more than once. Right-handers should work clockwise (or right to left) round a boat, thus brushing from left to right into the existing work (Illus. 174).

Illustration 173   Sanders

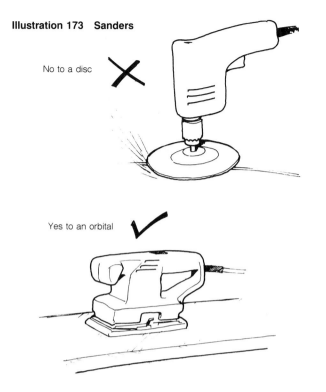

No to a disc

Yes to an orbital

Illustration 174   Direction of Painting

When masking for clean edges to paintwork, do not leave the tape in position for more than the time it takes the paint to go tacky, otherwise it can prove very difficult to remove, especially if it gets wet. On the other hand, try to remove the tape too soon and the paint peels off with the tape.

Bottom painting can be executed with a paint roller. The slightly dimpled look to the finish hardly matters on all but high performance craft. And do throw the rollers away after use, particularly when they have been used to apply antifouling or black varnish (an inexpensive steel boat bottom finish).

Where applying a number of layers of paint, more especially primers, it is usual to alternate the colours and note their sequence in the ship's log (what's that?). At a future date, when carrying out painting maintenance, this record enables an owner to know how many layers of paint have worn off.

Whichever manufacturer's products are chosen it is ESSENTIAL that their instructions are followed to the letter.

To sum up:

DO NOT — smoke when painting or preparing surfaces.

DO — ensure adequate ventilation throughout the boat when painting the interior.
— flat down gloss enamel/topcoats between applications.

The above are general notes. There follows more detailed extracts in respect of painting the six shell materials covered in this book. Note that quantity calculations are dealt with at the end of the Chapter and that the number of applications mentioned hereunder is only an average.

Teak Oil Vis à Vis Varnish For finishes below decks I prefer teak oil to varnish for as much of the woodwork as possible. In the long run it saves the beastly job of stripping varnish and remains relatively easy to freshen at any time of the year.

When varnish is used, mix the initial coat with up to 50% thinners and the next few coats with progressively less thinners. In between applications lightly stroke with wet and dry paper after which wipe down the surface with the tak-rag, prior to applying the next coat. The final three to five coats are unthinned, the last being brushed on with as few strokes as possible and all in one direction only.

Teak oil requires the same initial surface treatment as varnish but is infinitely easier to apply, requiring, say, three coats, the first thinned out some 20%.

Varnish, and for that matter most other paints, should not be applied on any day when the night temperature is likely to drop dramatically. Moisture precipitation may occur and 'blooming' afflict the most painstaking efforts. Teak oil does not lift and bloom as easily as varnish.

As a last word on this subject, if my advice is anything to go by, do not use polyurethane varnish for exterior work — there have been, and no doubt will continue to be, so many 'foul-ups', despite instructions seemingly being followed to the last letter.

Deck Surfaces External deck surfaces may well require treatment if the craft is not to look like a floating bath. If it can be afforded, the areas enduring heavy foot traffic look very well finished with a non-slip deck covering. One company produces a composition material of cork, rubber plus a 'mystery' ingredient. Marvellous stuff which comes in 1200mm x 900mm (4ftx3ft) sheets. Rather than apply solid sheets it looks better, and works out cheaper, to lay it in defined, cut out shapes leaving small areas of deck showing (Illus. 175a). Before leaving the subject of composition deck covering, it is stuck down with a contact adhesive, so do obey the instructions and place weights on the outlines whilst the adhesive sets, otherwise it tends to bubble (Illus. 175b).

Other areas, not subject to so much wear and tear, can be painted but this treatment requires care and preparation. Circumscribe the area to be painted with masking tape. Don't paint right up to the cabin side or toe-rails as it looks more professional to place the tape so as to leave a strip of deck, ensuring the painted areas have rounded, not sharp corners. Similarly, when deck painting around the handrails and deck fittings, position the masking tape to leave an inch or so clear (Illus. 176a).

If the deck is GRP degrease, very lightly wet and dry, apply one coat of glassfibre primer and two coats of deck paint which can be purchased with the anti-slip constituent 'built-in'. Should a builder require to add a little more 'non-slip', then a flour shaker filled with silver or 'budgie' cage sand does trick.

GRP

Hulls Degrease the area to be painted after which thoroughly wash with clean water. Any sign that the water is forming droplets and the degreasing will have to be done again. Continued failure to break down and remove the mould polish and or release wax and it will be necessary to very lightly wet and dry paper the surface and clean with a thinners. Fill defects with an epoxy filler, fair off, and apply one coat of antifouling primer and two coats of antifouling.

An alternative painting programme, especially where osmosis protection is in mind, involves utilising a two-pack, solventless, clear epoxy. The surface should be first cleaned and degreased with a multipurpose cleaner and degreaser, followed by a careful rub down with a 180-220 wet and dry paper, after which the surface must be thoroughly washed. Then apply one coat of epoxy

Illustration 175   Composition Deck Covering

175a

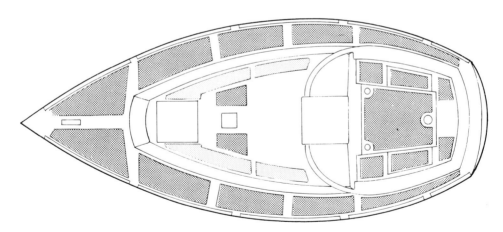

Composition deck covering

Deck paint

Corners rounded off & masked up so white GRP margin left visible

175b Weight down the cut-outs to save bubbling

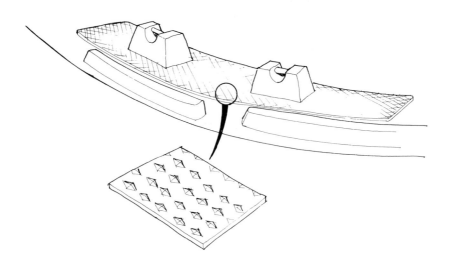

primer with a brush or roller, allowing to dry prior to, where necessary, filling with an epoxy resin filler and rubbing down lightly with a fine 280-320 grade wet and dry paper. Wash with clean, fresh water and, when dry, apply a second coat of epoxy primer followed by a pigmented coat of epoxy primer and three coats of antifouling. Depending on the instructions and time lapses, the last coat of epoxy primer may have to be followed by a straightforward glassfibre primer before the antifoulings are brushed or rollered on. Phew!

Boot Topping This water-line stripe is best applied on to the antifouling priming coats. The easiest method is to prepare and prime the hull up to the top of the planned boot topping line. Then paint in the boot topping after which antifoul up to the bottom of the boot topping. Naturally use masking tape to delineate the paint parameters (Illus. 176b).

Bilges Wash and apply a multipurpose cleaner and degreaser after which wash again and allow to dry completely before treating with a bilge paint.

On the other hand it is now considered advisable to treat GRP hulls from the inside out, as it were, and apply similar treatment to the bilges as is applied to the hull exterior. If this course of action is chosen, it is necessary to apply a multipurpose cleaner and degreaser, rub down (or flat out) with a 180-200 grade wet and dry paper, wash, allow to dry and paint with two coats of epoxy primer, the second being pigmented.

STEEL

It is mandatory that all surface rust and millscale i removed prior to painting and welds must be thoroughl cleaned out. To achieve this aim an operator has number of options to hand including these listed below in a descending order of effectiveness:

Sandblasting; abrasive disc; power tool wire brushing and 'handraulic' wire brushing.

If sand blasting is out of the question, carry out a mi: of the last three — that is, hand, or power tool wire brushing and grinding to clean back to bare, shiny metal AND DO wear goggles — it is very macho without bu may well necessitate a visit to the eye department of the nearest hospital!

Above Water-line After thoroughly dusting, speedily apply a coat of metallic based yacht primer, stop up with epoxy filler and rub down as necessary. Ensure the surface is dry and then build up a further three coats of yacht primer, followed by an undercoat and two topcoats.

Below Water-line Treatment is as above but substitute an underwater primer and apply some five coats prior to antifouling with two coats of the selected colour.

Incidentally, I am a great devotee of Black Varnish for the underwater of steel hulls.

Decks Follow the *Above Water-line* schedule up to anc

Illustration 176   Masking For Painting

176a Decks

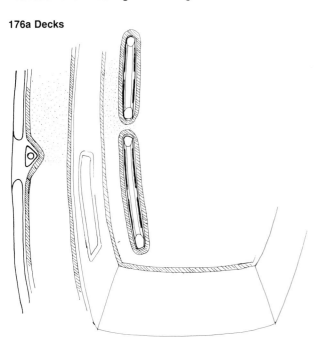

176b Hull

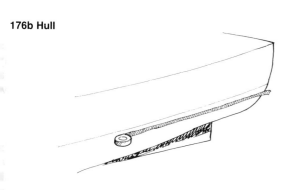

including the last coat of primer, after which apply several coats of deck paint.

Bilges Follow the *Above Water-line* schedule (presumably not bothering to fill any imperfections) up to and including the last coat of primer, after which slap on two coats of bilge paint.

PLYWOOD & TIMBER

The following descriptions cover craft that both flex (clinker and carvel built boats) and those categorised as rigid (plywood, double diagonal and moulded boats). Note that the application of varnish is dealt with elsewhere in this Chapter.

If it is necessary to sand down the surface, use a 80-120 grade sandpaper followed by a further sanding with 180-220 grade sandpaper. Remove all traces of sandpaper dust and make sure the surface is dry, wiping down with a tak-rag. Only 'oily' timbers, which include teak and iroko, require an initial application of thinners to counteract the natural oils. Timber craft kept in fresh water greatly benefit from being treated with a wood preservative, inside and out, prior to any other paint applications. The first coat of wood primer should be thinned to the point where it is rather wishy-washy. Follow with two coats of unthinned primer, after which trowel cement and sand back with a 280-320 grade paper, where required, and thoroughly clean. Then:-

Topsides Apply another coat of primer, at least one, but preferably two undercoats and two topcoats.

or

Below Water-line Apply two coats of primer after which trowel cement any further imperfections, wet and dry paper back, followed by another application of primer and two coats of antifouling.

Decks As for *Topsides* but substitute two coats of deck paint for the undercoat and topcoat.
or

Bilges Apply two coats of primer and two coats of bilge paint.

FERROCEMENT

Any old paint that comes to hand cannot be used on a ferro craft, due to the high alkaline content of the mortar used in the construction. This restricts paints to those based on epoxy coatings (or chlorinated rubber).

Hull The hull should have cured for at least one month before thoroughly wire brushing all over to remove any efflorescent salts. Then 'stone' the hull with a constantly wetted, medium grade carborundum stone followed by a sanding with 180 grade wet and dry paper. Wire ends showing through must be punched in and stopped with a filler, after which, etch the hull with a solution of one part phosphoric acid to four parts of water, applied with a large stiff distemper brush or broom. Wash and leave a week to dry. Then apply one coat of epoxy primer with a brush or roller, allowing to completely dry prior to, where necessary, filling with an epoxy resin filler and rubbing down lightly with a fine 280-320 grade wet and dry paper. Prior to applying a second coat of epoxy primer, wash with clean, fresh water. After which, paint on a pigmented coat of epoxy primer and three coats of antifouling. Depending on the instructions and time lapses, the last coat of epoxy primer may have to be followed by a straightforward primer before the antifoulings are brushed or rollered on.

Hull Freeboard & Topsides Proceed as for the *Hull* but follow the epoxy primer with an undercoat and substitute two coats of gloss paint for the antifouling, lightly flattening down between each coat.

Decks Proceed as for the *Hull*, but only apply two coats of two-pack epoxy primer. Follow these with two coats of undercoat and two of deck paint, the first of which must be applied between three and seven hours of the last coat of epoxy primer, depending on the temperature at the time. If there is a greater interval of time, apply a coat of glassfibre etch primer to give a good key for the next coat of paint.

Bilges Do not paint internally, especially with an epoxy coat, at the same time as externally painting — blistering may well occur. Initially treat the internal areas with the phosphoric acid/water mix, then apply a 15% thinned coat of epoxy primer followed by three undiluted coats of primer.

ALUMINIUM

Generally aluminium requires thorough degreasing. This can be achieved by either:
(a) low pressure, aluminium oxide grit blasting followed by the immediate application of an epoxy primer, to which an undercoat can be directly applied. Then proceed, as appropriate, below
or
(b) rub down with a fine to medium abrasive after which, painstakingly clean with a cloth soaked in a multipurpose cleaner and degreasing agent. After the prescribed time the surfaces must be thoroughly washed with fresh water, allowing to dry prior to applying a coat of self etch primer.
Then:-

Topsides Follow either of the above preparations with three coats of alloy primer. Where necessary, fill with a trowel cement between the second and third coats of the primer after which apply two coats of undercoat and one or two coats of gloss yacht enamel.
or

Below Water-line Follow the above preparations with five coats of suitable underwater primer and two coats of antifouling.
or

Decks Follow the above preparations with two coats of deck paint.
or

Bilges Follow the above preparations with two coats of bilge paint.

CAST IRON KEELS

They require vigorous cleaning, preferably with an electric powered rotary wire brush, after which strenuously, hand wire brush local areas and sandpaper all over. Voids must be filled with trowel cement and the whole treated with an anti-oxidisation liquid. Follow with five coats of metallic primer and two applications of antifouling.

QUANTITIES

As a general indication to the amounts of paint required the empirical formulae that follow give a guide.

Topsides: The area (in square meters) = (overall length + beam) x (2 x the average freeboard).

Decks: The area = (overall length + beam) x ¾ — (coach roof, cockpit and hatches).

Underwater: Racing Craft. The area = water-line length x (beam + draft) x ½
Cruisers. The area = water-line length x (beam + draft) x ¾.
Motor Sailers. The area = water-line length x (beam + draft).

Use the tables below to give the approximate requirements

The area in square metres
per 750 ml tin

Primers:	Glass fibre	7½
	Wood	7½
	Steel (2 pack)	10

| **Undercoats:** | | 7½ |

| **Topcoats/enamels/gloss:** | | 8 |

| **Antifoulings:** | | 6 |

| **Varnish:** | | 7½ |

| **Deck paint:** | | 7 |

250 mls = 0.005 galls; 500 mls = 0.11 galls;
1 litre = 0.22 galls; 2½ litres = 0.55 galls;
5 litres = 1.1 galls.

17

CRUISING EQUIPMENT, INSTRUMENTS, SAFETY EQUIPMENT & 'BOLT ON' GOODIES FOR SEAGOING CRAFT

The seemingly ever greater number of firms supplying an ever increasing and widening range of instruments, safety equipment and 'bolt on' goodies must induce a bemused and befuddled state of mind in the average boat owner.

In this Chapter I intend to keep the suggestions and details to broad and basic outlines. The items are listed under headings indicating the degree of necessity. Naturally this 'league table' may be the subject of dissension but that is the nature of making lists of the best 'this' or the first 'that'.

Planned cruising grounds must be considered in determining the necessity of this or that piece of equipment. For instance, if engaging in ocean voyaging, a Satellite Navigation System may be considered necessary but would be a waste of time and money for cross channel work and possibly for negotiating the Shropshire Union Canal . . .!

MANDATORY EQUIPMENT

Boat Anchors

A very wide choice including Danforth and variations; plough and variations; Bruce; folding grapnel and fisherman anchors, to name but a few (Illus. 177).

I don't recommend either the folding grapnel or fisherman anchors for boats in excess of say 6m (20ft) in length. The required size and weight of an anchor are determined by the craft's length and proposed cruising grounds. See Chapter Eighteen for a table of anchor size to boat length and planned cruising grounds.

Anchor Chain & Warp

It is usual to have a comparatively short length of chain and bend it on to anchor warp of polyester 3 strand rope. Ensure the chain is calibrated and tested.

Fenders

They should be as large as looks sensible when in position but do check they can be stowed away in the cockpit lockers. Consider fitting hull protectors (sounds rather like a cricket box) or chafe canvas (Illus. 178) to save unsightly marks and abrasions of the hull.

Boat Hook
A choice of telescopic or ash pole and galvanised head jammed on one end. At least one company markets a patent end fitting which aids picking up marker and mooring buoys.

Deck Scrub & Mop
Bull brigade, but necessary for cleaning the decks.

Scoop Bailer
Essential for cleaning unwanted bilge water out of lockers, removing oily engine slime and childrens' unnoticed seashells and seaweed (unnoticed that is until the smell leads to further investigation).

Hand bailers have been known to remove an unbelievable quantity of water when the fear of sinking is upon a crew!

Canvas Bucket
Complimentary to the bailer. Ensure both have securely attached lanyards.

Over Boom Cover, Cockpit Spray Hood & Dodgers
Useful and worthwhile 'extras' to a cruising yacht's inventory include well fitting cockpit dodgers, a spray hood and an over boom cockpit tent (Illus. 179). The tent is more than useful in enabling the skipper to shelter stores and sails in the cockpit when moored up, sleep an extra hand as well as being able to leave the main companionway open in order to increase the cabin through ventilation.

If coloured 'Day Glo' orange they double up as a signalling and marker cloth.

Radar Reflector
Follow the manufacturer's instructions and hoist as high as possible.

Fire Extinguishers
The minimum is one dry powder, of not less than 1.5kg (3 lbs), for the galley, plus a fire blanket to smother flaming frying pans, and one BCF (Halon Gas) 1.5kg (3 lbs) extinguisher for use on electrical wiring and electronic equipment fires. A word of warning is that BCF gas, if used in confined spaces, gives off toxic fumes.

Additionally, it is worth considering fitting a BCF fire extinguisher mounted in the engine compartment. If fitted with a heat detector the extinguisher automatically 'fires off' when a pre-set temperature is reached (usually 80°C).

First Aid Kit
Do ensure the box contains items personal to the crew,

bearing in mind that proprietary kits often exclude the most basic items such as aspirin and a wide swathe of plaster.

Illustration 177   Anchors

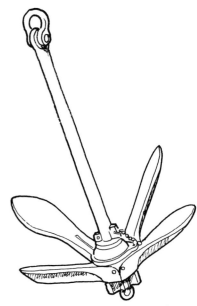

Folding grapnel

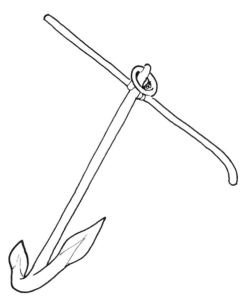

Fisherman

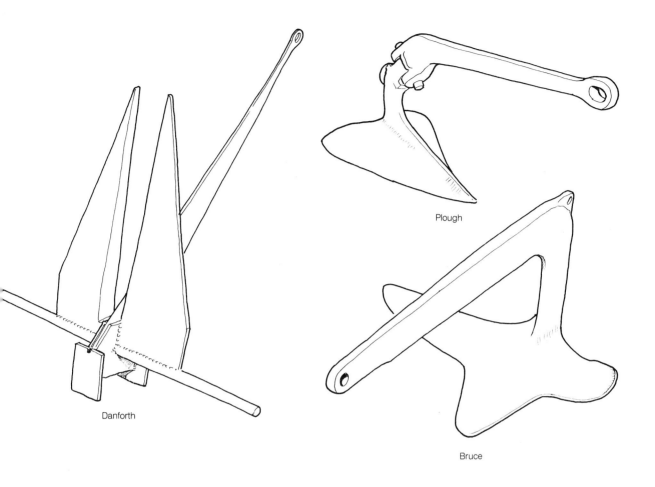

Plough

Danforth

Bruce

Illustration 178   Fender Chafe Canvas

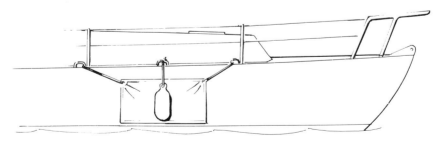

Saves hull marks & abrasions

Flares

The inventory must include at least one of the 'coastal' packs. Why not splash out and include an RORC flare pack contained in a plastic, screw topped container (resembling one of those old fashioned sweet jars).

Do not stow flares away under a berth or somewhere 'real' convenient, but in an easily accessible, cockpit locker. Consider a line throwing rocket and a buoyant orange smoke canister. Well, it could happen to you!

Torch

Two in number, rubber coated and fitted with leakproof batteries.

Dinghy & Liferafts

The choice is between an inflatable or a rigid dinghy, preferably of moulded GRP with built in buoyancy. Much depends on the depth of an owners pocket (again) and size of the craft. Inflatables can be tucked away, but are more expensive than rigid dinghies, which are not so easy to stow on board, usually trailing aft on a painter (of which make sure the fastenings and rope are very, very secure!).

If fortunate enough to be able to afford a small outboard motor to power the dinghy, consider stowing it on a bracket fixed to the pushpit (Illus. 180a). Also fit a transom or rudder mounted outboard bracket which provides the mounting for auxiliary power should the main motor malfunction (Illus. 180b).

Spare Water Container

It may seem unnecessary but a two gallon water can may well be the difference between a 'fair' to 'middling' trip if the boat's water supply becomes contaminated or runs out. Also useful where the shore water point is nowhere near the quayside.

Flags

The Ensign and International code flag 'Q' are a minimum.

Lifebuoys

Two are better than one. Why not obtain the horseshoe type, complete with — if the financial strain can be borne — a flashing light, whistle and a drogue (to stop excessive drifting of the lifebuoy) all mounted on the pushpit in one of those neat, stainless steel holders.

Other Items

Consider fitting a pair of spreader chafe guards to save wear and expensive damage to hard sheeted genoa's and or a wildly flapping mainsail.

Rather than fitting proprietary, plastic covered stainless steel guard rails consider the option of Parafil. This is not only less expensive but easier to use as it can be cut to any length and 'swaged' to special, manually fastened compression end fittings.

Illustration 179   Covers, Hoods and Dodgers

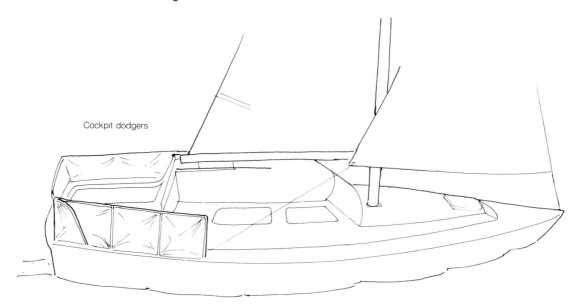

Cockpit dodgers

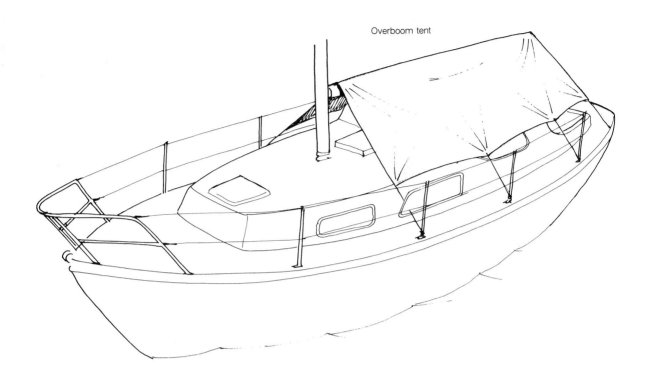

Overboom tent

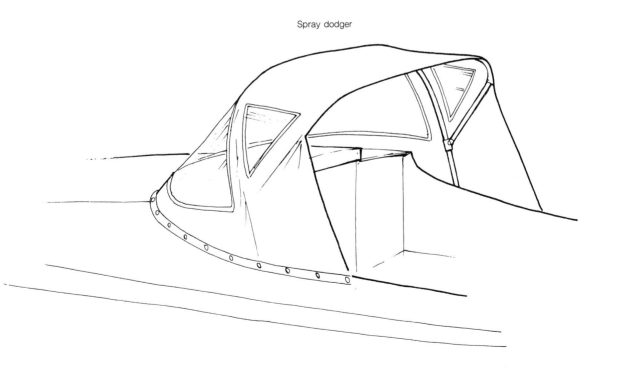

Spray dodger

PERSONAL

Life Jacket
One per person. I prefer the more expensive version with a built in safety harness.

Knife & Lanyard
Stainless steel complete with a shackler in the body and a spike.

Sail Bag
Containing a change of underwear, run-ashore-slacks, shirt and windcheater, a good set of separate top and bottom 'oilies', yellow 'wellies', oiled fisherman's socks and sweater, deck shoes, a neck towel and woolly hat. Consider thermal underwear if prone to feeling the cold and don't forget a toilet bag containing personal medical requirements.

Sleeping Bag
Complete with an inner, cotton liner.

Illustration 180   Outboard Motor Mountings

180a   Outboard motor pushpit mounting

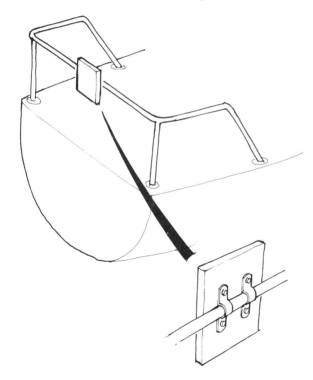

180b   Transom mounted bracket

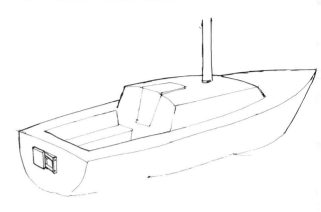

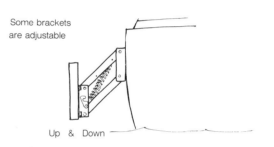

Some brackets are adjustable

Up & Down

Rudder mounted brackets

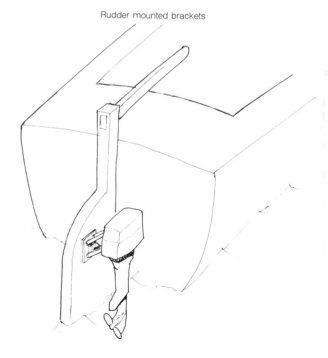

ADDITIONAL MANDATORY EQUIPMENT

Kedge Anchor

Compass
a) Hand held.
b) A choice of bracket, binnacle, flush or porthole mounted.

Echo Depth Sounder
Heaving' the lead was fine in the days of unlimited crew but when short handed and in need of quick, accurate information there is no substitute for a good, reliable depth sounder. They are now available in ever increasing degrees of complexity including digital readouts and pre-set alarms. If unable to afford 'repeater' stations, and wishing to keep the system simple, fit the unit on a swing out bracket mounted on the entrance hatch frame (Illus. 181).

Illustration 181   An Echo Sounder Swing Out Bracket

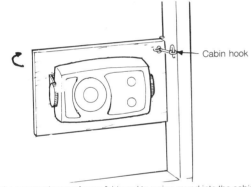

Cabin hook

Mounted on the companionway frame & hinged to swing round into the cabin & fasten on the main cabin bulkhead

Log
For speed and or distance travelled through the water. An alternative is the trail speed log hung over the transom.

Portable Direction Finding Radio
The direction finding facility is usually indifferent but does indicate that the radio is designed for marine use and the important task of easily receiving weather forecasts and shipping transmissions, as well as the normal wavelength stations.

Hand Held Radio Direction Finder (RDF)
Gives an approximate position. This type of equipment is getting progressively more sophisticated.

Chart Table
Parallel rules, single handed dividers, navigation plotter, almanac, tidal stream atlas and a log book.

NECESSARY EQUIPMENT but not mandatory

Clock & Barometer
Often available as a set for bulkhead mounting.

Binoculars
Normally specified 7 x 50 for marine use (Magnification x 7 and 50mm object lens diameter).

USEFUL (but not essential) EQUIPMENT

Engine Hours Run Meter
Useful as long as the engine is not left running for periods, whilst tied up alongside.

Clinometer
For angle of heel — well it's nice to know how far over the craft has been!

Ventimeter
To measure wind speed — well it's nice to know, if only for the same reason as having a clinometer. In any case the information gained, with possible elaborations, makes for good bar yarns.

Fog Horn
Gas canister or 'lung' operated.

Set of Signal Flags

'NICE TO HAVE' EQUIPMENT

Two Way Loud Hailer
Very useful, when close to, for ship to ship and ship to harbour wall conversations.

Wind Speed Direction & Close Hauled Indicator
Almost a necessity to get the very best performance in all wind conditions and at all points of sailing. If a number of instruments are being fitted, including the above and, say, speed and distance travelled logs, it is probably best to pick one system and fit a matched instrument console.

VHF Radio
The microchip revolution has really brought the cost of multi, fixed channel two-way radios within the reach of most boat owners. The range is averagely horizon sight distance plus 10% to 15%. Two small craft with aerials positioned fairly low down can probably be in contact up to 8 miles plus, whilst a small craft in touch with the Coastguard on a fairly high headland could communicate for up to 25 miles as can a couple of 8½m (28ft) yachts with masthead mounted aerials.

Installation hints include consulting an expert but failing that:-

(a) use a tailored length of the correctly screened coaxial cable
(b) ensure the power cable run to the relevant battery is as short as possible
(c) ensure the battery is well charged
(d) fit the recommended aerial
and
(e) run the coaxial cable as clear as possible of the cables of other electronic navigational aids.

Automatic Pilot

If contemplating cross channel cruising and/or short handed, the auto pilot or tiller pilot are a great boon and can steer a better course than any human being. It won't steer round things though!

LUXURIOUS

Radar & Satellite Navigation Systems

If you can afford one you won't need my advice.

Composition deck covering, applied in rounded section & leaving portions of the GRP deck showing, gives a pleasing look to the uncluttered and clean looking superstructure.

A well engineered & finished main saloon facing aft. Particularly of note are the sole to deckhead stainless steel tube supports doubling up, on the one side, as the table pillar & on the other, as a convenient 'arm grab'; the sturdy internal deckhead & cabin bulkhead grabrails; the solid companionway steps & the sensibly proportioned dropboard hatch.

18

TABLES, CONVERSION FORMULAE & USEFUL NAMES AND ADDRESSES

Hose Clips

Pipe clips are extremely confusingly sized by the various manufacturers and the list below will be of some help in sorting out the ridiculous situation. Use ONLY stainless steel clips.

000	⅜″ — ½″	9 — 13mm
M00	⅜″ — ⅝″	9 — 16mm
00	½″ — ¾″	13 — 19mm
0	⅝″ — ⅞″	16 — 22mm
0X	¾″ — 1″	19 — 25mm
1A	⅞″ — 1⅛″	22 — 28mm
1	1″ — 1⅜″	25 — 35mm
1X	1⅛″ — 1⅝″	28 — 41mm
2A	1¼″ — 1⅞″	32 — 48mm
2	1½″ — 2⅛″	38 — 54mm
2X	1¾″ — 2⅜″	44 — 60mm
3	2″ — 2¾″	50 — 70mm
3X	2⅜″ — 3⅛″	60 — 80mm

Machine Screws

Due to standardisation over recent years, the metric equivalent of the machine screws listed below should be used as imperial sizes may be more than double the cost.

British Standard	Approximate Metric Thread equivalent	Clearance Drill Size	75% Tap Thread Drill Size
$\frac{3}{16}$″ (.1875)	M5	$\frac{7}{32}$″	$\frac{3}{32}$″
¼″ (.25)	M6	$\frac{17}{64}$″	$\frac{7}{32}$″
$\frac{5}{16}$″ (.3125)	M8	⅜″	$\frac{17}{64}$″
⅜″ (.375)	M10	$\frac{7}{16}$″	$\frac{21}{64}$″
½″ (0.5)	M12	$\frac{9}{16}$″	$\frac{7}{16}$″

Metal & Wire Gauge Equivalents

It is useful to have the tables to hand as there is nothing more infuriating than being unable to communicate with a supplier or to have gauge numbers with no way of converting them to really useful equivalents, such as thickness. This usually occurs at a weekend according to Murphy's Law.

Metal Gauge Number	Imperial Thickness	Metric
	inches	mm
1	0.3	7.61
2	0.276	7.00
3	0.252	6.39
4	0.232	5.88
5	0.212	5.38
6	0.192	4.87
7	0.176	4.46
8	0.160	4.06
9	0.144	3.66
10	0.128	3.25
11	0.116	2.94
12	0.104	2.64
13	0.092	2.34
14	0.080	2.00
15	0.072	1.83
16	0.064	1.62
17	0.056	1.42
18	0.048	1.22
19	0.040	1.01
20	0.036	0.91
21	0.032	0.81
22	0.028	0.71
23	0.024	0.61
24	0.022	0.56
25	0.020	0.51
26	0.018	0.46
27	0.016	0.41
28	0.014	0.36
29	0.013	0.33
30	0.012	0.30

Standard Wire Gauge	Imperial Thickness	Metric
	inches	mm
30	0.0124	0.314
29	0.0136	0.345
28	0.0148	0.375
27	0.0164	0.416
26	0.018	0.457
25	0.020	0.508
24	0.022	0.558
23	0.024	0.609
22	0.028	0.711
21	0.032	0.812
20	0.036	0.914
19	0.040	1.016
18	0.048	1.219
17	0.056	1.422
16	0.064	1.625
15	0.072	1.828
14	0.080	2.032
13	0.092	2.336
12	0.104	2.640

11	0.116	2.946
10	0.128	3.251
9	0.144	3.657
8	0.160	4.064
7	0.176	4.470
6	0.192	4.876
5	0.212	5.384
4	0.232	5.892
3	0.252	6.400
2	0.276	7.010
1	0.300	7.620
0	0.324	8.229
2/0	0.348	8.839
3/0	0.372	9.448
4/0	0.400	10.16
5/0	0.432	10.97
6/0	0.464	11.8
7/0	0.500	12.70

Nobility Table

	Material	Voltage potential
Least noble	Magnesium alloy	− 1.6
	Zinc	− 1.10
	Galvanised iron	− 1.05
	Aluminium	− 0.75
	Mild steel	− 0.70
	Cast iron	− 0.65
	Lead	− 0.55
	Brass*	− 0.27-0.29
	Magnese bronze	− 0.27
	Copper-Nickel	− 0.25
	Silicon bronze	− 0.18
	Monel*	− 0.08-0.20
Most noble	Stainless Steel*	− 0.05-0.20

*The actual nobility depends upon the exact alloy composition of the metal.

To eliminate corrosion in sea-water it would be necessary to achieve a voltage difference of only 0.20 volts — so anodic protection is the answer.

Water pipe equivalents:-

³⁄₈″ 12mm)   ¾″ 22mm)not inter-
½″ 15mm) inter-   1¼″ 35mm)changeable &
1″   28mm) changeable 1½″ 42mm)require a
2″   54mm)   conversion coupling

Note Gas & fuel pipe sizes are still measured in Imperial sizes.

Plywood board equivalents:-

⅛″ 4mm
¼″ 6mm
³⁄₈″ 9mm
½″ 12mm
¾″ 18mm

Sandpaper grades:-

60-120	Very abrasive and used to remove burnt off paintwork. Scores the surface.
80-200	Abrasive and used to prepare wood for a coat of primer.
220	Used to prepare a surface for an undercoat.
280-320	Used to prepare a surface for a topcoat or a first coat of varnish.
400	Used to cut back the first topcoat or a subsequent application of varnish.
400-600	Used to remove blemishes in the topcoat of enamel paint or varnish.

Skin fitting equivalents

1/2″	13mm
3/4″	19mm
1″	25mm
1 1/4″	32mm
1 1/2″	38mm
2″	50mm

Timber thickness:- (approx.)

1/2″	13mm
5/8″	16mm
3/4″	19mm
7/8″	22mm

1″	25mm
1 1/4″	32mm
1 1/2″	38mm
1 3/4″	44mm
2″	50mm
2 1/2″	63mm
3″	75mm
4″	100mm
5″	125mm
6″	150mm

Note. The above sizes are for sawn timber. Planed timber looses about 1 1/2mm ($\frac{1}{16}$″) per planed surface, so a board ordered '25mm (1″) planed thickness' finishes up at about 22mm ($\frac{7}{8}$″)

Woodscrew drilling sizes:-

		Screw gauges*				
		6	8	10	12	14
Softwoods.	pilot drill	-	$\frac{1}{16}$″	$\frac{5}{64}$″	$\frac{5}{64}$″	$\frac{7}{64}$″
	clearance drill	-	$\frac{3}{32}$″	$\frac{5}{32}$″	$\frac{5}{32}$″	$\frac{7}{32}$″
Hardwoods.	pilot drill	$\frac{5}{64}$″	$\frac{3}{32}$″	1/8″	1/8″	$\frac{5}{32}$″
	clearance drill	$\frac{5}{32}$″	$\frac{3}{16}$″	$\frac{7}{32}$″	1/4″	1/4″

* To ascertain a screw's gauge, measure the diameter of the head of the screw, using a ruler marked in sixteenths (of an inch), multiply the measurement by two and subtract two from the result.

Pipe & Hoses

General Types	Bore Sizes	Outside dia.	Comments & Usage
Clear PVC, non toxic pipe	13mm-38mm (1/2″-1 1/2″)	19mm-48mm (3/4″-1 7/8″)	Water supply and occasionally delivery. Kinks and collapses, so must not be used on suction runs. Also cannot be used where fluids are hot, nor should fuels be piped in this hose. Can be 'persuaded' to distort.
Spiral reinforced plastic pipe	19mm-30mm (3/4″-1 1/2″)		Three general types. Very and medium stiff, with moulded in spiralling, and flexible, thin wall with external spiralling. Does not kink but conversely can be difficult to get round tight bends. Used for both suction and delivery pipe runs. Heat must be used to ensure pipe clips have properly tightened down. Will not easily distort.
Low pressure rubber pipe	13mm, 19 & 25mm (1/2″, 3/4″, & 1″)		Calor gas piping from a bibcock to, say, a gimballed cooker.
Seamless copper tube	1/8″-3/4″		Calor gas and fuel pipe runs.
Reinforced, clear fuel pipe	1/4″, $\frac{5}{16}$″, 3/8″ & 1/2″		Suitable for petrol or diesel fuels.
Synthetic delivery pipe	13mm-25mm (1/2″-1″)		Hot water supply.
Reinforced rubber heater hose	13mm-25mm (1/2″-1″)		Engine water cooling inlet pipe.

Skin Fittings, Pipes & Hoses For Various Fittings

Skin Fittings

General Types	Sizes	Comments & Usage
Nylon	13mm-50mm (½"-2")	Above water-line
Gunmetal	13mm-50mm (½"-2")	Above and below water-line. Usually fitted with a gate valve and serrated tail or bent elbow.
Seacock-toilet	20mm & 38mm (¾" & 1½")	Below water-line. Engineered with tapered valves.
Seacock-engine water strainer	13,19 & 25mm (½", ¾" & 1")	Below water-line. Engineered with a mesh filter.

N.B. Thru' hull skin fittings must be fitted with the nut tightened down on adequate internal backing pads. Do not forget to place sealant on both the skin fitting and the backing pad.

Skin Fittings & Pipe Usage

General	Thru' hull skin fitting, attachments & pipework
Sinks:	Gunmetal complete with gate valve and serrated tail. If the outlet is close to the water-line fit a non-return valve. PVC non-toxic pipe.
Gas locker drain:	Nylon. PVC non toxic pipe Alternatively the drain from the gas locker can be run in seamless pipe and connected to a gunmetal skin fitting via a short link length of PVC pipe.
Automatic bilge pumps: including shower tray pumps:)	Gunmetal complete with gate valve, serrated tail, non return valve. PVC pipe unless the run might kink, when fit spiral reinforced pipe.
Bilge & galley pumps:	Nylon Suction line: spiral reinforced pipe. If a long run fit a non-return valve. Delivery line: PVC pipe unless the run might kink, when fit spiral reinforced pipe.
Cockpit drains:	Cockpit sole: Nylon Thru' hull: Gunmetal complete with gate valve, serrated tail or bent elbow. Spiral reinforced pipe. N.B. Double pipe clip.
Cockpit seat & scupper drains	Nylon both ends unless the scupper drain outlet (of the scupper drains) is close to the

water-line (allowing for heel) when gunmetal skin fittings complete with gate valves and tail must be used. Spiral reinforced pipe.

*Sea toilet	Toilet seacocks. Spiral reinforced pipe N.B. Double pipe clips must be fitted.
Engine cooling water intake	Engine water strainer seacock. Reinforced rubber heater hose. N.B. Double pipe clips must be fitted.
Engine exhaust pipe (water cooled)	Exhaust thru' hull skin fitting (specific manufactured item) or gunmetal skin fitting c/w gate valve and tail. Specialist exhaust hose.

On a general note, DO NOT use proprietary rain water pipework and adhesive (as I have seen with unbelieving eyes) — the sea-water dissolves the adhesive with interesting results.

NB British Waterways Board Regulations specifically forbid these items. See Chapter Eight.

SAMPLE FASTENING SCHEDULE FOR AN 8½-9m (26-28ft) YACHT

Item Deck Fittings & Quantity	Fastening Quantity & Description
Mast heel, Pot, T-bar or Tabernacle	4 76mm x 13mm (3" x ½") stainless steel (SS) machine screws (MS), hex. head complete with (c/w) washers and nuts.
Bow bollard	6 50mm x 6mm (2" x ¼") SS, MS, csk. head c/w washers & nuts
4 Mooring cleats	16 50mm x 6mm (2" x ¼") SS, MS, csk. head c/w washers & nuts
3 Cockpit sheet cleats	12 40mm x 19mm (1½" x ¾") SS MS, csk. head c/w washers & nuts
Chain pipe	3 40mm x 5mm (1½" x $\frac{3}{16}$") SS, MS, csk. head c/w washers & nuts
Chain plates	35 40mm x 6mm (1½" x ¼") SS, MS, csk. head c/w washers & nuts
	& 7 50mm x 6mm (2" x ¼") SS, MS, csk. head c/w washers & nuts

or
Rigging Eyes — 14 8mm ($\frac{5}{16}$ ") SS, nuts & washers

Pulpit/Pushpit 8x16 10mm (⅜") SS, nuts & washers

Stanchion bases — 18 50mm x 6mm (2" x ¼") SS, MS, csk. head c/w washers & nuts

Grabrails — 12 90mm x 19mm (3½" x ¾") SS, MS, csk. head c/w washers & nuts

Gunwales — 200 50mm x 6mm (2" x ¼") SS, MS, pan head c/w nuts & washers

Transom gunwale — 10 76mm x 5mm (3" x ¼") SS, MS, csk. head c/w washers & nuts

Bow roller — 8 50mm x 6mm (2" x ¼") SS, MS, csk. head c/w washers & nuts

Main & Genoa sheet tracks — 30 40mm x 5mm (1½" x $\frac{3}{16}$ ") SS, MS, csk. head c/w washers & nuts

Fore-hatch surround — 30 19mm x 4mm (¾" x 8) SS, self tapping screws (self tappers)

Fore-hatch surround to coach roof — 40 30mm x 4mm (1¼" x 8) SS, self tappers

Internal Fitting Out

Toilet door frame — 6 1¼" x 8 brass, csk. wood screws
& 10 1½" x 8 brass, csk. wood screws

Toilet sole frame — 14 1½" x 8 brass, csk. wood screws

Toilet sole — 10 1½" x 8 brass, csk. wood screws

Toilet fore & aft bulkhead — 15 1" x 8 brass, csk. wood screws

Toilet door plinth — 3 1½" x 8 csk. wood screws
& 6 1" panel pins, brass

Toilet base — 3 50mm x 6mm (2" x ¼") SS, MS, csk. head c/w washers & nuts

Toilet valves — 6 50mm x 6mm (2" x ¼") phosphor bronze bolts c/w washers & nuts

Toilet sink fixing — 4 ¾" x 6 SS, csk. wood screws

GRP mouldings to bunk bearers — 52 1" x 8 brass csk. wood screws

Toilet compartment fashion piece — 4 1" x 8 brass csk. wood screws

Dinette drawer framing — 11 1¼" x 8 brass csk. wood screws
3 1" x 8 brass csk. wood screws
& 3 ¾" x 6 brass csk. wood screws

Forward berth — 8 1" x 8 brass csk. wood screws

Drawer frame — 6 1¼" x 8 csk. wood screws
& 6 ¾" x 6 brass csk. wood screws

Toilet sink — 7 1¼" x 8 brass csk. wood screws and cups

Hanging locker mast support block — 2 2" x ¼" SS, MS, csk. head c/w washers & nuts

Shelf fiddles — 15 1" x 8 brass csk. wood screws

Shelf supports — 15 1¼" x 8 brass csk. wood screws

Toilet inlet & outlet pipes — 4 25mm (1") pipe clips, SS,
& 4 38mm (1½") pipe clips, SS. Note both are double clipped

Galley porthole, 2 Forecabin windows & 2 Saloon windows — 64 12mm x 5 mm (½" x $\frac{3}{16}$ ") SS, MS
& 64 Collars

Shelves: 1 main port cabin, 2 forward cabin — 15 2" x 8 brass csk. wood screws

Sliding door frame — 4 2" x 8 brass csk. wood screws

Shelf battens — 4 1½" x 8 brass csk. wood screws

Cupboard bottom — 11 1" x 8 brass csk. wood screws

Facing strip — 13 ¾" x 6 brass csk. wood screws

Table blocks — 4 1" x 8 brass csk. wood screws

Berth table blocks — 6 40mm x 5 mm (1½" x $\frac{3}{16}$ ") SS, MS head c/w washers & nuts

Galley forward bulkhead — 3 1½" x 8 brass csk. wood screws
& 4 ¾" x 8 brass csk. wood screws

Galley aft bulkhead — 3 ¾" x 8 brass csk. wood screws

Galley flap forward — 3 1½" x 8 brass csk. wood screws

Galley cupboard catch — 3 ¾" x 6 brass csk. wood screws

Back cooker shelf — 2 ¾" x 6 brass csk. wood screws

Back cooker panel fillets — 4 1¼" x 8 brass csk. wood screws

Galley sink bottom shelf — 6 ¾" x 6 brass csk. wood screws

Tiptoe pump — 3 ¾" x 6 chrome wood screws

Cupboard fashion pieces	8 ¾" x 8 brass csk. wood screws
Galley flaps	6 1¼" x 8 brass csk. wood screws
Galley formica top	3 1¼" x 8 brass csk. wood screws
Galley cupboard bottom	6 1¼" x 8 brass csk. wood screws
Galley cupboard (sliding)	8 1½" x 8 brass csk. wood screws
Capping inside galley cupboard	6 ¾" x 6 self tappers
Capping galley front cupboard	7 ¾" x 6 brass csk. wood screws
Cooker gimbals	6 ¾" x 8 brass csk. wood screws
Toilet door fashion piece, forward cabin	46 1" panel pins, brass
Wardrobe head frames	6 1¼" x 8 brass csk. wood screws
Engine box cheeks & frames	24 ¾" x 6 brass csk. wood screws
Chain locker access hatch	1 Brass ball catch (finger hole) & 4 ½" x 4 brass csk. wood screws
Toilet door	3 50mm x 25mm (2" x 1") brass butts 18 ½" x 4 brass csk. wood screws 1 75mm (3") barrel bolt 4 ½" x 4 brass csk. wood screws 1 Door catch & finger hole 2 ¾" x 6 brass csk. wood screws & 1 ½" x 6 brass csk. wood screws
Toilet door stops	10 ¾" panel pins, brass
Hatch lining curved section	5 1½" x $\frac{3}{16}$" SS, self tappers
Trim cappings forward	50 ¾" x 6 SS, self tappers
Dinette & galley cappings	28 ¾" x 6 SS, self tappers
Quarter berth capping	23 ¾" x 6 SS, self tappers
Hanging locker rail	4 ¾" x 6 brass csk. wood screws
Table blocks	8 1¼" x 8 brass wood screws
Overhead panel rails	4 1¼" x 8 brass csk. wood screws
Echo sounder bracket	2 50mm x 25mm (2" x 1") brass butts 2 90 mm (3½") brass barrel bolts 50 ½" x 4 brass csk. wood screws & 5 1" x 8 csk. wood screws
Transducer block	2 ½" x 4 brass csk. wood screws
Echo sounder to bracket	3 ¾" x 8 brass csk. wood screws and cups
Engine box side	3 1" x 8 brass csk. wood screws and cups & 2 ¾" x 6 SS, self tappers
Toilet sink outlet	2 25mm (1") SS, pipe clips
Toilet roll holder	2 ¾" x 6 brass csk. wood screws
Dinette table bolts	10 ¼" x 4 brass csk. wood screws
Dinette table barrel bolt	6 ½" x 4 brass csk. wood screws
Fresh water tank	5 25mm (1") SS, pipe clips & 1 50mm (2") SS, pipe clips
Galley plinth	5 1" x 8 brass csk. wood screws
Sole to deckhead support tube in way of galley bulkhead	3 1" x 8 SS, wood screws
Bilge pump thru' deck plate	4 40mm x 6mm (1½" x ¼") SS, MS, csk. head c/w washers & nuts
Dropboard hasp & staple	4 ¾" x 6 SS, self tappers
Sliding hatch stops	4 1" x 8 brass csk. wood screws
Engine box top	4 1½" x 8 brass csk. wood screws and cups
Dropboard cover strips	10 1" x 8 SS, self tappers
Dropboard bottom cover strip	4 ¾" x 6 brass csk. wood screws
Battery tray battens	12 1¼" x 8 brass csk. wood screws
Battery straps	4 1" x 8 brass csk. wood screws
Battery strap clips	12 ½" x 4 brass csk. wood screws
Gas bin	7 1" SS, self tappers
Galley flap barrel bolts	6 Screw cups & 8 ½" x 4 brass csk. wood screws
Fire extinguisher	2 ¾" x 8 brass csk. wood screws
Sole bearers	9 ½" x 8 brass csk. wood screws
Fwd. cabin sole	20 ¾" x 6 SS, self tappers

Lap floor joints	30	1″ x 8 brass csk. wood screws
Engine box frame	5	32mm x 5mm (1¼″ x $\frac{3}{16}$″) SS, MS, c/w nuts & washers
	& 6	1″ x 8 brass csk. wood screws
Engine box cheek	6	40mm x 5mm (1½″ x $\frac{3}{16}$″) SS, MS, c/w washers & nuts
Engine box starboard cheek	6	1½″ x 8 brass csk. wood screws
Chrome catches	10	¾″ x 6 SS, roundhead wood screws
Barrel bolts	10	½″ x 4 brass csk. wood screws
Engine box berth front	3	¾″ x 8 brass csk. wood screws and cups
Dropboard frame	20	¾″ x 8 brass csk. wood screws
Dropboard frame support rail fwd.	5	1¼″ x 8 brass csk. wood screws
Sliding hatch frame underside	10	1″ x 8 brass csk. wood screws
Sliding hatch frame topside	10	1¼″ x 8 brass csk. wood screws
Sliding hatch runners	18 & 8	1″ x 8 brass csk. wood screws Screw cups
Gas bottle fixing eye plates	4	1″ SS, self tappers
Gas pipe clips	20	½″ x 6 SS, self tappers
Flag socket	4	40mm x 5mm (1½″ x $\frac{3}{16}$″) SS, MS, c/w washers & nuts
Cockpit seat hinges	32	¾″ x 8 brass csk. wood screws
Cockpit seat batten timber	82	¾″ x 6 brass csk. wood screws
Winch pads	8	1¼″ SS, self tappers
Cockpit sheet winches	8	50mm x 6mm (2″ x ¼″) SS, MS, c/w washers & nuts
Anchor chocks	6	25mm x 6mm (1″ x ¼″) SS, MS, c/w washers & nuts
Dropboard frame cover strip	4	1½″ x 8 brass csk. wood screws
Engine insulation battens	4	1¼″ x 8 brass csk. wood screws
Plate rack	2 & 2	1″ x 8 brass csk. wood screws screw cups, brass
Water filler	4	40mm x 5mm (1½″ x $\frac{3}{16}$″) SS, csk. head MS, c/w washers & nuts
Cockpit	18	½″ SS, self tappers

locker hasp and staples

Engineering

Rudder to stock	4	50mm x 10mm (2″ x ⅜″) Hex. head bolts c/w nuts & washers, steel
Skeg fastening	3	75mm x 10mm (3″ x ⅜″) Hex. head bolts c/w nuts & washers
Engine holding bolts	8	1½″ x $\frac{5}{16}$″ galvanised coach screws
Rudder anode	1	30mm x 10mm (1¼″ x ⅜″) bolts, steel c/w nuts & washers.
Sterntube	4	75mm x 10mm (3″ x ⅜″) phosphor bronze, MS, csk. head.

plus numerous stainless steel pipe clips, nuts & bolts & screws.

USEFUL CONVERSION FORMULAE & TABLES

To convert Pounds (lb) to Kilogrammes (kg) multiply by 0.4536 and kilogrammes to pounds multiply by 2.205

Water 1 litre weighs 1.00 kg/2.2 lb.
1 gallon weighs 4.53 kg/10 lb.

Gallons to litres: Multiply by 4.546
Litres to gallons: Multiply by 0.22
1 cu ft holds 6¼ gallons & weighs 62.3lb
To convert cubic feet to cubic metres multiply by 0.028

The central figure in the table represents either of the two outside columns, as the case may be i.e. 1 gallon = 4.546 litres or 1 litre = 0.22 gallons.

Litres		Gallons
4.546	1	0.220
9.092	2	0.440
13.638	3	0.660
18.184	4	0.880
22.730	5	1.100
27.276	6	1.320
31.822	7	1.540
36.368	8	1.760
40.914	9	1.980

Petrol 1 litre weighs 0.73 kg/1.61 lb.
1 gallon weighs 3.36 kg/7.4 lb.

Diesel 1 litre weighs 0.84 kg/1.85 lb
1 gallon weighs 3.86 kg/8.5 lb.

Measurements

To convert inches to centimetres (cm) multiply by 2.54 and centimetres to inches multiply by 0.393

1 inch = 25.4 millimetres (mm)
1 foot = 30.48 centimetres (cm)
1 yard = 0.9144 metre (m)

1 mile = 1.6093 kilometres (km)
1 millimetre = 0.03937 inch
1 centimetre = 0.0328 foot (ft)
1 metre = 1.094 yards (yd)
1 kilometre = 0.62137 mile

The central figure in the table represents either of the two outside columns, as the case may be i.e. 1 inch = 2.54 centimetres or 1 centimetre = 0.394 inches.

Centimetres		Inches
2.540	1	0.394
5.080	2	0.787
7.620	3	1.181
10.160	4	1.575
12.700	5	1.969
15.240	6	2.362
17.780	7	2.756
20.320	8	3.150
22.860	9	3.543

Metres		Yards
0.914	1	1.094
1.829	2	2.187
2.743	3	3.281
3.658	4	4.374
4.572	5	5.468
5.486	6	6.562
6.401	7	7.655
7.315	8	8.749
8.230	9	9.843

Speed
To convert knots to miles per hour, multiply by 1.15

Distance
To convert miles to kilometres multiply by 1.609 and kilometres to miles multiply by 0.621

Temperature
To convert Centigrade to Fahrenheit divide by 5, multiply by 9 and add 32. To convert Fahrenheit to Centigrade deduct 32, divide by 9 and multiply by 5.

Electrics
Amps equals watts divided by volts.

Cable/Current Requirements

Possible Item	Current requirement in amps (approx)	Conductor specification in mm		Cable Ref. Numbers [*]	
		Single core	Twin Core	Single core	Twin core
Gauge lamps	6-8	14/0.30	2x14/0.30	PV2a76/1	PV2a 76/2
Interior lamps	9-12	21/0.30	2x21/0.30	PV2b76/1	PV2b 76/2
Larger lamps (such as search lights)	17.5	28/0.30	2x28/0.30	PV376/1	PV3 76/2
Battery supply	27.5	44/0.30	2x44/0.30	PV3a76/1	PV3a 76/2
Dynamo	42	84/0.30	-	PV3b12/1	-
Alternator	60	120/0.30	-	PV3c12/1	-
Starter motors	135	266/0.30		-	PV336/1
	170	37/0.90		-	PV436/1
Electric winch	300	61/0.90		-	PV536/1

[*]These are Ripaults reference numbers.

Anchor, Chain & Warp Sizes, Weights & Lengths for Patent Anchors

DANFORTH & PLOUGH Anchors:

Boat Length:	up to 6m (20ft)	up to 7m (24ft)	up to 8m (27ft)	up to 9m (30ft)	up to 10.4m (34ft)	up to 13.4m (40ft)
Coastal Cruising						
Anchor Weight	4/5kg (10lb)	7kg (15lb)	10kg (22lb)	14kg (30lb)	16kg (35lb)	25kg (55lb)
Chain Link — diameter	6mm ($\frac{1}{4}''$)	6mm ($\frac{1}{4}''$)	8mm ($\frac{5}{16}''$)	8mm ($\frac{5}{16}''$)	10mm ($\frac{3}{8}''$)	11mm ($\frac{7}{16}''$)
length	3m (10ft)	3½m (12ft)	4¼m (14ft)	4½m (15ft)	6m (20ft)	9m (30ft)
Polyester 3 Strand warp diameter	8mm ($\frac{3}{8}''$)	10mm ($\frac{3}{8}''$)	12mm (½'')	16mm ($\frac{5}{8}''$)	18mm (¾'')	20mm (¾'')
length	15¼m (50ft)	18¼m (60ft)	21⅓m (70ft)	32m (105ft)	39½ (130ft)	45¾m (150ft)
Overall chain & warp length	18m (60ft)	22m (72ft)	25m (84ft)	36m (120ft)	45m (150ft)	55m (180ft)
Offshore Cruising						
Anchor Weight	7kg (15lb)	10kg (22lb)	14kg (30lb)	16kg (35lb)	18-25kg (40-55lb)	27kg 60lb)
Chain Link diameter	6mm ($\frac{1}{4}''$)	8mm ($\frac{5}{16}''$)	8mm ($\frac{5}{16}''$)	10mm ($\frac{3}{8}''$)	11mm ($\frac{7}{16}''$)	13mm (½'')
length	6m (20ft)	7½m (24ft)	8m (26ft)	9m (30ft)	10½m (35ft)	12m (40ft)
Polyester 3 Strand warp diameter	10mm ($\frac{3}{8}''$)	12mm (½'')	16mm ($\frac{5}{8}''$)	18mm (¾'')	20mm (¾'')	24mm (⅞'')
length	21⅓m (70ft)	29¼m (96ft)	37¾m (124ft)	45m (150ft)	53⅓m (175ft)	61m (200ft)
Overall chain & warp length	27m (90ft)	36m (120ft)	45m (150ft)	55m (180ft)	64m (210ft)	73m (240ft)

BRUCE Anchor

Boat Length:	up to 7m (24ft)	up to 9m (30ft)	up to 10.4m (34ft)	up to 13.4m (40ft)	up to 15.4m (47ft)
Coastal Cruising					
Anchor weight	5kg (11lb)	7.5kg (16.5lb)	10kg (22lb)	15kg (33lb)	20kg (44lb)
Chain Link diameter	6mm ($\frac{1}{4}''$)	7mm ($\frac{5}{16}''$)	8mm ($\frac{3}{8}''$)	9mm ($\frac{3}{8}''$)	10mm ($\frac{7}{16}''$)
length	2¾m (9ft)	3m (10ft)	3⅓m (11ft)	3½m (12ft)	4m (13ft)
Polyester 3 Strand warp diameter	10mm ($\frac{3}{8}''$)	12mm (½'')	14mm ($\frac{5}{8}''$)	16mm ($\frac{5}{8}''$)	18mm (¾'')
length	19¼m (63ft)	33½m (110ft)	42⅓m (139ft)	51¼m (168ft)	60m (197ft)
Overall chain & warp length	22m (72ft)	36m (120ft)	45m (150ft)	55m (180ft)	64m (210ft)

PLEASE NOTE: The above are only RECOMMENDATIONS and NO LIABILITY can be accepted for ANY DECISION based on these figures. The conversion between Imperial and Metric sizes is approximate.

Easy Conversions

Metres into yards . . . add one-tenth
Yards into metres . . . deduct one-tenth
Kilometres into miles . . . multiply by 5 and divide by 8
Miles into kilometres . . . multiply by 8 and divide by 5
Litres into pints . . . multiply by 7 and divide by 4
Pints into litres . . . multiply by 4 and divide by 7
Litres into gallons . . . multiply by 2 and divide by 9
Gallons into litres . . . multiply by 9 and divide by 2
Kilogrammes into pounds . . . divide by 9 and multiply by 20
Pounds into kilogrammes . . . divide by 20 and multiply by 9

USEFUL NAMES AND ADDRESSES

Chapter Two

GRP supplies:

Strand Glassfibre Ltd, (apply to head office for the closest depot). Brentway Trading Estate, Brentford, Middx. TW8 8ER. Tel. 01 568 7191 Local suppliers and boat builders

Gelcoat protection & osmosis treatment:

*International Paints, Yachts Division, 24-30 Canute Rd, Southampton, SO9 3AS Tel. (0703) 226722

Two-pack foam:

Strand Glassfibre Ltd. *See* above for address.

Chapter Five

Cold castable resin/iron ballast system:

Barton Abrasives Ltd, Bagnall St, Great Bridge, Tipton, West Midlands, DY4 7BS. Tel. 021 557 9441

Adhesives & fillers:

Simpson-Lawrence (apply to head office for the closest depot). 218-228 Edmiston Drive, Glasgow, G51 2YT Tel: (041) 427 5331/8.

Sowester, South Western Marine Factors Ltd, PO Box 4, 43 Pottery Rd, Poole, Dorset. BH14 8RE. Tel. (0202) 745414.

Sealants:

Adshead Ratcliffe & Co. Ltd, Derby Rd, Belper, Derbyshire DE5 1WJ. Tel. (0773) 826661.

*Ralli-Bondite Ltd, Arnside Rd, Waterlooville, Hants. PO7 7UJ. Tel. (0705) 251321.

Chapter Nine

Masts & spars:

*Kemp Masts Ltd, St. Margarets Lane, Titchfield, Fareham, Hants. PO14 4BG. Tel. (0329) 41900.

Chapter Ten

Propeller shaft coupling:

Halyard Marine Ltd, 2 Portsmouth Centre, Quatremaine Rd, Portsmouth, Hants. PO3 5QT. Tel: (0705) 671641

Sterngear & other engineering supplies:

Carvel Developments, Bedford Engineering Works Houghton Rd, Bedford. Tel. (0243) 54781

T. Norris (Ind) Ltd, 6 Wood Lane, Isleworth, Middx. Tel. 01 560 3453

Chapter Eleven

Morse & Teleflex Cables:

South Western Marine Factors Ltd, Controls Dept, 5/7 Uddens Industrial Estate, Ferndown, Dorset BH21 7LF Tel: (0202) 892542

Engine water coolant pumps:

*Cleghorn Waring & Co. (Pumps) Ltd, 9-15 Hitchin St, Baldock, Herts. SG7 6AH. Tel. (0462) 893838

Indirect engine cooling:	E.J. Bowman (Birmingham) Ltd, Chester St, Birmingham B6 4AP Tel. (021) 359 5401
Engine exhaust systems:	A.N. Wallis & Co, (W.H. Den Ouden), Greasley St, Bulwell, Nottingham, Notts. NG6 8NJ. Tel. (0602) 2271154.
Engine electrical equipment:	*Lucas Marine Ltd, Frimley Rd, Camberley, Surrey, GU16 5EU Tel. (0276) 63252
Galvanic/anodic protection:	M.G. Duff Marine Ltd, Chichester Yacht Basin, Birdham, West Sussex PO20 7EW Tel. (0243) 512777.

Chapter Twelve

Wiring:	Local auto-electrical factors.
Electric cables & connectors:	*Ripaults Ltd, Southbury Rd, Enfield, Middx. EN1 1UE. Tel. 01 804 8181.
Wiring & marine electrical electrical supplies:	E.C. Smith & Sons (Marine Factors) Ltd, Units H & J, Kingsway Industrial Estate, Kingsway, Luton, Beds. LU1 1LP. Tel. (0582) 29721
Marine electrical fittings:	Simpson-Lawrence & South Western Marine Factors. See above for addresses.

Chapter Fourteen

Bottled gas:	Calor Gas Ltd, Appleton Park, Riding Court Rd, Datchet, Slough SL3 9JG. Tel. (0753) 40000.
Calor gas fittings & appliances: caravan galley fittings & chemical toilets:	Joy & King, 6 Wooburn Industrial Park, Wooburn Green, High Wycombe, Bucks, HP10 OPF. Tel. (06285) 30686.

Toilets:- chemical:	See above for address.
seagoing toilets & gate valves:	Simpson-Lawrence & South Western Marine Factors. See above for addresses.
Water & bilge pumps: pressure water systems:	*Munster Simms Engineering Ltd, Old Belfast Rd, Bangor, Co. Down, N. Ireland, BT19 1LT Tel. (0247) 461531

Chapter Fifteen

Headlinings, berth cushions & other materials:	Toomer & Hayter Ltd., 74 Green Road, Winton, Bournemouth, Dorset. Tel. (0202) 515789

Chapter Sixteen

Paints:	*International Paints, Yacht Division. See above for address.
Deck coverings:	James Walker & Co., Lion Works, Woking Surrey. GU22 8AP Tel. (0483) 757575

*The companies marked with an asterisk have been very helpful and in some instances have given a great deal of assistance.

GENERAL

Sell's Marine Market — The Boating Fact Finder, 55 High St, Epsom, Surrey KT19 8DW. Tel. (03727) 26376.

British Waterways Board, Melbury House, Melbury Terrace, London NW1. Tel. 01 262 6711.

Inland Waterways Association, 114 Regents Park Rd, London NW1 8UQ. Tel. 01 586 2510.

R.Y.A., Victoria Way, Woking, Surrey GU21 1EQ. Tel. (04862) 5022.

Thames Water Authority, Thames Conservancy, Nugent House, Vastern Rd, Reading RG1 8DB. Tel. (0734) 593333.

INDEX